The Rage of Edmund Burke

THE RAGE OF EDMUND BURKE

Portrait of An Ambivalent Conservative

ISAAC KRAMNICK

Basic Books, Inc., Publishers

NEW YORK

Library of Congress Cataloging in Publication Data

Kramnick, Isaac.
  The rage of Edmund Burke.

  Includes bibliographies and index.
  1.   Burke, Edmund, 1729?–1797—Political science.
2.   Burke, Edmund, 1729?–1797.   3.   Political scientists
—Great Britain—Biography.   I.   Title.
JC176.B83K7   320.5'2'0924   [B]   76-43466
ISBN: 0–465–06829–4

TO

Rebecca, Jonathan, and Leah

CONTENTS

PREFACE

FEW write of Burke with qualification or reservation. His contemporary Sir Gilbert Elliot insisted in 1791 that Burke's attack on the French Revolution "contains the fundamental elements of all political knowledge." On the other hand, a few months earlier an angry Thomas Jefferson had described Burke's condemnation of the Jacobins as "evidence of the rottenness of his mind." In the nineteenth century, one finds the historian Lecky commenting on Burke's writings that the "time will never come in which men would not grow wiser by reading them." Lecky's contemporary Woodrow Wilson thrilled to Burke's extraordinary imagination. It was, he wrote, one that "takes your breath and quickens your pulse. The glow and power . . . rejuvenates your faculties." In our own age, the editors of Burke's speeches see in them the holy creed inspiring the defense of "Western Christendom" against the "Moscow enslavement of 1917."

In the last thirty years Burke has assumed nearly legendary status. He has emerged as the prophet of Conservatism, unsung perhaps in his own time, but very much the voice of Tory wisdom for a latter-day conservative movement. One need only mention his name today to suggest an attitude, a stance, an entire world view. This book seeks to rescue Burke from the overly worshipful embrace of those who usually write on him. It assumes that he is a much more complicated and interesting figure and thinker than conventionally depicted, and that his message for today is by no means as clear as his disciples would have us believe. On the other hand, his stature and importance as a historical figure, it will be argued, is really much greater than envisioned even by his champions.

It is the relationship between Burke's life, personality, and social thought that will be studied here. This approach will involve linking his biography and state of mind to his actions, writings, and speeches, and it requires rather extensive use of his private letters. This study is, in fact, rooted in Burke's recently published correspondence, a wholly new source of data of critical importance in understanding the man and his ideas. The central purpose of the book will be to clarify Burke's ideological posture by questioning the assumption of his romance with the ancien régime, the traditional order. His personality is the key to this reassessment, and from his letters it will be seen that the more complicated ideological picture that will be offered of Burke is in turn related to critical private issues.

In some respects, it will be a new Burke that emerges from these pages. This may bother some, but my hope is that it will be intriguing and interesting as well. Reasonable people can differ on some of the lines of argument found in the book—on Burke's sexuality, for example, or on the basic ambivalence of his personality revealing itself in ideological tension. The former is based primarily on exegetical treatment of materials that are by no means self-evident. The latter, while fundamental to the whole study, is an organizing and interpretive construct of my own creation, imposed from without on a life history. While some may find these arguments not to their liking, they are, I think, well within the pale of interpretive insight. My speculations are usually based on extensive textual documentation and this reluctance to argue without evidence accounts, I am afraid, for the overly rich diet of direct Burkean citations found here.

Several words are in order on how this study came to be. For some time now I have been concerned with eighteenth-century England as the critical era of transition during which the bourgeoisie replaced the long dominant aristocracy. In an earlier work I looked at the response of men such as Bolingbroke, Pope, and Swift to the earliest stages of the passing of the old order. I then turned my attention to research on the actual bearers of this transformation, the middle-class radicals who in industry, science, politics, and culture changed England irrevocably from the years 1760 to 1800. While preparing a study of these bourgeois radicals I constantly had to confront their great contemporary, and apparent antagonist, Burke. Convention dictates that he stood the foil to all they represented. But there was too much in Burke that smacked of these, his very enemies, for me to be comfortable with this interpretation. At this point fortune intervened. I was asked to write a review article of the nine volumes of Burke's correspondence, finally completed after some fifteen years of ongoing publication. It was in reading these letters that I came to see Burke as the more complicated ideological figure I present here. What Burke offers, I now suggest, is nothing less than a pivotal insight into that great turning point in our history—the transformation from the aristocratic to the bourgeois world. He does this not only in his ideas, but also in himself. He personifies this transformation. It is in this that his importance and even his greatness consist.

Most of the original manuscript for this study was completed within the elegant and hospitable walls of Cornell's Society for the Humanities. I should like to thank its directors during that period, Henry Guerlac and Eric Blackall, for the delightful community over which they presided. Various parts of the manuscript were initially tried out on a variety of audiences. I am indebted to these forums and the questioners there whose comments and criticisms were of great value. Among them, I include Cornell's Group for Applied Psychoanalysis, headed by Dr. Howard Feinstein, McGill University's History of Political Thought group, Geoffrey Hartman's program in Psychoanalysis and The Humanities at Yale, the 1975 Chicago conference on the History of Political Thought, and the Eighteenth-Century Studies Bicentennial Conference in Philadelphia.

For readings of early drafts of the manuscript I thank Dan Baugh of Cornell, Peter Hughes of the University of Toronto, Stanley Hoffman, and, as always, Judith Shklar of Harvard. For readings and discussions on psychoanalytic matters, I offer appreciation to Karen Slavin Brody of New York City and to Dr. Richard Munich and Dr. Leonard Zegans, both of New Haven, Connecticut. Thanks are also due to the review editor of *The American Political Science Review* who graciously watched as his intended review article turned into a book; to David Danelski who first proposed that metamorphosis; and to Ted Lowi who brought together author and publisher. Martin Kessler of Basic Books has consistently been an astute reader and critic of the manuscript and its tendency to inflation. Arline Blaker deserves special thanks for her impressive deciphering skills which allow people like me, who can't think at the typewriter, to still write books in longhand.

There is, finally, my family. Miriam Brody Kramnick consistently questioned the enterprise. Her insightful and constructive criticism often forced me to rethink and redo what I felt was already thought out and done. But perhaps no questions can have been as challenging as those put to me by my children, Rebecca, Jonathan, and Leah. They have confronted me and my absorption in Burke with the same curiosity and skepticism that they turned on the weightier issues that they saw absorbing the adults around them in the middle 1970s. To them I dedicate this book with all my love.

Ithaca, New York
March 6, 1977

The Rage of Edmund Burke

INTRODUCTION

The Burke Problem

EDMUND BURKE was an angry man. His was the first and most articulate voice to repudiate the French Revolution and in so doing he gave birth
to the intellectual tradition of conservatism. At the heart of conservatism is
rage—fury at those who would tamper with the stability and peace of the
order that already is. In his most well-known book, *The Reflections on the Revolution in France,* in his parliamentary speeches, and in a long series of essays
and letters, Burke angrily lashed out at the middle-class radicals of France
and England who were destroying the aristocratic world, which, according to
Burke, was the glory of Europe. His rage knew no limits as he denounced the
upstart bourgeoisie who undermined the beautiful harmony of the ancien
régime. He condemned the Jacobins (English and French) who sought to
govern in the place of those great oaks, the aristocracy, that God had set over
men as their natural rulers. He was contemptuous of the revolutionaries' lack
of reverence for the past, for tradition, for old institutions, ancient ideas and
prejudices. He was consumed with anger at their rationalism, and their
science which cut through the miasma of mystery which he saw hovering
over the social and political world. "The age of chivalry was gone," Burke
wrote, and "that of sophisters, economists, and calculators had succeeded."

This is the conventional image of Burke, the heroic figure burning with
anger, lashing out at the planners, the ideologues, the revolutionaries who
dared reconstruct the social order in their prideful zeal. This image is
very much alive and with us today as in the 1790s. There has, in fact, been a
major revival of interest in Burke during the last twenty-five years. This important and unexpected Burkean renaissance was fueled in part by the use
made of him by cold-war anti-communists who saw his defense of Christian
Europe against French revolutionary fanaticism as a stirring example to the
western democracies engaged in ideological warfare against atheistic commu-

nism. Much more significant, however, is the role Burke has come to play in recent years as the inspirational hero for a conservative resurgence in Anglo-American intellectual circles. His repudiation of radicals who seek to eliminate inequality and injustice and of utopians who seek to establish true freedom, has attracted to him many in recent years who are angry with social planning and naive liberalism. He speaks for a new conservatism today that is convinced of the complexity and fragility of social institutions and of the inevitability of sin and suffering. Burke gives to this new conservatism a respectable and most appealing prophet.

Conservatism was born, the legend goes, with Edmund Burke. No less than John Locke and Karl Marx, prophets of liberalism and communism respectively, Burke seems secure as one of the few seminal minds who have shaped the ideological contours of modern political debate. Secure he may be, but this book argues that to label him father of conservatism tells but half the story. This argument stands Burke on his head, replacing the Tory prophet with the ambivalent radical. There are two Burkes and doing the man and his works full justice requires a revision of his conventional image.

The two Burkes can be seen struggling with each other in the long letter Burke wrote in 1795, two years before his death, to Bedford, the great English Peer. During his long career Burke had often written to and about the aristocracy. All England, indeed, all Christendom, knew that in Edmund Burke the privileged classes had a chivalric champion eager at the slightest insult to their class to defend his betters with speech or pen. At his lévee, King George III had been overheard whispering his thanks to Burke for his great support of "the cause of the gentlemen." Pope Pius VI in a letter to Burke had praised his "defense of the cause of right . . . of civilization." [1] The ranks of privilege could not have hoped for a more articulate and persuasive defender. Master of English prose as have been few other politicians or writers on politics, Burke's dazzling language was at the service of those who were, as God had intended them, his natural superiors. As he prepared his letter to Bedford through his mind might have passed other passages he had written about the aristocracy. There was, for example, the now-celebrated letter to the Duke of Richmond in 1772, in which Burke had offered the metaphor of the tree, so favored by conservatives ever since. The product of generations of slow and imperceptible growth with its roots set deep in stable, unchanging, yet nurturing earth, the tree would become the symbol of conservative continuity. Beside the towering tree that was Richmond, the lowly Burke was nothing.

Persons in your station of life ought to have long views. You people of great families and hereditary trusts and fortunes are not like such as I am, who whatever we may be by the Rapidity of our growth and of the fruit we bear, flatter ourselves that while we creep on the Ground we belly into melons that are exquisite for size and flavour, yet still we are but annual plants that perish with our season and leave no sort of traces behind us. You, if you are what you ought to be, are the great Oaks that shade a country and perpetuate your benefits from Generation to Generation.[2]

Such sentiments were far from Burke's mind in 1795, however. In his *Letter to a Noble Lord* he offered an attack on Bedford so vicious that contemporaries were astounded. No self-deprecating deference to a Great Oak here; Burke chopped away at each and every one of the roots of Bedford's fame. Bedford, of the great Russell family, had just criticized Burke's acceptance of a government pension upon leaving Parliament after nearly thirty years' service. Burke, in turn, had no love for Bedford, one of the Whigs who still supported Fox and the French Revolution—a "new whig" from whom Burke had angrily disassociated himself. But Burke's reply to Bedford went far beyond the internecine conflicts of the crumbling Whig Party. It was a vicious and personal attack on the Duke and, interestingly enough, a self-conscious justification of Burke's own career and actions. Burke juxtaposed, on the one hand, his own hard-won achievements based solely on industry and merit for which he had been rewarded by Pitt's pension with, on the other hand, the Duke's privileged life, and the rewards granted him by English Society for no discernible achievement, for nothing other than being the descendant of an earlier Russell who himself had done nothing in particular to merit honors from Henry VIII other than having been a loyal follower while Henry, like the later Jacobins in France, ransacked the monasteries and redistributed the booty to his henchmen. There are few more revealing passages in Burke's published writings than this bitter indictment of Bedford. It is also a personal apologia from an aging Burke seeking in 1795 to give meaning and integrity to his long life.

I was not, like his Grace of Bedford, swaddled and rocked and dandled into a legislator. . . . I possessed not one of the qualities nor cultivated one of the arts that recommend men to the favor and protection of the great. I was not made for a minion or a tool. . . . At every step of my progress in life (for in every step was I traversed and opposed) and at every turnpike I met, I was obliged to show my passport, and again and again to prove my sole title to the honor of being useful to my country, by a proof that I was not wholly unacquainted with its laws and the whole system of its interests both abroad and at home. Otherwise, no rank, no toleration even, for me. I had no arts, but manly arts. On them I have stood, and please God, in spite of the Duke of Bedford . . . to the last gasp will I stand. . . . I have done all I could to discountenance their inquiries into the fortunes of those who hold large portions of wealth without any apparent merit of their own. . . . The grants to the house of Russell were so enormous as not only to outrage economy, but even to stagger credibility. The Duke of Bedford is the leviathan among all the creatures of the crown. He tumbles about his unwieldy bulk, he plays and frolics in the ocean of the royal bounty. Huge as he is, and whilst "he lies floating many a rood" he is still a creature. His ribs, his fins, his whalebone, his blubber, the very spiracles through which he spouts a torrent of brine against his origin, and covers me all over with the spray, everything of him and about him is from the throne. Is it for *him* to question the dispensation of the royal favor? . . . My merits, whatever they are, are original and personal; his are derivative. It is his ancestor, the original pensioner, that has laid up this inexhaustible fund of merit which makes his Grace so very delicate and exceptious about the merit of all other grantees of the crown. . . . Why will his Grace by attacking me, force me reluctantly to compare my little merit with that which obtained from the Crown those prodigies of profuse donation by which he tramples on the mediocrity of humble and laborious individuals? [3]

There is a striking difference in tone between Burke's comments on Bedford and those in the letter to Richmond. It is nowhere more apparent than in Burke's characteristic use of metaphor. One Duke is worshipped as the great tree that shelters and nurtures a grateful people; the other is ridiculed as a ponderous mass of blubber, frolicking in a sea of royal corruption, spewing forth disdainful spray. What does one make of this apparent inconsistency? What happens to Burke the great apologist for privilege? To be sure, the essay does not call for an end to Bedford's wealth or power. Indeed, it ends with a ringing defense of traditional rights and status against the levelling ideology of Jacobinism. But there can be no mistaking the essay's very explicit defense of self-made man and the implied critique of the aristocratic principle of inherited and thus unearned rank and status. In retailing attitudes such as these, this essay of Burke's reads a close kin to much of the ideological writing he so despised.

Radical bourgeois thought in the early years of the Industrial Revolution has this as its central ideological theme. Dominating radical writing is a ringing defense of self-made men (and women in Wollstonecraft's case), men of merit and talent, men of hard and useful work in contrast to men of privilege and rank, idle and unproductive men, men of leisure and lineage. The development of this bourgeois ethos would rip apart the facade of a stable and harmonious social structure and in pitting the middle class against the aristocracy and gentry would expose the class conflict rampant in industrial England. Wordsworth saw this. He wrote in 1817:

I see clearly that the principal ties which kept the different classes of society in a vital and harmonious dependence upon each other have, within these thirty years, either been greatly impaired or wholly dissolved. Everything has been put up to market and sold for the highest price it would bring. [4]

At the center of this market selling their skills and talents were social upstarts, the likes of Arkwright, Watt, Boulton, Wedgewood, and Burke— showing his passport. The ideology of the upstart bourgeoisie would ultimately transform England and create in its green and pleasant lands satanic mills and the first great middle-class civilization. It was fast happening in Burke's day, and its immediate political objective was to oust men of privilege from their control of the State and to replace them with more virtuous self-made men of talent and merit.

We are, in fact, familiar with this ideological conflict partly because convention has it that Burke himself stood as a bulwark against this very transformation, which he epitomized as the passing of the "age of chivalry." Yet Burke evokes in this *Letter to a Noble Lord* the very spirit of his despised Jacobin and bourgeois antagonists. His is the cry of Beaumarchais's Figaro, who but a few years earlier had asked of his Count Almaviva:

Just because you're a great lord, you think you're a genius. Nobility, fortune, rank, position—you're so proud of these things. What have you done to deserve so many rewards? You went to the trouble of being born, and no more.[5]

So, indeed, it appeared to some of Burke's readers in 1795. The conservative *Monthly Review* responded immediately to Burke's *Letter,* drawing its own conclusions as to the meaning of the attack on Bedford.

By exhibiting an odious and detestable picture of the means by which great hereditary fortunes have been raised, it is calculated to change the respect of the multitude for property into disgust; to let loose their enraged passions on that wealth which is the object of their perpetual envy, and to lend even to rapine itself some of the features and lineaments of justice. . . . Mr. Burke calls the Duke of Bedford's estates "landed pensions" an expression reconcilable to no system but that of Mr. Godwin.[6]

Another contemporary drew the same conclusion. Wasn't Burke's essay an example of radical ideology, he asked? Perhaps he recognized it as such, for but a few short years before he had himself written poetry for the Jacobin cause. Already turned against the revolution, a puzzled yet perceptive Coleridge reviewed Burke's *Letter to a Noble Lord* in the first number of his new journal, *The Watchman,* on 1 March 1796.

The attack is on the Duke of Bedford for enjoying the senatorial office by hereditary right, or (to use Mr. Burke's own words), for being "nursed, and swaddled, and dandled, into a legislator," for his immense property, which overshadows and "oppresses the industry of humble men." . . . This is not the only instance to be met with in the course of Mr. Burke's writings, in which he lays down propositions, from which his adversaries are entitled to draw strange corollaries. The egg is his: Paine and Barlow hatch it.

Which is it, then, Burke as Burke, or Burke as Paine, Barlow, and Godwin? Is Burke the champion of a privileged aristocratic order or, like Paine equating "nobility" with "no-ability," is he one of the radical bourgeoisie found in the Jacobin camp? He is, in fact, both. Coleridge in a flash of inspired insight saw through the man, but he never went further to explain what instances, what propositions, or what corollaries. The beginning of wisdom in understanding Edmund Burke is here in discerning his basic ambivalence to the two great ideological currents whose confrontation dominated his age.

Much of Burke's life was a charade, and most of those who worship him today notice only the half of it. While he hated the ambitious Jacobins who saw themselves repudiating received notions of natural superiority and subordination, he also shared some of their aspirations. It was a precarious act for the Irish outsider in a closed English aristocratic world to pull off. One part of Burke loyally served and defended his betters while another despised and sought to replace them. Perhaps more than anyone else in his age Burke epitomized the love/hate ambivalence that the assertive bourgeoisie felt toward their aristocratic betters. The anxious guilt produced by their attack on those whom they had been socialized to revere evoked the reactive formation of love which appeased this guilt. This love was itself enhanced by their everexisting and powerful envy of the great. Far from being a doctrinaire apologist for one set of values, confidently throwing himself into a holy cause— the defense of the past—undaunted by doubt and misgivings, Burke was in fact an ambivalent and tortured man. Torn by personal misgivings about his own place in society, some of his most basic personal inclinations seem, in fact, to have been not that far removed from those of the very radicals against whom he thundered.

The complexities of Burke's social thought were in turn reflective of deep confusion over personal identity. Behind the public creed lurked nagging issues of private need. Never secure about the boundaries between rightful initiative and ambition, on the one hand, and shameful overstriving, on the other, Burke's life was a constant vacillation between assertion and self-denigration. The source for much of this conflict lay with unique events in his childhood and the legacy of his troubled relationship with his father.

No surprise, then, that Burke's ambivalent social and ideological identity was paralleled by serious confusion and doubt about his sexual identity. His adolescence and early manhood were characterized by painful efforts at coming to terms with sexual passion in general and making sexual object choices in particular. At the age of fifteen his letters reveal Burke committing himself to a lifelong struggle against passions and inclinations that he sees working within and which he takes to be part of a diabolical plot tempting him to self-destruction.[7] This came to a head in an identity crisis in his early twenties when Burke virtually withdrew from society and turned inward in an effort to sort out these tumultuous issues which divided him against himself. Plagued by internal doubt, he was wracked with the constant pain of repressed private tension, tension unresolved and unremitting. In later life Burke wrote of hidden personal problems that he would rather forget, indeed, from which he had fled in the frenzied diversion of an active public life. The letter, written in 1779 to his childhood friend Dick Shackleton, speaks of a series of political setbacks that Burke had just suffered and of his thoughts on leaving political life because of them. But he would not, Burke wrote; to do so might invite even more serious discomfort.

So little satisfaction have I that I should not hesitate a moment to retire from publick Business—if I was not in some doubt of the Duty a man has that goes a certain length in those things; and if it were not from an observation that there are often obscure vexations and contests in the most private life, which may as effectually destroy a man's peace as anything which happens in publick contentions.[8]

The psychic cost of holding in check these vexations and contests, his ideological and personal ambivalence, was great for Burke. Throughout his life he was subject to deep depression, followed often by manic fits of activity. It is clear from his correspondence, for example, that at twenty-one and at thirty-seven he experienced nervous collapses. His alternation from depression to manic hyperactivity was evident quite early in his life. He wrote to Shackleton when he was fifteen of his "sallies of passion" when he would feverishly study without rest and of other times when he would lie idle doing nothing for days.[9] Bouts of depression came upon him often, and it was the most he could do to keep from succumbing. In September 1774 he offered a candid description of this in a letter to his patron the Marquess of Rockingham.

Sometimes when I am alone, in spite of all my efforts I fall into a melancholy which is inexpressible, and to which if I gave way, I should not continue long under it, but must totally sink. Yet I do assure you that partly and principally by the force of natural good spirits, and partly by a strong sense of what I ought to do, I bear up so well, that no one who did not know them could easily discover the state of my mind or my circumstances.[10]

Writers on Burke have seldom investigated those "obscure vexations and contests in the most private life," which destroyed his peace and which Burke himself related to his public career. G. M. Young, the English essayist, did suggest in 1948 that understanding the passion, the vehemence, and the frenzy of Burke required looking at "a deeper source." He suggested that the importance in Burke's writings of family and "domestic relationships" might be a place to turn in understanding Burke's ideas.[11] Young left off at this point, however, and turned from two sentences of novel advice to pages of conventional exegesis and praise of Burke. The recent publication of Burke's complete correspondence, however, makes it easier for an investigator now to relate Burke's private need to his public creed. What the letters provide, along with a new reading of Burke's published speeches and writings, is an impression of Burke as a deeply troubled and ambivalent man. Moreover, Young's surmise was more accurate than he could ever have known. Burke's "domestic relationships," in his youth, adolescence, and early adulthood turn out to have been of profound significance in shaping his troubles and ambivalence.

Ambivalence is not a word one usually associates with Burke. He is outspoken and dogmatic, perhaps inconsistent, but certainly not ambivalent. Burke has for many quite adequately handled the issue of his consistency himself. In his *Appeal from the New to the Old Whigs* (1791) and in his *Letter to a Noble Lord* he argued the underlying consistency in his advocacy of the American colonies, his attacks on the Crown around 1780, and his repudiation of the French Revolution. By ambivalence, however, something quite different is meant here. It suggests that basic to Burke's personality were conflicts over identity and motivation, conflicts which, in turn, expressed themselves in his politics. This is what led him at one and the same time to despise Bedford and all he stood for and to defend His Grace with purple prose from the Jacobins who shared this hatred.

Burke's social, political, and ideological attitudes as expressed in public life—in Parliament, in his correspondence, and in his essays—reflect and in turn are heavily influenced by personal and private concerns, concerns of identity and self-image which originated in childhood and adolescence and which persisted throughout his adult life. At the center of Burke's life and thought is an unresolved ambivalence between his identification with what might be called the aristocratic personality on the one hand, and the bourgeois personality on the other. This is a dichotomy of more than economic or social dimensions; it has, as we shall see, cultural and sexual overtones as well. Crucial to the evolution of this ambivalence were Burke's complicated attitudes to his mother and father, authority in general, his "cousin" Will and wife Jane, and to such issues as ambition, industry, status, merit, privilege, action, aggression, passivity, masculinity and femininity. This personal ambivalence is of importance in more than simply biographical terms. Burke's relationship with his father, the youthful relationship with Dick Shackleton and more significantly with Will Burke, were, along with other features of his private world, of great importance in shaping his political vision. Concerns with themes of masculinity and femininity leap from his writings and speeches on India and France, for example. His political and social thought is in many ways a public coming to terms with "the obscure vexations and contests in the most private life."

No adequate alternative exists for explaining certain parts of Burke's life and thought, the frenzied passion and obsessiveness of his attack on Hastings or the Jacobins, for example, or the fascination with America and the simultaneous attack and defense of the great, than turning to the relationship of this public creed with his private need. Similarly, there is no other adequate explanation of the extent to which Burke's preoccupation with sexuality enters into his writings and speeches—the graphic morbidity, for example, with which he repeatedly described in Parliament the torture of virgins in India or the frequency of jokes to his colleagues on the order of boastful lovers comparing in the morning how many times they'd "done it"—than by looking at his private life. Deep and persistent tensions arising from issues of ideological and sexual identity conflict left him on occasion in melancholic fits of depression; they also helped shape the content of his social and political ideals. They would, for example, inform his bleak view of human nature, the nightmarish preoccupation in his writings on India and France with cannibalism, parricide, sexual aggression, violence, death and destruction. Like Augustine before him and Freud after, Burke saw the horrific potential for greed, exploitation, and lust that lay just beneath the veneer of civility and it is against this background that his conservative justification of repressive government must be read. Government, he wrote in the *Reflections on the Revolution in France,* was a power outside of individuals which thwarted, subdued, and put chains on passion and appetite.[12] This legitimization of government was informed no doubt, in part, by Burke's repudiation of the facile optimism of the Enlightenment, his desire to restore a sense of original sin and evil. But there also lurks behind it Burke's awareness of how powerful these frightening and disruptive passions and appetites were within himself and how difficult and painful it was to keep them under control.

Investigating the relationship between Burke's private and public self indeed stands him on his head. No longer the dogmatic ideologue that conventional wisdom portrays, Burke emerges a figure of uncertainty and ambivalence. No longer the conservative prophet, Burke emerges the ambivalent radical. This new Burke is a much more interesting and important historical figure than the defender of the faith so venerated by generations of conservatives. But traditional Burke still deserves a hearing, if only to set the stage for the revisionist views which make up the heart of this study. We begin, then, with a review of Burke's political and philosophical world view, giving some attention both to the social and intellectual tendencies he reacted against, as well as to how the conventional view of Burke as patron saint of conservatism has evolved to the present day. Only after having done that can one turn to an alternative reading of the man and his work.

CHAPTER 1

Mythic Burke: The Prophet of Conservatism

THE FRENCH REVOLUTION and its apocalyptic promise marked the passing of the age of chivalry and with it, according to Burke, the end of the glory of Europe. But the old order did not suddenly fall; it had been chipped away for decades. For some thirty years the radical bourgeoisie had been assaulting the turrets and moats of the aristocratic edifice, and for some thirty years Edmund Burke's conservatism had served the hard pressed ancien régime. His conservatism was not simply a reaction to the Revolution in France. It was a life-long response to what he perceived as dreaded tendencies of his age. *The Reflections on the Revolution in France* elaborates and develops themes and concerns he had articulated throughout his career. While it is the most poignant and dramatic statement of these ideas, indeed, one of the most moving and ably written political testaments in the western tradition, its themes had been rehearsed for decades, as far back, in fact, as Burke's college years. What the Revolution did was confirm his most horrible fears, that what the bourgeois radicals—the sophisters, economists and calculators— would wreak, was not a new dawn but a hellish nightmare of chaos and confusion, destruction and death.

BOURGEOIS RADICALISM AND THE SUBVERSION OF
THE ANCIEN RÉGIME

England in the second half of the eighteenth century was characterized, as one modern historian has noted, by a striking combination of "modernity and aristocratic domination." [1] Burke, the most articulate defender of the aristocracy, singled out one group as the major modernizing agent in his England—the sectarian Protestant dissenters. He was right. While many strains of English life, including even parts of the aristocracy itself, contributed to the modernity that threatened the old order, the cutting edge of change came from these dissenters. They were the secular prophets, the vanguard, of a new social order and played the decisive role in transforming England into the first bourgeois civilization.

By the 1770s and 1780s large numbers of the English dissenters, the subdued descendents of the nonconformist sects that had waged revolution under Cromwell in the seventeenth century, had already emigrated to America. Those Baptists, Presbyterians, Independents, Unitarians and Quakers who remained in England constituted only seven percent of the population. But this seven percent destroyed aristocratic England and its traditional values. [2] It was at the heart of the progressive and innovative nexus that linked scientific, political, cultural, and industrial radicalism. The dissenters played an innovative role vastly disproportionate to their numbers. While they made up 7% of the population, for example, (90% were Anglican), these non-conformists contributed some 41% of the important entrepreneurs between 1760 and 1830. The names that conventionally symbolize the Industrial Revolution are virtually *all* dissenters. The mnemonic scheme used by generations of English schoolchildren to personalize the Industrial Revolution, for example, the three W's, Watt, Wilkinson, and Wedgewood, were dissenters to a man.

The dissenters played a central and crucial role in scientific and political innovation as well. This is best personified in the career of Joseph Priestley, who more than anyone else qualifies as the principal architect of bourgeois England. Radical in politics, laissez-faire theorist in economics, innovator in science and technology, founder of the modern Unitarian movement, Priestley schooled England's "new men" of business in the series of dissenting academies at which he taught, while personally serving as the critical link between virtually every aspect of the progressive and innovative bourgeois nexus. Brother-in-law to Wilkinson, friend of Price and Wollstonecraft, "guide, philosopher, and friend of Boulton, Watt, and Wedgewood at Birmingham," [3] he was "Gunpowder Joe" to Burke and the Church-and-king mob that burned his laboratory and home in 1791, sending him to finish his days in dissenter's paradise—America.

In their academies the dissenters armed the children of the bourgeoisie with a new learning and a new anti-aristocratic political ideal. Priestley was quite outspoken in his belief that only the educated youth of the middle class could perpetuate the wondrous potential of the new bourgeois civilization. This was the message of his lecture to the parents and supporters of the academy at Hackney in 1791. His concern, he noted, was for the young "in the middle classes of life." He urged them to work for the abolition of all "useless distinctions . . . and a general release from all such taxes and burdens of every kind, as the public good does not require. In short, to make government as beneficial and as little expensive and burdensome as possible." [4]

Priestley envisioned a minimal and noninterfering state. This flowed quite easily from his commitment to religious freedom, for there was a close relationship in the dissenting world view between religious dogma and the political and economic concerns of the bourgeoisie. Matters of religion and of conscience were held to be totally beyond the competence of the magistrate. Dissenting clergy and political writers insisted that the power of government be limited strictly to preserving the peace and protecting property. This constant invocation of the principle of religious laissez-faire, the withdrawal of the state from the realm of belief, soon became appropriated by secular arguments for economic laissez-faire. The centuries-old restrictions on economic activity inherited from medieval Christian dogma, a guild-dominated feudalism, and Tudor paternalism were under attack by the entrepreneurs of industrializing England.

Individualism was as crucial for Priestley in the economic realm as in the religious realm. Man should be "left to himself." All the restrictions on individuals should be undone so that they could "revert to that natural condition of man from which we have departed." [5] Where he applied this most clearly was in his attack on the Poor Laws, which for the bourgeoisie were one of the most onerous of the old order's interferences with economic liberty. In his attack on the Poor Laws he captures beautifully the emerging bourgeois attitude to the poor as well. "Some will become rich and others poor," he writes. The state has attempted too much in publicly providing for the poor. The poor become "improvident, spending everything they get in the most extravagant manner, knowing they have a certain resource in the provision which the law makes for them." They are not taught the necessity of prudence and foresight, they think only for the present moment, and are thus, he suggests, reduced to a condition lower than beasts. "Better," he recommends, "if government had not interfered in the case of the poor at all." All it does is take taxes from the industrious and encourage the idle. The deserving poor, he suggests, should, if need be, be taken care of by "the charity of the well disposed." [6]

Another, even more blatant, example of the state's having legislated too

much were the Test and Corporation Acts which interfered both with religious liberty and civil liberty. They violated the natural rights of believers
while intruding the state into the free competitive market of careers and
rewards by right due the talented and industrious. The ideological heart of
dissenting social thought is found here in its opposition to the restrictive
Test and Corporation Acts, for they violated the fundamental assumptions of
the ethos of the self-made individual and of society disinterestedly rewarding
people of merit and talent, people of hard and useful work. By excluding dissenters from holding public office the Acts were assailed as the major buttress
of an aristocratic order of received and unearned status and rank. They
rewarded idle and unproductive people of leisure and lineage. These intolerable Acts, Priestley wrote, rewarded "the gentlemen born," those "with family and connections respectable . . . of polished and engaging manners."
His is the bourgeois demand for careers open to the talented in his mocking
comment that "the door of preferment is so open to him (the gentleman
born) that he hardly needs to knock in order to enter." [7]

In their assault on the Test and Corporation Acts, Priestley and his dissenter friends, Anna Barbauld, John Aikin, Thomas Walker, and Thomas
Cooper, articulate the very essence of liberal-bourgeois social theory. In the
competitive scramble of the marketplace all citizens are equal in terms of
their opportunity to win; no one has built-in advantages of birth or status.
Freedom involves unrestrained competition and equality, an absence of built-
in handicaps. In the vulgar rhetoric of the bourgeoisie, life is competition, a
race for goods and offices, and in this race all have an equal opportunity to
win. It is indeed these very same dissenters who popularized the metaphor of
life as a race. [8]

The radical dissenters of Burke's day were men and women of property.
The English Jacobins, indeed, worshiped private property. They may have
had little respect for ancient baronial estates, but they were bourgeois to the
core. Along with their dissenting religion they learned respect for property
quite literally in their infancy. In his *Memoirs* Priestley, for example, writes
of an incident that happened when he was five. He was playing with a pin.
His mother asked him where he had gotten it and the youngster answered
from his uncle. "She made me carry it back again; no doubt to impress my
mind, as it could not fail to do, with a clear idea of the distinction of property, and the importance of attending to it." [9] His mother died when he was
six. The adult Priestley remembered only two things about her, the incident
of the pin and that she had taught him the creed of the Protestant Assembly.

The adult writings of these bourgeois radicals represent a self-conscious
glorification of the mission of the middle class in British politics. Before
James Mill and legions of Victorian apologists for the bourgeoisie, radicals of
the late eighteenth century made the case for the superiority of men and
women from the virtuous and industrious middle ranks. And who was more

middle class than the dissenters? John Aikin wrote of his radical associates, "Your natural connections are not with kings and nobles. You belong to the most virtuous, the most enlightened, the most independent part of the community, *the middle class.*" [10] His sister Anna Barbauld was equally as insistent that the dissenters were fortunate to be "in that middle rank of life where industry and virtue most abound." [11] Mary Wollstonecraft lamented that women were not more like middle-class men. "The middle rank," she wrote, "contains most virtue and abilities." It is where "talents thrive best." Indeed, her *Vindication of the Rights of Woman* was written specifically, as she put it, for "those in the middle class, because they appear to be in the most natural state." [12]

Not only was the middle class more virtuous and more industrious, it was also the happiest. There are interesting echoes of Jefferson's "pursuit of happiness" in Richard Price's observations on the good fortune of the Americans. America is lucky, he wrote in 1784, because the "happiest state of man is in the middle state between the savage and the refined, or between the wild and the luxurious state." [13] Priestley, too, was convinced that middle-class existence was the most felicitous. For several years in the late 1770s he lived in the great house of Lord Shelburne as librarian to this aristocratic patron of bourgeois radicalism. Price had held the job before Priestley and later Shelburne would champion Jeremy Bentham. Looking back in his *Memoirs* on his years as resident intellectual for the great, Priestley noted that he was above temptation.

I was not at all fascinated with that mode of life. . . . . These people are generally unhappy from the want of necessary employment; on which accounts chiefly there appears to be much more happiness in the middle classes of life, who are above the fear of want, and yet have a sufficient motive for constant exertion of their faculties, and who have always some other object besides amusement. I used to make no scruple of maintaining that there is not only the most virtue and most happiness, but even most true politeness in the middle classes of life.[14]

Asserting the superiority of the middle class involved not only putting down those above, but also, as we have already noted in Priestley, criticism of those below. The Aristotelian praise of the mean was sanctified by religion when the Cambridgeshire dissenting minister Robert Hall compares the Georgian middle class with the early converts to Christianity. Like them "they were drawn from neither the very highest nor the very lowest classes. The former are too often the victims of luxury and pride, the latter, sunk in extreme stupidity. They were from the middle orders, where the largest portion of virtue and good sense has usually resided." [15] This parallel between the early Christians and the middle class produced by the Industrial Revolution was constantly evoked. They both had great historical missions as messianic agents of regeneration and rebirth. Joel Barlow, the American entrepreneur who spent the 1790s in England and France pursuing profits and radical politics, expressed this theme in his *Advice to the Privileged Orders in the Several States of Europe* (1792).

In mercy to them all, let the system be changed, let society be restored, and human nature retrieved. Those who compose the middle class of mankind, the class in which the semblance of nature most resides are called upon to perform this task . . . It will require some time to bring the men who now fill the two extremes in the wretched scale of rank to a proper view of their new stations of citizens. Minds that have long been crushed under the weight of privilege and pride or of misery and despair are equally distant from all rational ideas of the dignity of man. But even these classes may be brought back by degrees to be useful members of the state.[16]

It was primarily against the "weight of privilege and pride" that middle-class radicals, "the useful members of the state," waged war. The fundamental sin of the privileged order was their violation of what Cooper, the dissenting industrialist, called the "principle of talent." Government required "talents and abilities," which were not assigned at birth, but which manifested themselves in personal merit and achievement. While the privileged ruled the state,

the business of the nation is actually done by those who owe nothing to their ancestors, but have raised themselves into situations which the idleness and ignorance of the titled orders incapacitate them from filling.[17]

These men of "meritorious attainment" were the bearers of an ideology of equal opportunity. The bourgeois radicals demanded political reform in order to destroy forever the aristocratic world of ascribed status. The demands of the reformers that the suffrage be extended to industrial and commercial wealth, that the new manufacturing centers like Manchester and Birmingham be granted parliamentary representation, that expensive aristocratic institutions be streamlined or eliminated, that dissenters be free to serve as municipal and governmental officials, all boil down to the bourgeois demand of careers opened to the talented. A public order managed by men of merit and achievement would in turn reward others for industry and effort. Poor laws would be abolished, taxes decreased, government withdrawn from the market and the pulpit, luxury discouraged, thrift and other middle-class values encouraged.

One activity greatly encouraged in the new order would be science. Bourgeois science was closely linked to radical politics. Its practitioners were themselves good bourgeoisie who in a closed aristocratic society of privilege and rank sought radical social changes, not the least of which were greater social and political rewards and power for themselves and their industrial friends. But science was also a powerful tool in the bourgeoisie's effort to demystify the universe. Here, too, its impact was radical. The ancien régime and the aristocratic political world was defended by Burke and others because

of its very mysterious and superstitious essence—the dark shadowy eminences of kings, queens, and lords, with their cloaks of mysterious authority,
crowns, scepters, and thrones. Government, it was held, was also a mysterious, complicated, and arcane realm. Only those born to it could understand
and manipulate it. Science expelled superstition from the heavens and could
expel the mysteries that lay heavy on aristocratic society. Its new and corro-
sive ideals were truth, efficiency, and utility. Science seemed to give reality
to the radical's unbounded faith in progress, the belief in perfectibility and
the elimination of pain and suffering. It was in science as in politics that the
unrestrained pride of man took flight seeking even to rival the gods. The radical millennial role of science is aptly illustrated by a fascinating aside in a
letter Wedgewood wrote his partner. Commenting on some recent electrical
experiments, he was moved to note:

I am much pleased with your disquisition upon the capabilities of electricity, and
should be glad to contribute in any way you can point out to me towards rendering
Doctor Priestley's very ingenious experiments more extensively usefull, and whatever is the result of your father thoughts, and the Doctor's experiments on this subject, I am ready, so far as I can be concerned, to ratify and confirm your resolutions.
But what daring mortals you are! to rob the Thunderer of his bolts,—and for
what?—no doubt to blast the oppressors of the poor and needy, or to execute some
public piece of justice in the most tremendous and conspicuous manner, that shall
make the great ones of the earth tremble! [18]

This is the radical bourgeois nexus at work. In Wedgewood's mind science
was automatically linked with anti-aristocratic politics—making the great
tremble.

In the bourgeois radical camp one person, more than any other, made
the great of the world tremble. Tom Paine, the transatlantic revolutionary,
lifted the ideology from its English context and gave it universal and metahistorical meaning. Burke wrote of Paine that he sought to destroy "in six or
seven days" the feudal and chivalric world which "all the boasted wisdom of
our ancestors has labored to bring to perfection for six or seven centuries." [19]
Part of Paine's achievement was indeed to mock the past so venerated by
Burke. For Paine it was "the Quixotic age of chivalric nonsense." [20] He
ridiculed the ancient principles of British society, beginning in *Common Sense*
with the useless and unproductive monarchy.

In England a king hath little more to do than to make war and give away places;
which in plain terms, is to impoverish the nation and set it together by the ears. A
pretty business indeed for a man to be allowed eight hundred thousand sterling a
year for, and worshipped into the bargain! Of more worth is one honest man to society and in the sight of God, than all the crowned ruffians that ever lived. [21]

Is there anything more absurd than the hereditary principle, Paine
asked, "as absurd as an hereditary mathematician, or an hereditary wise man

and as ridiculous as an hereditary poet-laureate?" What mattered was not a man's pedigree but his productivity. Government required "talents and abilities," yet its offices were filled by a nobility which, according to Paine, really meant "no-ability." [22] The aristocracy were unproductive idlers, parasites who lived off the work of the industrious classes. No one would miss them in a reconstructed rational society.

Why then does Mr. Burke talk of his house of Peers, as the pillar of the landed interest? Were that pillar to sink into the earth, the same landed property would continue, and the same ploughing, sowing, and reaping would go on. The aristocracy are not the farmers who work the land, and raise the produce, but are mere consumers of the rent; and when compared with the active world are the drones . . . who neither collect the honey nor form the hive, but exist only for lazy enjoyment. [23]

The recurring theme of Paine's attack on aristocratic and monarchic government is that it was expensive. American government was cheap, and so was peace. This, above all, recommended them to men of common sense. The English, Paine wrote, should copy the Americans. He is one of the purest ideological spokesmen for the bourgeoisie, calling for them to take over the state. The demand is expressed in the language of economic determinism; the political order, he insists, must mirror the realities of economic power.

Whether the forms of maxims and governments which are still in practice, were adopted to the condition of the world at the period they were established, is not in this case the question. The older they are, the less correspondence can they have with the present state of things. Time and change of circumstances and opinions have the same progressive effect in rendering modes of government obsolete, as they have upon customs and manners. Agriculture, commerce, manufacturers, and the tranquil arts, by which the prosperity of nations is best promoted, require a different system of government, and a different species of knowledge to direct its operations, than what might have been required in the former condition of the world. [24]

Having taken over the state the bourgeoisie would proceed to simplify and streamline its institutional apparatus. The size of government would be reduced dramatically and it would be made inexpensive. This is, in fact, at the heart of what Paine meant by the end of tyranny. The new order would have no costly royal family and no aristocratic retainers subsidized in unnecessary wars and padded civil bureaucracies. Government would do little since society was by and large self-regulating, and social harmony was spontaneous. Paine's is the perfect expression of the liberal-bourgeois theory of the state. It serves strictly limited purposes.

Every man wishes to pursue his occupation, and to enjoy the fruits of his labors, and the produce of his property in peace and safety, and with it the least possible expense. When these things are accomplished, all the objects for which government ought to be established are answered. [25]

Enterprising individuals left alone by government would not produce a completely egalitarian social structure, however. Good bourgeois liberal that he was, Paine saw the postrevolutionary order free of the aristocracy but still characterized by economic differentiation. "That property will ever be unequal is certain," he wrote in 1795. This is not unjust, but simply a result of "industry, superiority of talents, dexterity of management, extreme frugality, and fortunate opportunities." [26]

It was ostensibly against such sophistery of Paine and Price, and the economics and calculations of a Priestley that Burke raised the proud, albeit tattered, banner of chivalry. It was he who, in declaring "if I must, my choice is made, I will have Louis XVI rather than Monsieur Brissot or Chabot; rather George III or IV than Dr. Priestley," [27] became the champion of the aristocratic order and bulwark against the transformation sought by bourgeois radicals.

BURKE'S CONSERVATISM BEFORE 1789

The intellectual core of bourgeois radicalism was its aggressive use of older liberal principles of natural right, freedom, and equality. Efforts to reform the existing society, economy, and polity and to build an ideal and perfect order were fueled on the energy provided by these normative principles. In their name the new day would come. It was in response to this faith that Burke's conservatism developed. A fundamental component of his counter-revolution was a ruthless skepticism about the role of abstract ideals, and a priori reasoning in general, and, in particular, in the realm of philosophy and social life. This was apparent as early as the 1740s during Burke's undergraduate years at Trinity College, Dublin. During these years and in the early 1750s the young Burke produced religious and philosophical notes and essays which were strikingly anticipatory of his later views. His skeptical attitude toward abstract reason and speculation was apparent, for example, in his early denunciation of "great subtleties and refinements of reasoning (which) . . . like spirits . . . disorder the brain and are much less useful than ordinary liquors of a grosser nature." One such useful and more common liquor which should guide men's social inquiries, he suggested, was custom. It was "to be regarded with great deference." There were "general principles operating to produce customs," which were surer "guides than our theories." [28]

It was in his *Vindication of Natural Society* that one first finds full-blown Burkean skepticism applied to conservative ends. Written in 1756, six years after Burke had settled in England, this essay, along with his treatise on aesthetics, *On the Sublime and Beautiful,* published that same year, symbolized Burke's decision to abandon the study of law and to set upon a career of public writing. On the basis of these two essays Burke won his entrée into London intellectual and bluestocking circles. Horace Walpole and Mrs. Montagu were impressed. His writings struck them as "sensible," even "elegant" and "ingenious." [29] What seemed particularly ingenious about the *Vindication* to his contemporaries was Burke's satiric assault on the prestigious Lord Bolingbroke. Burke's essay is an extended argument on the alleged advantages of a natural society with no political institutions and no law. According to a preface which he added to his second edition, Burke's purpose was to defeat Bolingbroke by *reductio ad absurdum.* The speculative rationalism of Bolingbroke's Deism and natural religion if applied to politics would work "with equal success for the subversion of government." The culprit was "the abuse of reason," "the fairy wand of philosophy." There is an "extreme danger of letting the imagination loose upon some subjects," Burke suggested. Rational investigation into the "foundations of society," the search for speculative "reasons made clear and demonstrative to every individual" leads abstract man to "attack everything the most excellent and venerable." [30]

In addition to introducing Burke's lifelong conviction that abstract speculation was dangerous to the status quo, the *Vindication* announces another persistent preoccupation of Burke's, his respect for the given ranks of God's creation. God has structured the universe in a hierarchy of descending orders, according to Burke. Against Bolingbroke's alleged leveling tendencies Burke revived the imagery of God's "Chain of Being," which had so fascinated the Elizabethan humanists and Augustan poets. [31] "The editor," Burke wrote in the preface, is fearful of "a mind, which has no restraint from a sense of its own weakness, of its subordinate rank in the creation." [32] Here in his preface of 1757 one finds Burke's first indictment of the hubris of Enlightenment man. He was, by the age of twenty-eight already, as Alfred Cobban put it, in revolt against the eighteenth century. [33]

The "sensible" and "ingenious" Burke soon became a member of the innermost circles in the London literary and artistic world. He met Johnson, Reynolds, Goldsmith and Garrick, and in 1763 they founded "The Club," where conversation would thrive for decades. The life of leisure was soon abandoned, however, first for a return to Ireland as secretary and assistant to William Hamilton, himself Chief Secretary to the Lord Lieutenant for Ireland, and then for a career in Parliament. In 1765 Burke became private secretary to the great Whig magnate Lord Rockingham and shortly thereafter he was elected to the House of Commons in the service of Rockingham's interests. The Whigs, far from being a united party, were a collection of factions clustered around the dominant personalities of Rockingham, Bedford, Temple, and the elder William Pitt. Burke emerged the intellectual spokesman of the Rockingham connection, for whom he wrote two important pamphlets in 1769 and 1770 directed just as much at the other Whigs as they were at George III and his ministers.

Burke's *Observations on a Late Publication Intitled* (sic) *the Present State of the Nation* and his *Thoughts on the Cause of the Present Discontents* offered the first major theoretical defense of party government in the western constitutional tradition. Commons should be controlled not by personal connections and interests, not by the "King's friends," Burke wrote, but by men "bound together by common opinions," by men who were in a party together because they shared the same principles, who were "united for promoting by their joint endeavors the national interest, upon some particular principle in which they are all agreed." [34]

What England needed, then, to cure its discontent was a change of leadership, the elevation of the men around Rockingham to the control of government. Only when such as these principled men from the first ranks of the aristocracy governed would peace and order return, according to Burke. This would become the characteristic conservative reflex; men, not systems, are at fault; changes in leadership, not changes in law. There were, of course, some who called for more radical solutions, for an extensive parliamentary reform increasing the membership in the Commons, for a Place Bill that would strike at royal corruption by outlawing Government officers from sitting in Parliament, or for a Triennial bill that would limit the life of a Parliament to three years and not seven, thus providing for more popular control of the Commons. Burke rejected all these proposals for reform and in these pamphlets announcing the theory of party are intimations of the Burkean conservatism that would conventionally be identified with much later years. He criticized reformers, for example, who sought "abstract, universal, perfect harmony" in government, and who assumed it could be achieved by "the infallibility of laws and regulations." [35] His reply to the radicals in London led by Horne Tooke and Catharine Macauley, "The Bill of Rights people," as he called them, was that they were ridiculous to "expect perfect reformation." They should leave "speculative questions" out of politics. He contrasted to these philosophical politicians prudent statesmen, who knew that "all that wise men ever aim at is to keep things from coming to the worst." [36]

This warning offered in 1770 to those who sought structural change in the name of reform is one Burke would make over and over again in his career and one which conservatives repeat to this day in his name. It is crucial, he wrote, "to know how much of an evil ought to be tolerated, lest by attempting a degree of purity impractical" one will instead of getting rid of the evil produce "new corruptions." [37] Efforts at reform often lead to worse ills because society is so complex, so unpredictable, so fragile. Change in one place might produce an undesirable response elsewhere.

One principle the Rockingham Whigs cared very strongly about was justice in America. Burke warned his colleagues in a remarkable set of speeches in 1774 and 1775 about the dangerous course being pursued by the British Government.[38] He was neither a rebel nor a revolutionary. He never advocated American independence and there was no inconsistency with his later denunciation of the French Revolution. The Americans were not innovators or zealous ideologues, in his opinion. The English government had simply revoked their traditional privileges. What he called for was a return to this former relationship. That some Americans saw the Revolution as much more, as even an effort to establish a *novus ordo seclorum,* does not blunt the traditionalism inherent in Burke's espousal of their cause. His speeches and writings on America reveal, in fact, not only no inconsistency with his later attitude to the French, but an amazing and articulate display of the very conservative attitudes that convention would associate with Burke much later in his career.

Burke's recurring plea was that his colleagues "leave the Americans as they anciently stood. . . . They and we, and their and our ancestors have been happy under that system." He approached the whole American question, he told Commons, "with a profound reverence for the wisdom of our ancestors." The government was guilty of innovation and Burke's mission was to "persuade you to revert to the ancient policy of this Kingdom." [39]

Price and Priestley might defend the Americans in the name of the natural rights of free men, but not Burke. "Abstract liberty, like other mere abstractions is not to be found." It is nothing more than a metaphysical speculation, and while "some amongst us who think our constitution wants many improvements," did in fact, strive for perfect and complete liberty, Burke is certain that they, too, ultimately know their limits. Men "consider what we are to lose as well as to what we are to gain." In this calculation he is certain that interest wins out over "delusive geometrical accuracy." [40] The bulk of mankind, Burke insists, "are not excessively curious" about theories of government and the nature of freedom when they are happy. It is, he goes on, a sad symptom of disorder and trouble when people turn to theorizing about government.[41] It is the eternal longing of the conservative for the elimination of rational thought from politics which Burke proclaims here. It is best when ideology and theory are not applied to social questions.

Burke's writings and speeches on America were a testing ground where he first tried out many of the conservative guns he would later train on the French or even sooner on the English radicals. Burke left no doubt that in his mind his defense of the Americans was no more than a noble effort to restore the traditions of the past. In a striking Burkean passage he defended himself in the speech of 22 March 1775 against the charge that his reform plan for the colonies was novel. The flavor is vintage Burke complete with characteristic metaphors, but written twenty years earlier than one would suspect.

It is the language of your own ancient acts of Parliament. It is the genuine produce of the ancient, rustic, manly, homebred sense of this country. I did not dare to rub off a particle of the venerable rust that rather adorns and preserves, then destroys, the metal. It would be a profanation to touch with a tool the stones which construct the sacred altar of peace. I would not violate with modern polish the ingenuous and noble roughness of these truly constitutional materials. Above all things, I was resolved not to be guilty of tampering, the odious vice of restless and unstable minds. I put my foot in the tracks of our forefathers, where I can neither wander nor stumble.[42]

As we have noted, there were, however, many men and women in Burke's England with restless and unstable minds busy tampering and polishing the rough spots off the constitution. It was against them that Burke now turned his conservative arsenal. The first skirmish was on the nature of representation. Burke set himself firmly against the radicals' delegate theory of the representative's function. A persistent theme in radical circles of the period was the notion that the Member of Parliament was a mere agent for his constituents who simply carried out their authoritative instructions and obeyed their definitive mandates, even to voting contrary to the Member's own judgment. This vision of the representative's basic accountability had roots deep in the writings of seventeenth-century radical Commonwealthmen and in the debates of the Civil War and the later Exclusion effort of 1681.[43] In some radical circles in the eighteenth century the demand was made for written pledges on future votes, tally sheets on votes, and electoral reprisals for breach of the trust which bound the Member of Parliament to subordinate his own preference to the mandate of his constituents. Against this radical conception of representation Burke articulated what has become the classic conservative ideal. In characteristic style he did this in the context of a set of concrete incidents.

When asked to represent Bristol in 1774 Burke was under some pressure from its rather advanced and progressive Whig community to acknowledge his agreement with their conception of his office. But Burke would have no part of their radical views. A representative ought to give great weight to his constituents' "wishes," he conceded. He ought even to look ceaselessly after their interests, "but his unbiased opinion, his mature judgment, his enlightened conscience, he ought not to sacrifice to you." Government was not a matter merely of will or superior force, but of reason and judgment. The Members of Parliament, once elected, were there to exercise their superior and disinterested wisdom and judgment on the general good. They did not speak as "ambassadors from different and hostile interests," nor "as an agent and advocate" for particular local purposes. Their responsibility was to the "general reason of the whole." Once chosen, he answered his radical questioners, he would not be a "Member of Bristol," but "a Member of Parliament."[44]

To Burke's mind an alarming number of Englishmen wandered from the tracks of their forefathers in the early 1780s. Among those tampering

with the received constitution were the radical intellectuals who criticized
the unrepresentative quality of the Commons, its archaic and irrational basis
in a limited suffrage. There were other activist tamperers as well. In the
Constitutional Societies of the new Midland cities and in the London Society
for Constitutional Information papers were written and meetings called to
demand the reform of Commons and the extension of the vote to the broad
base of the propertied middle class. In Yorkshire the gentry were mobilized
by Christopher Wyvill and their cause soon spread to other counties where
men like Capell Lofft and John Jebb forged an Associational Movement
calling for additional county representation. All the while there persisted a
Middlesex and London radicalism never stilled from the earlier Wilkes crises
and the Rights of Man Association. From its spokespeople, Horne Tooke,
Catherine Macauley, and her brother, the city Alderman Sawbridge, there
came yearly motions and petitions for triennial or annual parliaments, Place
Bills, and, of course, extension of the suffrage. The middle class tamperers
even had their share—a small one, to be sure—of restless and unstable aristocratic sympathizers. The Duke of Richmond and the Earl of Shelburne could
usually be counted on for moral support, or an occasional pamphlet or parliamentary speech.

Burke's response to the political reforms sought by the English
bourgeoisie is symbolized by the dramatic speech he made in the House of
Commons 7 May 1782. It was perhaps the most brilliant, and certainly one
of the most purely conservative, of Burke's great lectures to his colleagues. A
full seven years before the French Revolution it contained each and every
theme that he would later turn on the Jacobins. He ridicules the reformers
for their belief in natural rights, the notion "that every man ought to govern
himself . . . that all other government is usurpation." Arguments from a
natural right of self-government have no limits, he insists. They are metaphysical abstractions oblivious to and subversive of the real basis of right
which is history as the codifier of national experience and tradition. Rather
than bring the Commons before the bar of speculative theories of natural
right, one should treat it with the respect due its age. Its legitimacy is
prescriptive. Prescription, a fundamental concept of Burke's conservatism, is
the natural and dutiful reverence to any institution that has existed through
the ages and persists to the present day. The House of Commons, Burke
shouts, was "not made upon any given theory," but simply evolved to what
it now was, and in this evolution was embedded the wisdom and good sense
of the past.[45]

In this speech Burke repudiates the fundamental liberal belief that institutions are produced by the willful choice of specific individuals. The liberal envisions society as made up of autonomous individuals free and independent of one another, free of corporate affiliations, free of history and the
past. A crucial dimension of this autonomy is the ability to establish volun-

tarily political and social institutions. These, according to the liberal, are products of choice and contract, and not given to free and equal individuals by either God or the past. Since men willfully create their institutions it follows that they may change or perfect them. Reform is thus an expression of the basic voluntarism of the liberal universe.

That social and political forms are the product of time and of peculiar circumstances, tempers, dispositions, habits, and customs is a notion foreign to Burke's radical enemies. In their minds they carry the Lockean myth as rendered by Defoe in *Robinson Crusoe*. Man is free and his world is the product of his willful creation. He is free of family, free of tradition, free of society, free of the past. This is what Paine meant when he described the American as "the Adam of a new world." In this freedom his entire world, his economy and his political institutions are his by voluntary choice, they are his "by actual election." It is more than radicals proposing the extension of the suffrage, then, that Burke attacks in this speech of 1782; it is the entire liberal world view that informs the very presumptuousness with which they even contemplate a reform of the Constitution and society.

Rail as he might against the furious and misplaced indignation of the English radicals in the 1780s, the rest of Burke's career would itself become a study in rage and furious indignation. What is remembered today of Burke in the 1780s, for example, is his fury at the English rule in India. Burke was obsessed by India. From 1780 to the end of his life he immersed himself in every aspect of its laws, its history and its culture.[46] Few Englishmen knew more about the subcontinent and few were more indignant at the impact and motivation of the English raj. No one expended as much energy and as much passion as did Burke in the decade-long impeachment proceedings against Warren Hastings, the governor general of the East India Company, who came to symbolize for Burke the crimes of England in India. Even at night Burke could not put to rest his obsessive concern with the Indians. He told the Commons in 1784 that the "cries of the native Indians," their groans of misery, "frequently deprived him of sleep." [47]

India was for Burke a vast stage on which the "dirty and miserable interferences of English politics" played havoc with some of his most basic social concerns.[48] The culprits in India, as in England in the 1780s, were restless and unstable minds tampering with traditional institutions sanctified by time and with the inherited order of rank and privilege presided over by God. Hastings' and the Company's most fundamental crime was their assault on the age-old social structure of India and on its traditions in general. It was particularly sinful because few peoples were as wedded to their past as the Indians who

still exist in a great old age, with all the reverence of antiquity, and with all the passion that people have against novelty and change. They have stood firm on their ancient base; they have cast their roots deep in their native soil.[49]

The most obvious victim of these English tamperers was the traditional ruling class of India. These men, "The first men of that country," illustrious in their birth, "opulent in fortune, eminent in situation," men who filled "the very first offices in that country," men who deserved the respect of all other men, were humiliated and subjected to the basest insults of Hastings and his irreverent cohorts.[50] And who were these Englishmen? They were "obscure young men," upstarts, men of no established rank who "tossed about, subverted, and tore to pieces . . . the most established rights, and the most ancient and most revered institutions of ages and nations." [51] This horrified reaction to the rise to prominence, to positions of power and authority, of obscure upstarts—the inversion of the traditional hierarchical order— would be a fundamental theme of Burke's conservatism (and a critical factor in the discussion below relating Burke's personality to his ideological convictions). It should be no surprise, then, that it is the upstart as bourgeois, as calculating economic man, as man of avarice and gain, that Burke characterizes Hastings and his lieutenants, those subverters of Indian traditions. The entire landed interest of India, Burke told the Commons, "was set up to public auction!" It was Hastings who stood behind this destruction of the ancient gradations of Indian social life. "Mr. Hastings set up the whole nobility, gentry, and freeholders, to the highest bidder." And who were the bidders? They were "every usurer, every temporary adventurer, every jobber and schemer," [52] that had come from England or from the bottom of the Indian social scale as camp followers of the East India Company.

THE COUNTERREVOLUTION OF EDMUND BURKE

The last seven years of Burke's life, when he could spare the time from his campaign against Hastings, were preoccupied with exposing and destroying the specter of Jacobinism that haunted Europe.[53] Jacobinism became an even greater obsession for Burke than "Indianism." His passion produced a prolific string of books, essays, long letters, pamphlets, and speeches in which one finds all the various doctrines and themes of modern conservatism, which as Hugh Cecil has written, emerged as a new ideology from the flames of the French Revolution.[54] It is in Burke that conservatism finds its prophet and in his writings over these last seven years of his life that conservatism finds its Bible.

As befits this most sacred of conservative texts, the *Reflections* was reactive. The pity was that Burke had even to write it; but he did, and in response to what he saw as the intemperate and unseemly remarks of the Reverend Richard Price in a sermon given in November 1789 at the dissenting chapel of Old Jewry. But the *Reflections* was much more than a response to Price's sermon. It was a passionate rebuttal to the evil principles of the French Revolution which Price applauded, as well as a renunciation of the whole world of Price and his ilk, a world in which ambition and self-centered disregard for the status quo had, in Burke's eyes, destroyed the glory that was aristocratic Europe. It was also a denunciation of all the millennial hopes that the Revolution had tapped in England.

If the Revolution was the great trauma that galvanized Burke and other conservatives, for the radicals it was testimony, testimony to the imminence of the millennium. It was, as Shelley saw it, "the master theme of the epoch in which we live." [55] On this master theme Blake, the young Coleridge, Wordsworth, and Southey wrote poems of revolution. Looking back on those years, Southey, by then respectable and Tory, wrote that "few persons but those who have lived" through the 1790s "can conceive or comprehend . . . what a visionary world seemed to open upon those who were just entering it. Old things seemed passing away and nothing was dreamt of but the regeneration of the human race." [56] All the poets echoed these sentiments. For Wordsworth "bliss was it in that dawn to be alive." For Blake, the friend of Wollstonecraft and Paine, "the times are ended . . . the morning 'gins to break." [57] For Hazlitt it was "that glad dawn of the day-star of liberty; that spring-time of the world, in which the hopes and expectations of the human race seemed opening in the same gay career with our own." [58]

Richard Price preached sermons on the imminent arrival of the kingdom of heaven. He informed his prosperous bourgeois audience that a heavenly city would be realized in this world. They were witness to "a progressive improvement in human affairs which will terminate in greater degrees of light and virtue and happiness than have yet been known." There was no doubt, he noted, that the "present day world is unspeakably different from what it was." Superstition was giving ground, "the world outgrowing its evils . . . anti-christ falling and the millennium hastening." [59] Price echoed what Hazlitt called "The spirit of the age." "We live in happier times than our forefathers." The "shades of night are departing," Price noted characteristically, "the day dawns." [60]

Joseph Priestley was ecstatic about the prospects for millennial regeneration. The French and American Revolutions were, according to Priestley, "unparalleled in all history." They opened a new and wonderful era in the history of mankind. They moved the world "from darkness to light, from superstition to sound knowledge and from a most debasing servitude to a state of the most exalted freedom." [61]

It was against this vision of secular perfection, of the absolute elimination of evil and misery that Burke reacted in the late eighteenth century. It is because he rejected this optimism and, in turn, insisted on the inevitability of sin, suffering, and imperfection, and did it in a prose style of compelling grandeur, that he has attracted to his name the legions of disciples that spread his teachings to this day.

The principal source of these teachings is Burke's *Reflections*. In it his basic tactic was to contrast the virtuous English and the radical French, which at the same time was to contrast virtuous English and radical millenarian English. Priestley and Price had abandoned the English past and this disrespect led ultimately to the crimes of the Jacobins. The English in 1688 had no "idea of the fabrication of a new government." Even in 1790, Burke suggests, such thoughts "fill us with disgust and horror."

Inferior men governed France and pushed their claims in England. "Are all orders, ranks and distinctions to be confounded?" Burke asks. This would "pervert" the natural order of things, to "set up on high in the air what is required to be on the ground." The radicals (French and English) are guilty of "selfish and mischievous ambition." [62] It is this basic component of bourgeois man, his ambition, which is undermining the age of chivalry and its corporate-feudal world view. Ambitious man would not find his self-fulfillment outside himself in guild, church, city, or in the secure knowledge that he kept to God's assigned place. Ambitious man was the individualist of liberal bourgeois ideology who would experience his individual dignity not as an expression of some ascribed role but as a personal achievement reflecting his own intrinsic talent and merit. Before such ambitious men the corporate medieval world would fall, and from it would grow the individualism of the bourgeois age. Burke saw all of this and he rejected the ideology of these sinful radicals, these men of "selfish and mischievous ambition." To be virtuous for Burke was "to be attached to the subdivision, to love the little platoon we belong to in society." [63] As the old order crumbles, the acceptance of one's place in it is transformed by Burke into loving the particular link in the Chain of Being that one occupies.

Burke takes the very vocabulary of the radicals and translates it back into the preliberal ethos of chivalry. Equality and happiness are transposed. They exist only in the old order where each one knows his place. Many a twentieth-century disciple of Burke like Edward Banfield and other critics of "the Great Society" have drunk deep at this particular Burkean fountain.

You would have had a protected, satisfied, laborious and obedient people, taught to seek and to recognise the happiness that is to be found by virtue in all conditions; in which consists the true moral equality of mankind, and not in that monstrous fiction, which by inspiring false ideas and vain expectations into men destined to travel in the obscure walk of laborious life, serves only to aggravate and embitter that real inequality which it never can remove; and which the order of civil life establishes as much for the benefit of those whom it must leave in an humble state, as those whom it is able to exalt to a condition more splendid but not more happy.[64]

Having rejected the liberal ideal of equality, the elimination of ascribed distinctions, Burke moves on to the liberal theory of government. In the liberal capitalist scheme of things government was a neutral arbiter, an umpire over the race for wealth. It was a necessary evil because autonomous self-directed individuals occasionally bumped into each other. Usually well-meaning and rational, individuals sometimes forgot themselves and interfered with one another's natural rights. On these occasions government was called in to protect the right of the aggrieved party. But liberal government was to do no more, neither dictate beliefs, nor lead citizens to a just or virtuous life. Government, for Burke, however, has much more to do than this passive policeman function. It is a positive tool of repression, in the real sense of the term. Burke rejects, as have generations of conservatives after him, the optimism and rationalism of the liberal theory of human nature. Deep reservoirs of evil and sin lurk in human nature, according to Burke, and government is necessary, not as an occasional umpire but as an indispensable external authority thwarting and repressing antisocial inclinations of individuals. To govern is to restrain man.

The source of Burke's ideal is, of course, religion. As the liberal optimism of the Enlightenment had been premised on the denial of original sin (about the only thing all the *philosophes* including Rousseau agreed upon), so Burke revives this staple of the chivalric world view. Government's function, he writes, is not to protect natural rights but to provide authority, constraint, and domination.

Society requires not only that the passions of individuals should be subjected, but that even in the mass and body, as well as in the individual, the inclinations of men should frequently be thwarted, their will be controlled, and their passions brought into subjection. This can only be done by a *power out of themselves*.[65]

That power is government. The focus has shifted away from the bourgeois liberal's preoccupation with freedom from government and his voluntaristic manipulation of his social environment and institutions based on the power within him.

Since government was not a mechanical umpire merely called upon when rights needed protection, but a positive agency constraining the evil tendencies inherent in human nature, it follows that it is much more than the simple, efficient, and cheap policeman envisioned by radical theorists. Its proper functioning required a deep understanding of human nature, rare skills acquired only with long experience. Governing, according to Burke, is "a matter of the most delicate and complicated skill." One can't simply renovate it, or reform it from some preconceived idea. To govern requires "more experience than any person can gain in his whole life." Cheap, simple, limited government is illusory, as is the notion of simple, swift, and radical social surgery.

The nature of man is intricate; the objects of society are of the greatest complexity; and therefore no simple disposition or direction of power can be suited either to man's nature or to the quality of his affairs. When I hear the simplicity of contrivance aimed at and boasted of in any new political constitution, I am at no loss to decide that the artificers are grossly ignorant of their trade, or totally negligent of their duty. The simple governments are fundamentally defective, to say no worse of them.[66]

The realism of the virtuous man is manifest in his ability to compromise, to temper his ideals with the realities and exigencies of the real world. The naive and idealistic radical has no appetite for trimming, according to Burke. He pursues his abstract rights of man wherever they may lead him, oblivious to the pain or unintended suffering they may cause. Virtuous man recognizes that one must strike compromises "sometimes between evil and evil." [67]

Radical man knows no limits, no boundaries to his excesses, which is well illustrated by the Jacobin attack on, and humiliation of, the queen of France on 6 October 1789. Burke's *Reflections* reach their literary, emotional, and theoretical crescendo in the passages Burke devotes to the queen. All his literary genius, all the frenzy of his fury is in the service of his consummate artistry as he manipulates the reader with this poignant and unforgettable tale of radical savagery. Roused from her peaceful sleep, this gentle soul "glittering like the morning star, full of life, and splendour and joy," is forced to flee her palace "almost naked." Her guards are butchered, and her rooms in that "most splendid palace in the world," were "left swimming in blood, polluted by massacre, and strewed with scattered limbs and mutilated carcasses." The queen and her husband flee Versailles, and have their subjects avenged this humiliation? They have not. It is this which prompts Burke to lament the demise of the ancien régime, its institutions and its values.

Little did I dream that I should have lived to see such disasters fallen upon her in a nation of gallant men, in a nation of men of honour, and of cavaliers. I thought ten thousand swords must have leaped from their scabbards to avenge even a look that threatened her with insult. But the age of chivalry is gone. That of sophisters, economists, and calculators has succeeded; and the glory of Europe is extinguished for ever.[68]

Burke moves immediately from this condemnation of the failure to respect the exalted rank of the queen to a basic repudiation of the liberal bourgeois notion of freedom. What he had begun in giving government a positive role in repressing the evil inclinations of unbridled individualism he completes now by a redefinition of freedom. In liberal theory freedom was the simple and empirical experience of the lack of constraint. It consisted in the independence and autonomy of the self-willing ego. Burke sees this very freedom as the death blow to the old order, and rightly so. It is this new notion of freedom that accounts for no one rising to champion the queen. What it has replaced is what freedom means for Burke, for Burke's theory of freedom differs profoundly.

Never, never more shall we behold that generous loyalty to rank and sex, that proud submission, that dignified obedience, that subordination of the heart, which kept alive even in servitude itself, the spirit of an exalted freedom.[69]

The corporate-feudal world of hierarchy where everyone knew and loved his little platoon is thus revived in Burke's assault on the new age of sophistery, economists, and calculators. Burke's notion of freedom denies the very basis of the new bourgeois ideal. The exalted freedom of a hierarchical social structure is in reality the absence of "selfish and mischievious ambition." Man is free in his little platoon, subordinate and obedient to those above him, in the sense that he is free of striving, free from ambition, free from the restless anxiety associated with ambition. Man is free from competition. His exalted freedom is the serenity and peace of mind that comes from knowing and loving his place. Man is free who has neither ambition to lift himself above his platoon or to topple and replace those set above him like the queen.

What has passed is a social order characterized by what Burke calls "a noble equality"—a far cry from liberal notions of equality. Noble equality recognizes rank, and "the gradations of social life." It is the principle of "love, veneration, admiration, or attachment" to persons. It is the "old feudal and chivalrous spirit of fealty." The mechanistic and abstract philosophy of the rights of man, of individual freedom, has no respect for this nobler equality that unites in personal bonds people who are fundamentally unequal. Radical man levels all such noble distinctions, he dissolves all that softened private society with "the new conquering empire of light and reason."

All the decent drapery of life is to be rudely torn off. All the super added ideas, furnished from the wardrobe of a moral imagination which the heart owns and the understanding ratifies as necessary to cover the defects of our naked, shivering nature, and to raise it to dignity in our own estimations, are to be exploded as ridiculous, absurd and antiquated fashion.[70]

The theme of man's inadequacy, his basic limitation, is reintroduced. In his essence man is defective and imperfect. He requires "the pleasing illusions," the myths, and superstitions that make life livable and tolerable. The radical seeking to free man from the past, from tradition, myth, and religion and who sets him to live on his own light and reason is unaware of man's intrinsic weakness and fallibility. The rationalism and utopianism of the radicals is rejected here as is the basic Enlightenment assumption about the unbounded horizons of the empire of reason. It is the eighteenth century itself which Burke repudiates in his proud admission that

we are generally men of untaught feelings; that instead of casting away old prejudices we cherish them to a very considerable degree, and, to take more shame to ourselves we cherish them because they are prejudices; and the longer they have lasted, and the more generally they have prevailed the more we cherish them. We are afraid

to put men to live and trade each on his own private stock of reason; because we suspect that this stock in each man is small, and that individuals would do better to
avail themselves of the general bank and capital of nations and of ages. Many of our
men of speculation instead of exploding general prejudices, employ their sagacity to
discover the latent wisdom which prevails in them. If they find what they seek, and
they seldom fail, they think it more wise to continue the prejudice with the reason
involved, than to cast away the coat of prejudice, and to leave nothing but the naked
reason.[71]

It is all here, the cornerstone of Burke's counterrevolution, and with it a
great deal of the future conservative creed. The most basic assumptions in
the world view of Price, Priestley, Paine, Godwin, and the *philosophes* is
written off with the stroke of the pen. Man is not only ruled by evil passions, his rational capacity is also severely limited. Without the warm cloak
of custom, tradition, experience, history, religion, and social hierarchy—all
of which radical man would rip off—man is shivering and naked. Free man
from all mystery, demystify his institutions and his intellectual world, and
you leave him alone in a universe of insignificance, incapacity, and inadequacy. But he is free, as the radicals construe freedom. This is indeed where
their freedom leads, and why virtuous men pull about them their cloaks of
unfreedom. In this wardrobe there are, according to Burke, two basic outfits,
the "spirit of a gentleman and the spirit of religion, the nobility and the
clergy." [72] It is the prescription of aristocracy, the ancient and received institutions of hierarchy, and the prejudice of religion, the ancient and received
ideas of God and his mercy, which rescue man from his shivering fearful
self. They ennoble life; they rescue the individual by submerging his individ-
uality in the "general bank and capital of nations and of ages." Who is man,
then, to question his social institutions, to envy his betters, to seek perfection in this world? He is puny and ineffectual, Burke answers, meaningless
and irrelevent on his own. He is someone only when guided by "ancient
opinions and rules of life." Freed from the wisdom and experience of the
ages, ungoverned by prescription and prejudice, men are no more than a
"swinish multitude," or "little, shrivelled, meagre, hopping, though loud
and troublesome, insects of the hour." [73]

The bourgeois liberal saw the state as a mere contractual arrangement, a
voluntaristic creation of self-seeking and autonomous individuals concerned
primarily with the secure enjoyment of their property rights. But the state
was more to Burke, much more than the joint stock company arrangement of
liberal-bourgeois theory, which he ridiculed as the paltry vision of sophisters, economists, and calculators. The state was, he wrote, "better than a
partnership agreement in a trade of pepper and coffee, calico or tobacco, or
some other such low concern, to be taken up for a little temporary interest,
and to be dissolved by the fancy of the parties." [74] Men ought to look to the
state with more reverence than to the East India Company. Political and

social life involved more than the scramble of mortal individuals for wealth and profit, for self-fulfillment, oblivious to those who had lived before or who would live hereafter. Whatever the bourgeois liberal touched became, in Burke's mind, a matter of economics and commercial calculation. "Let us not," he pleaded in the House of Commons, "turn our everything, the love of our country, our honour, our virtue, our religion, and our security to traffic—and estimate them by the scale of pecuniary or commercial reckoning. The nation that goes to that calculation destroys itself." [75]

Calculating and reckoning man was irrevocably and misguidedly mired in the present. Focused on the individual and his rights he had no sense of continuity, of roots in the past or obligations to the future. Burke and conservatives after him turned to a partnership of generations that transcended individual egos. The state involved a contract serving nobler ends. It was a partnership between the living, the dead, and the yet unborn in all of life's dimensions: art, sciences, virtue and perfection. Individuals, then, can never be free and autonomous for yet another reason. They always bear with them the constraints of the past. They have duties and responsibilities to the past as well as to the future.

As generations are linked together by Burke so each state and the evolution of its organic continuity through time is itself part of the greater cosmic linkage that holds all creation together—"the great primaeval contract of eternal society, linking the lower with the higher natures, connecting the visible and the invisible world . . ." [76] Once again it is the divine Chain of Being which is the ultimate repudiation of the bourgeois-liberal world view. Here by "fixed compact" all physical and all moral natures are held "each in their appointed place." This law fixing the places of cultures, states, and social orders is not subject to the will of those who inhabit the links which submit to that law. Once again, like Shakespeare and Pope before him, Burke holds out catastrophe "if the law is broken, nature is disobeyed." If this should happen, if ambitious men abandon their platoons, then there will be a "world of madness, discord, vice, confusion, and unavailing sorrow." [77] Read for this, revolutionary France, or the prospect for England if virtuous Englishmen succumb to radical Englishmen.

So that madness, discord, vice, confusion and unavailing sorrow would not spread to England, Burke followed up *Reflections* with essay upon essay aimed at arming virtuous Englishmen against the seductive appeal of Jacobinism, foreign or domestic. In each he returned to the themes set out in his immensely successful *Reflections,* many of which he had been preaching for nearly thirty years. Well might Burke worry about the stamina of his virtuous Englishmen, for radical dissenters like Cooper and young Watt, sympathetic to the revolutionary cause, were being wined and dined in Paris. It was by no means clear that large numbers of the English would not be swayed by the pamphlets printed and meetings organized by sympathetic dissenters and radicals in the constitutional societies sprung up in each English city. This, as much indeed as the developments in France, is critical in understanding the frenzied tone of Burke's writings after 1790.

The government's response was repression and Burke did more than simply defend Pitt's muzzle on freedom of speech and assembly. He became the principal intellectual influence shaping English response to the radical menace at home and abroad. Burke did this primarily with his pen, for his break with Fox and his former Whig colleagues dramatically undercut his impact in Parliament.

In 1791 Burke published the work that stands next to *Reflections* in the corpus of his holy writ. *An Appeal from the New to the Old Whigs* is at one and the same time a particularistic defense of self and a universal restatement of conservative principles. On the first level it is Burke's response to the main body of Whigs who had sided with Fox and who now accused him of inconsistency in condemning the French. Outside of Parliament there were other critics, radical critics, who in their angry replies to *Reflections* also dwelt on what they took to be the inconsistencies in Burke's career. Burke denies the charges. Consistency was, he insisted, self-evident in his long career— the consistent defense of the mixed constitution which he had sworn to defend from restless and unstable tamperers. Whatever variation there was in his actions was simply due to defending whatever part of that constitution was under attack at a particular time. He defended the Commons from the people in his rejection of the radical theories of representation. So, too, the Commons had to be defended from the Throne and this he had done in his economical reform. His defense of America was no more than a defense of the ancient constitution from its violation by the king's ministers. Now, in the 1790s, he defended the Lords and the Throne from those in the Commons and in the countryside who would diminish or even eliminate their power. The king and the aristocracy were the latest victims of those who would tamper with the delicate balance of the constitution by tilting it too much in the direction of popular government. In this consistent allegiance to the mixed constitution it was he, he insisted, who was true to the traditional old Whig principles; those who followed Fox, he charged, were new Whigs, i.e., radicals.

The *Appeal* was more than simply a defense of self, however; it was also a stirring restatement of Burkean conservatism, second only to *Reflections* in its recitation of the creed. The contractualism and voluntarism of liberal bourgeois social thought is rejected in Burke's most specific and articulate evocation of the divine Chain of Being and its immobile, determined, and hierarchical ideal.

I may assume, that the awful Author of our being is the Author of our place in the order of existence; and that having disposed and marshalled us by a divine tactic, not according to our will, but according to his, he has, in and by that disposition vir-

tually subjected us to act the part which belongs to the place assigned us. We have
obligations to mankind at large, which are not in consequence of any special voluntary pact. They arise from the relation of man to man, and the relation of man to
God, which relations are not matters of choice.[78]

Two basic "places" are assigned mankind by God. There is the rank of
people, and there is the rank of "their proper chieftains," the "governing
part." Part of God's plan is the establishment of certain men, the aristocracy,
in a particular relation of authority above other men, "the common sort of
men." The men assigned to a superior place were "bred in a place of estimation." They were taught "to see nothing low and sordid" from early childhood. They "stand upon such elevated ground" and they have a broad view
of the many and complex affairs of men and society. They "have leisure to
read, to reflect." These men are formed by nature to have "the leading, guiding and governing part." [79] Misery is the fate of any society that does not
give particular importance to such natural aristocracy.

In the years that followed, Burke singled out the Protestant dissenters
as the principal enemies of the hierarchical principle. He rose in the Commons in May of 1792 to oppose Fox's motion removing proscriptions against
Unitarians. His Swiftian metaphor condemned the dissenters for their failure
to keep to their natural place. They transcend their God-given size, their
place in His creation. Their monstrosity was the defilement of nature. It was
the ambition of the bourgeois radicals that he indicted.

These insect reptiles, whilst they go on only caballing and toasting, only fill us with
disgust; if they go above their natural size, and increase the quantity, whilst they
keep the quality, of their venom, they become objects of the greatest terror. A spider
in his natural size is only a spider, ugly and loathsome; and his flimsy net is only fit
for catching flies. But, good God! Suppose a spider as large as an ox, and that he
spread cables about us; all the wilds of Africa would not produce anything so
dreadful.[80]

The trouble with the dissenters and all radicals, according to Burke, was that
they loved to discuss "the foundations on which obedience to government is
founded," a subject better left alone.[81] They were like professors in this respect, who played with words and abstract meaningless questions. His
speech opposing the reforms sought by the Unitarians elaborates this theme
in a contrast Burke draws between professors and statesmen. While the
credit is seldom given to Burke, the distinction he makes becomes a staple
conservative put-down of naive and unrealistic dreamers in politics. "The
professor in a university," Burke notes, thinks in "abstractions and univer-
sals" and only in terms of "the general view of society." The statesman, on
the other hand, has to combine circumstances with general ideas. "A statesman never losing sight of principles is to be guided by circumstances." Circumstances are, of course, infinite and complex. The professor is oblivious to

them. He "is not erroneous, but stark mad . . . he is metaphysically mad." [82]

The French Revolution, toasted by the dissenters, represented for Burke much more than a change in government or "the victory of party over party." It was the destruction of all civilized society. [83] The war with France was a religious crusade. It pitted "the partisans of the ancient, civil, moral and political order of Europe against a sect of fanatical and ambitious atheists which means to change them all." It was up to Pitt's government to preserve Christian Europe, and this could not be the fruits of a negotiated peace and the coexistence of diametrically opposed world views. England's divine mission required victory. Burke's conservative defense of Christian ideals culminates in a rationale for imperialism. Pitt's role, Burke pleaded, was not petitioner for a compromising peace, but to be "great and glorious; to make England, inclined to shrink into her narrow self, the arbitress of Europe, the tutelary angel of the human race." [84]

Burke's *Letters on a Regicide Peace,* the third of his critical conservative texts, written in 1793, contains more than simply this Manichean vision of a world divided between the forces of good and the forces of evil. Basic Burkean themes reappear, not the least of which is the inversion of the traditional and hierarchic social order brought about by the Jacobins. In the *Letters,* however, Burke is preoccupied with one facet of this inversion, the alleged Jacobin assault on the family. The family, so essential in aristocratic and Christian culture, is the very paradigm of hierarchy and established roles and place. Its sanctity is thus one of the cornerstones of the conservative social ideal. The family and marriage, Burke writes, were the inspirations of God which have contributed more than anything else He has done "towards the peace, happiness, settlement and civilization of the world." [85] Yet the monstrous Jacobins systematically wage war on these institutions. They have said that marriage is no more than a common civil contract. They have called for a repeal of the legal incapacities of bastards. They have granted divorces at the mere pleasure of either party and at a month's notice. In Paris, Burke reports, there was in 1793 one divorce to every three marriages. The Jacobins in discrediting marriage have sanctioned promiscuity. They have taught mothers to neglect their children and "children are encouraged to cut the throats of their parents." All the obligations of subordination and obedience are thus destroyed. The Jacobins, convinced that "women have been too long under the tyranny of parents and of husbands" have liberated them, oblivious to "the horrible consequences of taking one half of the species wholly out of the guardianship and protection of the other." [86] So much for the *code civil* and so much for Mary Wollstonecraft.

It is clear from Burke's *Letters on a Regicide Peace* that all such unnatural efforts "to reverse the order of Providence," could ultimately be traced to the "middle classes" who had become the "seat of all the active politics." They

were possessed by "the spirit of ambition" and "impatient of the place which
settled society prescribes to them." Moreover, they "were no longer to be
controlled by the force and influence of the grandees." There is no passage
that Burke wrote or spoke that illustrates more perfectly than this his brilliant insight into the social dynamics of his age. "The chain of subordination," he adds for good measure, "was broken in its most important link."

One text remains in the holy writ of Burke's conservatism. Seldom
noted, the *Letter to William Elliot, Esq.* (1795) is a little jewel and an appropriate source with which to end Burke's defense of the "Age of Chivalry." It
has the litany of by now familiar doctrine. But there is also a new theme. The
august yet pleasing presence that was England and Europe before the revolution in France would be no more unless there arose, Burke suggests, a heroic
savior, one man, vigorous, enterprising and persevering, who with the aid
of God would rescue the Age of Chivalry.[87] He would "arise to assert the
honour of the ancient law, and to defend the temple of their forefathers . . .
the piety and the glory of ancient ages." The times call for such extraordinary
actions. The chivalric hero will rescue monarchy from the madness of the
crowd. He will "reform, not by destroying, but by saving, the great, the rich
and the powerful." He will place "religion and virtue" above all constitu-
tions. This hero will not be motivated by kings nor elected by the people; he
will feel within himself an "inherent and self-existent power" to act daringly
enough in these critical times to rescue a civilization "on the very brink of
ruin." [88] Such was Burke's hope in his old age, a new Saint George who
would slay the sophisters, economists, and calculators.

But they would win, alas. No knight rose up. Providence sent other
men on horseback to change the face of Europe. Here lay the ultimate futility
of Burke's dream in the *Letter to William Elliot, Esq.* and at the same time the
dilemma that confronts all conservatives who seek to stem the tide of historical change. If God or Providence is author of that which is, has He not
decreed the bad with the good? If He is the awful Author of this imperfect
world has he not decreed such imperfections as the French Revolution and
the triumph of the bourgeoisie? Can one pick and choose the things one
prefers among all that God has made? In the perspective of God, today's
change is tomorrow's tradition. Today's progressive innovation is tomorrow's
oppressive status quo. So it would be, too, with the French Revolution and
the rule of the middle class.

THE MAKING OF A PROPHET: FROM HOLY WAR
TO COLD WAR

Woodrow Wilson, writing just before the centenary of Burke's death, wrote that Burke's every sentence was "stamped in the colors of his extraordinary imagination. The movement takes your breath and quickens your pulses. The glow and power of the matter rejuvenates your faculties." [89] Wilson was right. For generations pulses have been quickened and breath taken away by Burke's words; more often than not, the pulses and breath belonged to conservatives. [90]

Burke was, of course, soundly praised by members of the belles-lettres circles in which he moved after his literary and political debut in London. He was feted by the likes of Johnson, Garrick, and Goldsmith, on the one hand, and by bluestockings like Mrs. Montagu, Mrs. Carter, and Mrs. Veysey, on the other. Boswell, Walpole, Arthur Young, and Fanny Burney sang his praises. [91] They all were dazzled primarily by his reputation for spellbinding oratory in the Commons. It would be the French Revolution, however, and his response to it which made him a legendary figure.

The legend had begun in his own time. In seventeen days after its publication on 1 November 1790, 5,500 copies of his *Reflections* were sold. On 29 November the sales had reached 12,000, according to Burke's account. Within a year some 19,000 copies were sold in England. [92]

The establishment loved *Reflections* and with its response began the myth of Burke as heroic Tory defender of the faith. They rallied to what they had long sought—a resounding defense of their privileges and a clarion call for resistance to Jacobinism, to democracy and leveling in both France and England. William Windham, fast becoming a leader in the House of Commons, wrote that "never was there, I suppose, a work so valuable in its kind, or that displayed powers of so extraordinary a nature." It was a work, he wrote, quite "capable of . . . turning the stream of opinion throughout Europe." [93] George III is quoted as having said, "Burke's *Reflections* is a good book, a very good book; every gentlemen ought to read it." [94] At Oxford, the bastion of reaction, there was talk of awarding Burke an LL.D. "in consideration of his very able Representation of the True Principles of our Constitution Ecclesiastical and Civil." [95] *The Times* saw it as a welcome antidote to "all those dark insidious minds who would wish to level it in a similar manner with the French for the sake of their own selfish purposes." [96] Edward Gibbon, the great historian, agreed. *Reflections* was "a most admirable medicine against the French disease," which was making too much headway in England. He admired Burke's eloquence, and "adored his chivalry." He even forgave him his superstition. [97]

The mythic figure of Burke was fast taking form even in the last years of the eighteenth century. Two people crucial in helping to give Burke to history were poets who came to Burke guilt-ridden over their own early enthusiasm for Jacobinism. The young Coleridge, for example, had attacked in an ode of 1794 Burke's "wizard spell" in rallying Europe against Jacobinism. Years later he wrote of Burke as "a great man," a man of "transcendent greatness" and "of measureless superiority to those about him." He could not conceive "of a time or a state of things in which the writings of Burke will not have the highest value." He saw in Burke's writings "the germs of almost all political truths." [98] Wordsworth in 1799 wrote of "that great stage, where Senators, tongue-favoured men, perform." One senator he remembers above all. And so the legend of Burke who said "no" took shape.

> Genius of Burke! forgive the pen reduced
> By specious wonders, and too slow to tell
> Of what the ingenuous, what bewildered men,
> Beginning to mistrust their boastful guides,
> And wise men, willing to grow wiser, caught,
> Rapt auditors! from thy most eloquent tongue—
> Now mute, for ever mute in the cold grave
> I see him,—old, but vigorous in age,—
> Stand like an oak whose stag-horn branches start
> Out of its leafy brow, the more to awe
> The younger brethren of the grove. But some—
> While he forewarns, denounces, launches forth,
> Against all systems built on abstract rights,
> Keen ridicule; the majesty proclaims
> Of Institutes and Laws, hallowed by time;
> Declares the vital power of social ties
> Endeared by custom; and with high disdain,
> Exploding against Theory, insists
> Upon the allegiance to which men are born—[99]

The year before Wordsworth's *Prelude,* but one year after Burke's death, the Burke legend received its first important prose statement in the biography written by Robert Bisset. Burke's mission had been, according to Bisset, the heroic conservative one of holding men to institutions and laws hallowed by time and to the allegiances into which they were born. Burke had seen the dreaded nature of Jacobinism and "stopped the infection from spreading in his own country." Bisset's apotheosis of Burke renders him as the very chivalric savior he had himself pleaded for in *The Letter to William Elliot Smith, Esq.* "He was," Bisset wrote, "the champion who drove back the flames of Jacobinism from our battlements and fortresses; the preserver of our Church and State." [100]

In the nineteenth century, however, Burke the heroic and legendary figure, the conservative prophet, lay dormant. He was remembered more as the model of the prudential statesman whose teachings contained the essence of political wisdom. Even more than this, he was eulogized as a great master of the English language. Hazlitt, DeQuincey, and Arnold praised Burke's prose. According to Macaulay he was the greatest Englishman of letters since Milton.[101] Nineteenth-century biographers MacKnight and Prior went even further, the latter noting, for example, that it took "two thousand years to produce one Cicero and one Burke." [102]

One nineteenth-century biographer, however, did keep alive the myth of heroic Tory Burke and in doing so was an early example of a tendency in Burkeana that would flower in the twentieth century—the latter-day partisan use of Burke. George Croly was an Anglican minister actively opposed to the Chartist movement. It was a time, he felt, much like the last decade of the eighteenth century. His purpose in writing on and editing Burke in 1840, he informed his readers, was to compile "an anti-revolutionary manual of the wisdom of the wisest of men." Burke had been the genius behind "the forces that preserved society as it was," and his words could do that again against the new menace. Croly may well have been the first to refer to Burke's "renown as a prophet," as well as to use him as a weapon in counter-revolutionary politics. Until our own day few have written of Burke as the Reverend Croly did.

The politician was elevated into the philosopher, and in that loftier atmosphere from which he looked down on the cloudy and turbulent contests of the time, he soared upward calmly in the light of truth and became more splendid at every wave of his wing.[103]

Croly was an exception, however. The nineteenth century in general had little of Burke as prophet of reaction. He was perceived, on the contrary, as an exemplar of the school that dominated Victorian thought, utilitarian liberalism. This was in no small part due to the efforts of Burke's second great nineteenth-century biographer, John Morley. Morley was a liberal and a positivist, schooled like John Stuart Mill in the writings of Comte. His two biographies of Burke rooted him in the liberal cause, emphasizing his years of opposition to the Crown and especially his role in the American Revolution, "that part of his history about the majestic and noble wisdom of which there can be least dispute." [104] On the French Revolution there was indeed dispute. Morley avoided the problem by leaving the verdict to history, "to our grandchildren." [105] What attracted Morley to Burke was his conviction that Burke's political philosophy was at bottom Benthamite utilitarianism. It seemed this way to Morley because Burke had rejected natural rights and other abstract and absolute principles. His every utterance praised expediency and prudence at the expense of rigid adherence to ultimate values. Henry Buckle, Leslie Stephen, and William Lecky agreed; Burke was a utilitarian liberal.[106]

These Victorian liberals who wrote of Burke as in their camp were no less outspoken in their praise for him. It was in fact partly because of his alleged utilitarian affinities that they were so effusive. They considered utility, expediency, and prudential calculation to be the heart of politics and so it was that they saw in Burke a kindred spirit. While they had little taste for the gorgeous excesses of his prose, he was for them the theorist par excellence of political wisdom. Lecky wrote of Burke's writings that "the time may come when they will be no longer read. The time will never come in which men would not grow wiser by reading them." [107] Buckle described Burke as "one of the greatest men, and, Bacon alone excepted, the greatest thinker who ever devoted himself to English politics." [108]

What happened to Burke at the hands of the Victorian liberals is of crucial importance. It represents the first and most important step in the embourgeoisment of Burke, his capture by the bourgeoisie, and his enlistment to save their cause and their interests. His aristocratic biases as displayed in his writings on France and India are pushed to the side and his writings on America are pushed front and center. More important than this, however, was the realization that his empiricism, and his skepticism when severed from his "unfortunate" predilection for aristocracy, could serve the new status quo in which the bourgeoisie dominate. The age of chivalry was, indeed, dead and buried. The powers that be were now the triumphant bourgeoisie who had already themselves turned their backs on the French Revolution and the politics of upheaval. The romance of Jacobinism was appropriate only for the assertive and struggling bourgeoisie seeking to find its place in the sun. It might not even be necessary then to overlook Burke's writings on the Revolution. For it would come to pass that bourgeois liberals could find wisdom in this very tirade against their earlier struggle. It was after all, a plea for order, for stability, for submissive obedience to the powers that be.

One sees this deep conservative strain in the nineteenth-century liberal embrace of Burke at work in Woodrow Wilson. It is not surprising that Wilson, the professor of government enamored of English parliamentary politics, would gravitate so naturally to the pull of this House of Commons man. But it is the passion of Wilson's attraction which is so striking and which seems to bespeak some deeper response that Burke struck in the repressed conservative Presbyterian within the liberal Wilson. For Wilson, Burke's was the embodiment of racial wisdom, the instinctive common sense and practical soul of the Anglo-Saxon. An interaction with Burke was emotionally and physically stimulating. To read him was to hasten the pulse, quicken the breath. "Does not your blood stir at these passages?" he asks the reader.[109] Like his contemporaries, the liberal scholars writing on Burke in England, Wilson was struck by Burke's "concrete mind." His disdain for "abstract speculation," and for "system," appealed to him as did Burke's "practical" approach, and his preference for "expediency." [110] Unlike them, however, Wilson was not afraid to meet the French Revolution head on, and to shout

Amen to Burke's crusade against Jacobinism. "The things he hated are truly hateful," Wilson wrote of Burke. "He hated the French Revolutionary philosophy and deemed it unfit for free men, and that philosophy is in fact radically evil and corrupting." [111] That this liberal president could be so taken by Burke is additional evidence of the general historical process by which Burke was possessed and used by the triumphant bourgeoisie, a process, of course, intensified in the United States where the bourgeoisie lacked even an aristocratic enemy to overthrow. The bourgeoisie were no longer frightened off by Burke; indeed, some of their spokesmen were quite taken by his conservatism and how it could now serve their interests.

All would not be praise of Burke in the twentieth century, however. To be sure, Arthur Bauman could sing his praises in 1929 as the "founder of Conservatism," and in 1931 the Reverend Robert Murray could write that Soviet Russia needed a strong dose of Burkean wisdom to cure it of its miseries. [112] And those years also saw Alfred Cobban's brilliant and sympathetic characterization of Burke as gravedigger for the eighteenth-century Enlightenment. [113] But in these very same years a marked departure in the history of Edmund Burke occurred. Beginning in 1929 and 1930 Burke's reputation was subjected to what would become the most serious assault on it since the radical crew of Wollstonecraft, Priestley, Paine, Godwin, et al. had finished with it one hundred and thirty-five years earlier. Irony of ironies, the great maligner of Burke in the twentieth century turned out to be much like Burke, an outsider who had made it in England, and who had also out-Toried the native conservatives. The parallels are striking. As Burke had his Rockingham, so Sir Lewis Namier had his Churchill; as Burke's Catholic sympathies and Irish passion repelled some in the inner circle so did Namier's Jewishness.

All this notwithstanding, Namier and his disciples have since 1929 been the most outspoken detractors of Burke since Thomas Paine, but for very different reasons, of course. The burden of Namierite scholarship has been "to correct" the Whig conception of eighteenth-century history with its scenario of the villain George III set against the virtuous House of Commons. Standing very much in the way, then, of Namierite revisionism is Burke and the picture of George III he had circulated from the late 1760s in the Wilkes crisis, through the American crisis in the 1770s and into the '80s with his economical reform, and finally with his outspoken views on the king's insanity during the Regency crisis. Wrote Namier:

What I have never been able to find, is the man [George III] arrogating power to himself, the ambitious schemer out to dominate, the intriguer dealing in an underhand fashion with his ministers; in short, any evidence for the stories circulated about him by very clever and eloquent contemporaries. [114]

Namier had one particular clever contemporary in mind, Edmund Burke, as the author of the legend that George III was out to destroy the

Constitution. Burke's version of George's double cabinet was a fiction, according to Namier. Equally misguided was his notion of the "king's friends" and the "ascendency" of the Earl of Bute. These were the products solely of Burke's "fertile, disordered, and malignant imagination," Namier argued.[115] But the Namierite attack on Burke is even more fundamental than this, for at bottom it insists that he is guilty of hypocrisy and cant. Namierism is itself a profoundly positivist indictment of the role of ideas and ideals in eighteenth-century politics. To understand the structure of politics one looks not at what Bolingbroke or Burke wrote, not at party pamphlets and manifestos, but at connections and configurations of interests. Men were not moved by ideas or ideals but by interests. Politics was a game played by shifting connections of "ins" and "outs" who wove idea structures around these basic facts of political life. The ideas were meaningless, mere rationalizations for the position then held. What the Namierites are saying, then, is that Burke's writings and ideas are mere cant, high-sounding principles that were laid over the base opposition of the outs.

It is this much broader and more basic assumption about politics that informs the Namierite indictment of Burke as a weaver of legends. His ideals are seen as hypocritical cloaks thrown over the material and personal interests of faction and connection. According to Namier, then, Burke was consumed with "blatant egocentricity." He was "self-righteous," "hardly a reliable witness," and a "party politician with a minority mind." His political writings are filled with "arrant nonsense written with much self-assurance," informed and distorted by a "blinding rage." [116] The Namierites cavalierly brush aside the writings of Burke, so treasured by the generations.

Burke's writings admired beyond measure and most copiously quoted for nearly two hundred years, stand as a magnificent facade between the man and his readers. . . . When the trend of his perceptions is examined, he is frequently found to be a poor observer, only in distant touch with reality, and apt to substitute for it figments of his own imagination, which grow and harden and finish by dominating both him and widening rings of men whom he influenced.[117]

One might think Burke would never recover from the viciousness of the Namierite attack. But just when he seemed to be down and out, Burke was rescued by his American friends, who revived his reputation to heights never before experienced. The history of Burke since the Second World War is thus of two Burkes, an English version and an American version. In neither case is he regarded with scholarly detachment. His name evokes passion and polemics; one is for him or against him. He is despised by one school in England, and beatified by another in America.

The tremendous renewal of interest in Burke in America is wrapped up with the here-and-now dynamics of American politics. As one American Burkean aptly put it in 1967:

As everyone knows, an enormous revival of interest in Edmund Burke has taken place during the past twenty years or so, the period roughly, since the end of the Second World War. Scholars, to be sure, have always been interested in him, and he was widely admired for his style, and by some for his "practical wisdom," during the nineteenth century. But the point is that in our time he has come to be read not merely as one among a large number of other important figures in the history of political thought, but as a thinker of intense, of special, contemporary relevance. Burke is our contemporary, he is an *issue,* in a way that Locke is not, and Leibnitz is not, and even Mill is not.[118]

This evolution of Burke as himself an issue, the defining of one's own politics through coming to terms with his ideas, occurred in two separate stages in postwar America, the "Cold War conservatism" of the 1950s and early 1960s, which still thrives, and the more recent new conservatism of the late 1960s and the 1970s.

Nothing less than the defense of Christian civilization is the mission that American conservatives gave to Burke in the first blush of their love affair with him. The wooers, who included Russel Kirk, Ross J. S. Hoffman, Francis Canavan, S. J., Louis Bredvold, Peter J. Stanlis, and C. P. Ives, had uppermost in their minds the threat of world Communism.[119] "The rise of the doctrines of Karl Marx and Communism" is comparable in scale only "to the ascending movement of the doctrines of Rousseau and the kind of democracy that was called Jacobinism." As Burke saved Christendom then, so his words could do it now. "He has become relevant again." [120] For Russel Kirk the impact of the *Communist Manifesto* was to efface "in much of the world . . . that order governed by what Burke described as the spirit of religion and the spirit of a gentleman." [121] For Kirk, Burke is our mentor in puncturing "the overweening self-confidence of modern man." His wisdom and his example are a mighty bulwark "against the fanatic ideologue and the armed doctrine, the great plagues of our time." Because we are attacked by the same enemy, fanaticism, "the resonance of Burke's voice still is heard amidst the howl of our winds of abstract doctrine." [122] Burke was the inspiration America needed in the Cold War, according to Kirk.

Burke's ideas did more than establish islands in the sea of radical thought; they provided the defenses of conservatism, on a grand scale, that still stand and are not liable to fall in our time. . . . Our age . . . seems to be groping for certain of the ideas which Burke's inspiration formed into a system of social preservation.[123]

At the hands of Burke's Cold War disciples the French Revolution becomes a totalitarian forerunner of the modern Bolshevik State. As then, so now, free men must choose, as Burke put it, between "the fanatics of popular arbitrary power" and "a manly, moral regulated liberty." In this struggle men "will have their faith in liberty renewed by turning to the political writings of Edmund Burke.[124] What Americans had to combat in 1958, according to Stanlis, was what Burke had opposed throughout his life, the pride and self-confidence of the Enlightenment. Nothing short, then, of repudiating the basic American mentality is what Burke requires of America in the Cold War. "Unbounded confidence in logical reason, science, and progress pointed toward the Reign of Terror and political despotism." Naive optimism as well as scheming social projects are equally dangerous. America must repudiate her twentieth-century sophisters, economists, and calculators and acknowledge the dual constraints of sin and history. When all is said and done, however, there is one reason above all for mass conversion to Burke.

His reply to the totalitarian challenge of the French Revolution has a special significance to twentieth-century man. We, too, are confronted with Jacobin types of popular collectivism which would make society and the State everything and the individual nothing. We have witnessed the rise of impersonal leviathan states, claiming the sanction of the popular will, in which every local corporate interest and every personal human right is extinguished or exists solely at the discretion of a centralized Sovereign power. If the Commonwealth of Christian Europe is to survive and form the ethical norms of civilization throughout the world, all men, but particularly Americans, will have to learn the great lessons in Burke's philosophy.[125]

Historically, then, American Cold War conservatism was based on the reaction against the threat of international Communism. Intellectually, the Burke revival was also a reaction against the nineteenth-century liberal and utilitarian reading of Burke. The two are, of course, related. Burke had to be rescued from Morley, Buckle, et al., because the very expediency, relativism, and prudential quest for utility which they attributed to and praised in him is part of the modern menace of Bolshevism, whose most grievous barbarity is its renunciation of absolute moral values, at least those of the Christian, now bourgeois, West. Enter Burke the theorist of natural law. Based upon the meager evidence of Burke's Indian speeches and the towering intellectual influence in the conservative intellectual community of Leo Strauss, who was much more cautious in seeing Burke as classical natural law thinker than they were, the Cold War conservatives packaged a Burke foursquare in the tradition of Aristotle, Cicero and Aquinas. Kirk, Canavan, and especially Stanlis see Burke as turning upon the apostasy of the liberal Hobbes and Locke who had betrayed the true classical and Christian concept of natural law in their philosophies of egocentric natural and individual rights. Far from the philosopher of expediency, Burke emerges now as the philosopher of fixed eternal principles, of the moral laws of God which enjoin certain actions and require others.[126]

This new Burke is, to be sure, a valuable restoration to sanity. Burke deserves to be rescued from the utilitarian embrace of Bentham and Priestley. He is no Bentham, then, and the devotees of both can breathe more easily. But Burke is no Aquinas either, let alone a Cicero or a Grotius. What should be clear by now is that the Burke packaged in the 1950s and 1960s as a natural law theorist was less the result of a philosophical reading than a political one. What it did was link him even more fundamentally to the Christian crusade against Communism. It also served the interests of the large number of Jesuits in the Burke revival. It drew attention to the important religious roots of natural law thinking and posed it as a set of absolute standards against atheistic Communism which undermined all standards of civility and bourgeois morality and order as well.

While there were tremendous political benefits from a natural law Burke, there were certain political dangers, too. The Burke revivalists have erroneously assumed that natural law principles will always support traditional and prescriptive rights. Nowhere is it written, however, that God's higher law is the preservation simply of that which is or has been. There is just as much precedent for the invocation of God's higher and eternal principles in opposition to authority. Stanlis, for example, quotes approvingly the "memorable appeal to natural law" of James Otis in 1768, that "no laws can be made or executed which are repugnant to any essential laws of nature." [127] Does he approve of the same appeal to higher natural law over the state's lower legislative and executive actions when made in his own day by Martin Luther King, Jr. in the *Letter from a Birmingham Jail*? Otis's appeal to higher law was repeated by draft-card burners and opponents of the Vietnam War in 1968. Does Stanlis not see any connection to the Thomist heritage that some Jesuits in the antiwar movement did? Natural law arguments can serve conservative or radical ends, symbolized poignantly by the Jesuits in Burke's camp and in Berrigan's camp. To respond that the latter use is false natural law, that it is egocentric and oblivious to duty, to insist that natural law is always a conserver, as Stanlis and his colleagues seem to do, is to specify the content of God's higher law as the unquestioned support of existing authority. This they may do, but it is to invoke a natural law quite different from that of Cicero, Aquinas, and Hooker.

Another advantage of the Natural Law Burke, it might be noted, is that in linking him to the Christian and humanist past he is reunited with his aristocratic inclinations. There is thus the potential for a historically accurate Burke revival. Reading Kirk, Stanlis, and Canavan one senses this aristocratic nostalgia for an era when Christian and humanist men of letters, men of learning and breeding, dominated public life, unhindered by the swinish multitude below and their incessant demands upon which demagogues and totalitarian leaders prey. In such a time there would be no Bolshevism, not even the competitive egomania of a bourgeois civilization. But this is pure fantasy in America. There is no traditional ruling class to rally here, no broad-acred families to call back to their natural mission of chieftains guiding and governing the common sort. All there is to call upon is a commercial and legal elite. The paradox at the heart of Burke as natural law theorist in

America is that the higher laws and the prescriptive rights of that country are
all liberal in content. The conservative defending American traditions
against the Bolshevik menace is obliged to defend liberal institutions and
liberal ideology. Kirk, Stanlis, et al. might long for the gradations and hierarchy, the stable, ordered ranks of the lost Christian-humanist world, but in
America this can only be translated into the hierarchy of a bourgeois world
where the ranks are determined not by learning or birth but by wealth and
influence. Once again one must be struck by Burke's total capture by the
bourgeoisie in America. He serves their interests nicely.[128]

Defender of narrow class interests, or of cosmic and eternal laws, whichever he may be, Burke flourishes in America today. A thriving industry is
hard at work ever increasing his epic Tory proportions. The Burke factory has
produced in recent years numerous learned books and monographs, and even
a most distinguished learned journal. In such unlikely places as Rockford, Illinois; Detroit, Michigan; Alfred and New Rochelle, New York; and Lubbock, Texas, Burke scholars and conservative disciples man the assembly
line.[129]

There is another intellectual group active in America today for whom
Burke is of central importance, the new conservatives. They are not primarily interested in Burke for intellectual inspiration or prophecy in any
ideological confrontation with the evil that is Communism. He is of use to
them not in a crusade against world revolution but in a more pragmatic
response to the politics of the domestic American Left. Whereas the Cold
War Burkeans were by nature or creed conservatives to the core, many of the
new conservatives were formerly liberals or radicals who have moved right in
reaction to the militancy of blacks, students, and war protesters in the 1960s
or those who have come to conservatism after disillusionment with the Great
Society's efforts to eliminate poverty and prejudice from the American scene.
From their ivy-covered campuses and from the pages of *Commentary* and *The
Public Interest,* the new conservatives, much more established and well connected than the Cold War Burkeans, may not always refer to Burke or invoke
his name and principles but their reflexes are Burkean, and as the new conservative mood spreads and deepens conscious credit is increasingly being given
to Burke as the inspirational source of what is basically a politics of pessimism and fatalism.

Echoes of Burke are clearly discernible in the new conservatism's cult
of complexity, for example. Nathan Glazer writes that what he learned from
a stint of government service was that there were no simple solutions and
that society was complex.

It was a big country and it contained more kinds of people then were dreamed of on
the shores of the Hudson. I learned in quite strictly conservative fashion, to develop a
certain respect for what was; in a world of infinite complexity some things had
emerged and survived.[130]

Radical social programs, he writes, were misguided because their naive authors had no sense of "the lineaments of modern society." In the face of this impenetrable complexity their simplistic solutions were the heights of presumption and arrogance. They assume they "understand the causes of our ills," and that they know "how to get them right." It may well be that we know neither, replies the deradicalized realist Glazer.[131]

Burkean wisdom lives on in the writings of Irving Kristol, as well. Burke had argued that radicals often cause more harm by efforts to remake society than existed in the evil they were reacting against. Kristol agrees. "I have observed over the years that the unanticipated consequences of social action are always more important, and usually less agreeable, than the intended consequences." Behind radicalism, Kristol, like Burke, sees both a conspiracy of critical, nay-saying "men of letters," and the decline of religious faith, fueled in part by a self-proclaimed cultural and intellectual elite. Like Burke, Kristol faults these "men of letters" for their naive utopianism, their simplistic conviction that the world can be made right.

I also regard the exaggerated hopes we attach to politics as the curse of our age . . . to think we have it in our power to change people so as to make the human estate wonderfully better than it is, remarkably different from what it is, and in very short order, is to assume that this generation of Americans can do what no other generation in all of human history could accomplish.[132]

Kristol acknowledges his agreement with Burke on how fortunate it is that most people refuse to question their society and merely accept it as given.[133]

In the context of American politics the new conservative rejects the role of government as problem solver or perfection planner because he knows that in a complex world some problems cannot be solved and in a sinful world perfection is an illusory goal. Edward Banfield cautions against governmental intervention, suggesting that if you do not know what you are doing, do not do it at all. Problems of the inner city cannot be solved, so leave them be.[134] Daniel Patrick Moynihan argues, similarly, to get government out of race relations. By raising expectations unrealistically more evil is done than good. The problem is unsolvable, or conceivably bettering itself; what is needed is benign neglect.

But there is one area in which they plead for more government action, and this because of their very sense of man's inherent baseness. It is evident in the writings of James Q. Wilson, for example, and his insistence on a stronger governmental role in curbing crime. It revives the classic conservative model of the state, the state as avenging hangman, the state as represser of evil passions. The liberal is naive in his belief that good men are rendered criminal solely by environment and society. The modern realist appreciates that some men are by nature evil or sinful and that the law-and-order state must actively punish them, less as a deterrent than as just external deserts for their internal failure to curb themselves.[135]

The new conservatism thrives in the academy today partly because the campus has been one of the great targets of today's restless and speculative tamperers. Allen Bloom, for example, invokes his beloved Plato and Aristotle; but there is another wise man whose wisdom lurks behind Bloom's indictment of modern universities and the democratic societies they mirror. His fearful response to students reads like Burke's frenzied response to the levelling Jacobins.

The young are powerful in democracies for many reasons. Estates are not easily transferable within them, so the authority of fathers is diminished. The hierarchies from which the young are excluded and which characterize other regimes are absent in a democracy. The older people lose their special privileges; and, in the atmosphere of liberty, the bodily pleasures, of which the young are more capable, are emancipated and have a higher status. Equality renders most claims to rule over the young illegitimate: age, wisdom, wealth, moral virtue, good family, all are banished leaving only number, or consent, and force. . . . One of the ugliest spectacles is that of a young person who has no awe, who is shameless. . . . this generation has nothing left in God or man against which to measure itself.[136]

Bloom takes particular offense at the student and counterculture worship of genuineness and spontaneity—doing their thing. What is important for them, he writes, is that the ego be unrestrained and allowed to express and realize itself in whatever banal, vulgar, philistine, even criminal way it deems genuine and true. The culprit is what Jeffrey Hart, a purer academic Burkean than Bloom, has labelled the "radical theory of freedom," the philosophy of absolute negation, negation of all limits and barriers to freedom, all those false and artificial appearances that cloak the only meaningful reality which is natural free man.[137] Bloom and Hart, like Burke, see in this intense expression of selfhood a nihilistic emptiness, a foolish and tragic rejection of all those features of tradition, excellency, and inherited values that cover the weak and fragile solitary ego and which make possible if not the good life itself then at least a life of "ordinary tranquility," which Burke had said nearly two hundred years ago was the most one could hope for.[138]

In recent years the invocation of Burke by academics has even reached the popular press, with Andrew Hacker singing his praises in *The New York Times Magazine* and the late Alexander Bickel quickly following suit in *The New Republic.*[139] But Edward Banfield is the academic new conservative who seems to have read Burke the most carefully, to have understood him the most profoundly, and who most writes like Burke reincarnated. All the Burkean themes are woven together as Banfield ridicules all schemes to change and perfect American politics. It is vintage Burke that Banfield turns on today's restless and unstable minds.

A political system is an accident. It is an accumulation of habits, customs, prejudices and principles that have survived a long process of trial and error and of ceaseless response to changing circumstance. If the system works well on the whole, it is a lucky accident—the luckiest, indeed, that can befall a society . . . To meddle with the structure and operation of a successful political system is therefore the greatest foolishness that men are capable of. Because the system is intricate beyond comprehension, the chance of improving it in the ways intended is slight, whereas the danger of disturbing its working and of setting off a succession of unwanted effects that will extend throughout the whole society is great.[140]

Central, then, in the defense of the "weight of privilege and pride" by American intellectuals in recent years has been the towering presence of Edmund Burke. His mythic Tory proportions increase with each passing year's invocation of his conservative wisdom. He has become for many, as Jeffrey Hart put it, "a thinker of intense, of special, contemporary relevance." To what extent, however, is this apotheosis of Burke as source of timeless Tory insights justified? Is he, in fact, the man that conventional wisdom has preserved for today's conservatives? I think not. Behind mythic Burke exists a very different and infinitely more fascinating real Burke.

CHAPTER 2

Tory Prophet as Irish Schoolboy (1729–1749)

BURKE'S CAREER was the realization of the middle-class ideal. His life is the personification of the self-made man. Born to middling parents of no great means he rose by dint of his own wits, skills, and energy to great success and fame. Like many of his contemporaries who were making their mark in the early years of the Industrial Revolution and slowly undermining the foundation of English aristocratic social life, Burke, too, was a "marginal man." He was Irish with a Catholic mother and Protestant father, an Irishman who made his mark in the alien world of England. In appearance he also stood apart; his Irish accent was unmistakable, as were his puffy cheeks, red hair, and ready emotionalism. Like the careers of other marginals who made it, Burke's was a tale of ambition, anxiety, and achievement.

Burke's contemporaries knew little about his early years, and he preferred it that way. Outsider and upstart that he was, his origins were grist for the rumor mill, not the least example of which was the recurring tendency of his enemies to describe some fanciful Jesuit past in his Irish years. Burke's strategy was to tell nothing. He never wrote or discussed his youth. It was a strategy he had hit upon when only sixteen. He wrote then that "the only way to be safe is to be silent—silent in any affair of consequence; and I think it would not be a bad rule for every man to keep within what he thinks of others, of himself, and of his own affairs." [1] But Burke's critics were tireless and in his own words they pursued him "into the closest recesses of my life, and hunt even to my cradle in hope of finding some blot against me." [2] His critics found nothing to retail except the spurious Jesuit schooling, and

Burke, in turn, remained true to his principle of silence and safety in this respect. It is only from his private correspondence that one can reconstruct those close recesses of his life, even to his cradle.

"I AM A RUNAWAY SON FROM A FATHER"

Edmund was one of four surviving children born in 1729 to Richard Burke and Mary Nagle. He was the middle son with an elder brother Garrett, a younger brother Richard, and an older sister Juliana. Burke's letters indicate a stormy relationship with his Protestant father and a warm and loving relationship with his Catholic mother.[3] The most critical event in his early years was his separation from his father from the age of six to eleven. Burke was delicate and sickly as a youth, showing signs of the lung trouble that would later kill his son. He seldom played or exercised. While his peers frolicked he could usually be found lying on a sofa resting.[4] His father's house in Dublin was close by a canal and the dampness exacerbated his condition. As a result the six-year-old Burke was moved to his mother's relatives in the south of Ireland where he remained until he was eleven.[5] His father seldom could leave his legal affairs, but his mother visited her son and kin often in those years. Burke remembered his stay with his mother's family with great fondness. His correspondence is sprinkled with letters to, or warm memories of, distant Nagle relations.

He returned to Dublin for one year at age eleven and then set off for Quaker boarding school. Classmates remembered him as being rather fond of solitude, of being less lively and less physically active than the other boys.[6] He did make one friend at school, however—Richard Shackleton, three years his senior, and son of the master. Shackleton would remain one of Burke's closest friends and partners in a voluminous correspondence. Only when he entered Trinity three years later did Burke live in Dublin under his father's roof. Burke's father was a difficult and moody man who seems to have been particularly harsh to Edmund. A friend of Edmund wrote in 1747:

My dear friend Burke leads a very unhappy life from his father's temper, and what is worse, there is no prospect of bettering it. He must not stir out at night by any means, and if he stays at home there is some new subject for abuse. There is but one bright spirit in the family, and they'd willingly destroy it . . . Pity him, and wish a change, is all I can do. . . . Care, I believe, wears as many shapes as there are men, but that is the most intolerable which proceeds from want of liberty. This is my friend's case, who told me this morning he wants that jewel of life, "Peace of mind"; and his trouble was so great that he forms desperate resolutions.[7]

These resolutions often took the form of schemes to leave the unpleasant atmosphere of home and his father's temper. In August 1746 Burke wrote Dick Shackleton that he would love "spending a week or two with you, did not some disgrace and some anger perhaps from a certain quarter attend it." [8] December of that year found Burke's resolution even more specific. He announced his intention to move from home and live at Trinity. His father was furious, and, as Burke wrote Shackleton, insisted "that I should not live in the college." Burke persisted in his demands that he be allowed to leave. Finally his father gave in. Burke wrote to his friend, "He since changed his mind." [9]

Threatening to leave or run away seems to have become a conscious strategy on Burke's part for dealing with his father. It remained a part of his identity for many years. In 1757, after he had been living in London for several years, Burke met an expatriate Indian, and introduced himself as "Edmund Burke, at your service. I am a runaway son from a father, as you are." [10] India and Ireland are the manifest references, but the choice of language is revealing nonetheless. On occasion Burke contemplated flight to even more distant parts. Word got back to his father in 1755 that Edmund planned to seek his fortune in America. The senior Burke was enraged. Edmund, having heard of his father's anger and grief, wrote a letter to him that suggests the deeper motives in this strategy of leave-taking. Burke's threats to leave were designed to elicit the wrath of his father. This tactic allowed a coming to terms with the traumatic years of youthful separation by, in fact, reversing the roles. Only by his threatening to leave could Burke get his temperamental father to display any concern for him, concern and affection so desperately needed by the young Burke that he would willingly accept it even in the form of wrathful refusals to let him go. How else can one understand the contrite and almost relieved tone of Burke's letter to his father on this question of going to America?

I am, I own surprizd, and very much concernd that this proposal should prove any cause of grief or anger to you, certain I am that nothing ever was further from my inclination than the least intention of making it so. . . . I proposed it to you as I must and ought to propose to you everything I think to my advantage, with a view of having your advice. . . . I have nothing nearer my heart than to make you easy and I have no scheme or design, however reasonable it may seem to me that I would not gladly sacrifice to your quiet and submit to your judgement. . . . I shall, therefore, follow your wishes not with reluctance but with pleasure and nearly nothing has this long time chagrined me so much as to find that the proposal of this matter has been disagreeable to you. . . . I shall be ready to yield to it always and go to Ireland when you think proper. . . . I am in some trouble and anxiety about this matter but in real truth in all my designs I shall have nothing more at heart than to show myself to you and my mother a dutiful affectionate and obliged son.[11]

The threat to leave was made, the token of parental affection delivered, and the runaway son ended the exchange with guilt and reciprocal affection.

But Burke did not return to Ireland. The response from afar was all he wanted. When they were together their relations were too stormy. The senior Burke fought with everyone, even Edmund's beloved schoolmaster, the elder Shackleton. Edmund, writing to Dick Shackleton, was embarrassed "about my father's quarrel with yours." His explanation for the flare-up reflects both the strained relationship between father and son and the hint of special treatment for Edmund's siblings. The quarrel seems to have been over the elder Burke's sudden withdrawal of young Richard Burke from Shackleton's school, which angered the elder Shackleton.

But if I may guess at the reason of my father's bringing him to town (for you know I'm not his privy councillor) it was a desire of having Dick with him and my mother to town, for really he is fonder of him than he will own.[12]

Jealous over his father's preference for Garrett and Richard, Edmund seems also to have suffered financially from the growing split with his father. Edmund alone of the three sons went to university and tradition has it that he received an allowance of £100 per annum from his father. That is until it became clear in the early 1750s that Edmund was not going to follow in his father's footsteps in the legal profession, whereupon the allowance was angrily and abruptly ended.[13]

In contrast to this uneasy relationship between father and son, Burke seems to have felt only warmth and love toward his mother. Unlike her tempermental husband, contemporaries described Mary Nagle as shy, retiring, delicate, gentle, and the very soul of her family. Burke's childhood friend wrote that she was "the one bright spirit in the family." Young Edmund's early years were spent with her relations in the country, and it was she who visited often and apparently taught him to read.[14] Mary Nagle worshipped her frail, sickly son, and regarded him with a deep and abiding love. When he returned triumphantly to Ireland in 1766 after his election to the House of Commons she wrote to her niece:

My dear Nelly, I believe you think me very vain, but as you are a Mother, I hope you will excuse it. I assure you it is not the honours that are done him that makes me vain of him, but the goodness of his heart, than which I believe no man living has a better. I am sure there cannot be a better son. . . .[15]

Burke, in turn, felt no ambivalence toward his mother. Their relationship had none of the tension and complications of his dealings with his father. Nowhere in his correspondence are there signs of quarrels or disagreements with her. She had not deserted him nor did society expect her to counsel and influence his career. His feelings for his mother are evident in the letters written in 1746 when she was near death. Burke was incapacitated. He wrote to Shackleton:

In all my life I never found so heavy a grief—nor really did I well know what it was before, you may well believe this when I tell you that for 3 days together we expected her death every moment, and really I was so low and weak myself for sometime after that I could not sit down to write.[16]

Burke's ambivalent feelings toward his father and his adoration of his mother are not unexpected in someone who felt, among other things, that he had been deserted by his father for five years and who during those years remained close to his mother. Hateful anger was directed at the father for the desertion, for his temper, for his partiality to the other sons. But there was also a love for father, a longing for reciprocal paternal affection and paternal acceptance. This might take the form of wishful thinking, of masking the brutal reality of a hateful father, with a loving or worthy father—as if wishing could make it so. An interesting example of this occurred after his father's death. Dick Shackleton had written a biographical sketch of Burke's Irish background for a London journal in 1766. Burke was intensely upset by this, as we shall have opportunity to see on more than one occasion. For now, one feature of his reaction is of interest, his anger over Dick's description of his father. In a letter to Dick, Burke complained that he had depicted the elder Burke as much too inconsequential, indeed as too unsuccessful. "You say he was an Attorney of the Province of *Munster* in *moderate* circumstances," which, he went on, seems "to be saying he was an hedge Country Attorney of little practice." He was by no means so inconsequential, Burke insisted. He never practiced in the country, "but always in the Superior Courts"; moreover, he was also "for many years not only in the first rank, but the very first man of his profession in point of practice and credit," until illness reduced his practice. In addition, Burke went on, he was a generous and giving father, laying out for his education, "a thousand pound or thereabouts for me." He died with substantial wealth, too, Burke insisted, "worth very near £6,000." [17] It is a fascinating letter. We know, for example, that this last point is simply not true. The transcript of the senior Burke's will indicates he left an estate of about £1,500.[18] Everything else Burke often wrote about himself, about his humble origins and his father, also calls into question other features of the letter. But it should be read less as exaggeration and falsehood than as wishful thinking.

There is ample evidence that Burke, in fact, hungered for his father's love and affection. In 1758 he named his first son (and only one to survive) with his father's name, Richard. In 1760 after several years of estrangement Burke sent his father, through an intermediary, a copy of his essay *On the Sublime and Beautiful.* The elder Burke was pleased and sent Burke a hundred pounds. Burke was touched by this gesture and wrote to the intermediary:

I cannot express how much I am obliged to you for your kind and successful endeavours in my favour: of whatever advantage the remittance was, the assurance you give me of my father's reconciliation was a great deal more pleasing.[19]

Near the end of his life Burke would speculate at great length about what parents owe their children. These thoughts, as we shall note, were prompted by feelings of guilt on having pushed his son too far and not having cared enough for his interest. Writing in 1794 in the twilight of life, Burke still reflected in no small way the hopes of what young Edmund Burke wanted from his father. Parents, he wrote, "are but too apt to think more of what the children owe to them than what they owe to their children." Parents," he went on in his eulogy to his son, "are made for their children, and not their children for them." [20]

Throughout his life Burke's contemporaries agreed on little about him, except that he was unabashedly ambitious. His brother Richard noted that while he played Ned worked. He added, rather ruefully, that it was because of this that Ned "came to monopolize all the talents in the family." [21] Edmund's earliest letters reveal a preoccupation with success and fame, or as the editor of Volume I of Burke's recently published *Correspondence* puts it, "his desire to excel." [22] Writing to Dick Shackleton, Burke at the age of fifteen, vacillated between self-deprecating protestations of worthlessness before the superior friend, and prideful self-assertive boasting. It is a striking pattern and one that would be repeated in countless similar relationships in Burke's life. Shackleton, Burke insisted, for example, in one letter, could probably detect "a thousand errors in one sentence," of his, Burke's, schoolwork. [23] Burke also confessed his social inadequacies:

I am very much afraid that I shall never be able to attain to that becoming confidence which renders a person so agreeable in all companies he converses with; another thing Dear Dick to tell my own imperfections is, I am quite dumb in mixt company. [24]

His sense of inadequacy also extended to his studies.

I am too giddy, that is the bane of my life, it hurries me from my studies to trifles and I am afraid it will hinder me from knowing anything thoroughly. I have a superficial knowledge of many things but scarce the bottom of any. [25]

Burke's repeated references to his own inadequacies often left him defensive and fearful. Would Shackleton cease being his friend because of this, he often asked. He hoped not. He often expressed fears that his own tardiness in writing would jeopardize their friendship. Only Burke seemed to fret and worry about this. Yet, these early letters also show a proud and assertive Burke. He reported to Dick that the tutor interviewing him for a place at Trinity was very pleased and found him better than "three parts of my class." He did well at Trinity and wrote often to Shackleton with justifiable boasting. In June 1746 he wrote of having received a scholarship. He succeeded in his exams, and wrote of anticipating "still more success." [26]

Concerns of social status and place in society were another preoccupation in these early letters. In some of them Burke adopted an elaborately ironic pose. He was written to and signed his letters Edmund Burke, Esquire. These letters were written in a condescending manner as if from a man of rank to a social inferior. It was elaborate play-acting. In one such letter, he instructed Dicky to take care that his (Burke's) tenants pay their rent. He warned his young servant, Shackleton, to be diligent or else he would not receive the Esquire's (Burke's) munificence. Work hard for your great man and it would pay off; you will be rewarded, wrote the role-playing fifteen-year-old. It was an uncanny anticipation of Burke's own life-strategy, the strategy by which in his thirties and forties he would reach fame. The letter was signed with an injunction that Shackleton not "assume airs that don't become men of your condition; for this and all the numberless favours and kindnesses heaped on you by your imperious and haughty master, Edmund Burke, Esq." [27] Five days later Burke wrote again to Shackleton apologizing for the tone of the previous letter "stiling me Esqr a title that I have not the least right." [28] The reality principle asserted itself, but this notwithstanding, the charade must have continued for in March 1746 Burke ended a letter to Dicky with "write no more to Edmund Burke Esq. but to your humble servant and friend Edmund Burke." [29] And so the other side of Burke's ambivalence revealed itself, just as when he wrote to Shackleton claiming that Dick's letters were like "the company of some great man." "I read them and stay silent," wrote Burke. [30]

These letters indicate that by the age of fifteen Burke was already very much concerned with questions of his own status, rank and deservedness of place. Some philosophical ramblings in the letters to Shackleton illustrate this same preoccupation. He wrote about how often he reflected on "how little man is yet in is (sic) own mind how great." We all seem disposed to our place, yet "the servant destined to his use confines, menaces, and frequently destroys this mighty, this feeble Lord!" [31] Is it possible, the letters seem to ask, that Burke, lowly Burke, can be great? In a line of poetry sent to Shackleton, Burke, an ambitious sixteen-year-old, anticipated the future passport to his greatness:

> As merit which can ne'er be long concealed
> By its own lustre always is revealed. [32]

But one can never be certain that the just will receive their rewards. Young Burke was very much aware of the uncertainty and unpredictability of the wheel of fortune. This was a theme often heard in the new bourgeois age. Fortune and fame were here today and gone tomorrow; the market economy makes and breaks quickly and without apparent reason. Bourgeois man was constantly confronted by anxiety as he sought to make his mark and establish a fortune for his posterity. [33] In aristocratic society such social anxiety played a much less important role. Where status was ascribed by birth, achievement in the competitive marketplace, professional world, or public life was less significant in the formation of an individual's sense of identity. Regardless of ability, merit, or the vagaries of the economy or social order, one was relatively secure in one's position. Burke's early letters to Shackleton often evoke this concern with social uncertainty. He wrote at sixteen, for example, of a "great man highly favored by his Prince and possessed of all that is usually thought to constitute the happiness of a man, but as all human affairs are full of instability," he lost his fame, fortune, and was disgraced.[34] In such a world fortune and fame were not fixed. There was a chance, therefore, that even he, Burke, could succeed. His own desire for fame and place were not unusual, then, and ought not to trouble him. He wrote to Dicky "we live in a world where every one is on the catch." [35]

Like many dissenters and other middle-class achievers driven by the Protestant ethic, Burke came to terms with this anxiety over the uncertainty of success and status by alternating between an active and prideful self-assertion and abdication before forces of predestination. After moving to London he wrote Shackleton in 1751 that it was not clear what he would be—a great success, a "middling poet" or a "middling lawyer." But, he added, in a sense the outcome was beyond his determination; "so much is certain though the success is precarious; but that we must leave to providence." [36] The very same Burke who later would boast that his achievements were derived solely from his own passport could also write in 1769 several years after his initial triumph:

My own endeavors have been of so little service to me in my life, I am so much the creature of Providence, in every good event that has befallen me, that I have grown into perfect resignation in everything.[37]

In a letter to Shackleton from London in 1751 Burke noted that he was "just beginning to know something of what I am about; which till very lately, I did not." [38] He was very much aware of his driving ambition, and at war with his anxiety over providence's handling of his fate was a self-confident assurance that his destiny was fame and success. As early as 1747 he had, in fact, suggested in a letter to Shackleton that perhaps they were not ordinary Irish schoolboys, but that great things were in store for them.

Had anyone now overlooked our letters they should find five hundred faults, and think maybe, one part entirely ridiculous. But let us once get a reputation by our writings or otherwise, they shall immediately become most valued pieces, and all the faults construed into beauties.[39]

The most dramatic evidence, however, of this side of youthful Burke, his blissful self-confidence as well as undaunted ambition, is found in the early months of 1748. At the age of nineteen Burke wrote, edited, and published his own weekly periodical, *The Reformer*. It was an extraordinary, al-

beit seldom remembered, achievement. Patterned upon the *Spectator,* it ran
for thirteen issues in Dublin from 28 January to 21 April. Burke wrote virtually all of these issues himself, and, in his own words, the venture did well.
He wrote to Shackleton in February that "we have nothing to complain of
the sale of the Reformer, few things have sold better . . . the scribblers do
us the honor to take notice of us." [40] Dublin was no provincial backwater; it
was an intellectual and cultural center of major repute. Trinity College was
esteemed even more than Cambridge or Oxford in the eighteenth century,
and with Thomas Sheridan, the father of R. B. Sheridan and Theophilus Cibber, son of Colley Cibber, both active in its theater, it was a thriving dramatic center as well. In such a milieu the journalistic undertaking of the
nineteen-year-old Burke was brash and presumptuous. So, too, was his message, for as he wrote to Shackleton, "we talk in a manner that surprises
some." [41] In the journal Burke lashed out at the great, ridiculing their pretentions—cultural, intellectual, social, and political. In turn, he paraded
himself as an alternative source of truth and wisdom.

Burke's *Reformer* reads as vintage bourgeois criticism of the aristocratic
age. It was part of the broader ideological assault on the indolent and useless
great from self-made men of talent and genius. It was young Burke at his
ambitious bourgeois best who in the first number of the weekly took on the
aristocracy and the decadence and uselessness of its cultural ideals. The aristocratic theater was ripe for destruction, he wrote. Its frivolity and dullness
depraved the public mind, fostering "Vice and Folly." The destroyers would
be men of merit and talent, men of genius, who would, like Burke, have to
put aside their instinctive modesty. The aristocratic order had its priorities
wrong. It subsidized ludicrous and luxurious diversions, while useful i.e.,
moral and ameliorative enterprise was neglected. There could be "no excuse
for not encouraging men of Genius. One tenth of what is expended on Fiddlers, Singers, Dancers and Players," wrote the youthful Burke, "would be
able to sustain the whole circle of Arts and Sciences." [42]

The full flavor of Burke's ambition and bourgeois bitterness against the
great was revealed in *The Reformer,* number seven, published on 10 March,
1748. Here Burke, still the student at Trinity, exhibited a savagery in his
denunciation of the social and political advantages of the great that rivals the
passionate radicalism of a Tom Paine or a Joseph Priestley. Like many middle-class ideologues Burke conjured up the misery of the poor, but like them
his principal concern was more an end to the privilege and splendor of the
great than improvement of the poor. The language used in this seldom-noted
bit of Burke juvenilia is no doubt surprising. It is not the rhetoric usually associated with Burke. It is, on the contrary, Burke out to make his bourgeois
mark at the expense of an aristocratic order ripe for destruction. A nation's
wealth, the article asserted, was not reckoned in terms of "the splendid appearance or luxurious lives" of its well-to-do. "It is the uniform plenty dif-

fused through a people of which the meanest as well as the greatest partake."
To be sure, wise governments should "secure the lives and properties of those
who live under it"; but, speaking of the poor, Burke asked in 1748, "why
should it be less worth consideration to make those lives comfortable, and
those properties worth preserving?" The poor lived lives of utter misery and
degradation.

In this City Things have the best Face; but still, as you leave the Town, the Scene
grows worse, and presents you with the utmost Penury in the Midst of a rich Soil.
Nothing perhaps shews it more clearly, than that though the People have but one
small tax of Two Shillings a Year, yet when the Collector comes, for Default of
Payment, he is obliged to carry off such of their poor Utensils, as their being forced
to use denotes the utmost Misery; those he keeps, until by begging, or other Shifts
more hard, they can redeem them. Indeed Money is a Stranger to them; and were
they as near the *Golden Age* in some other Respects, as they are in this, they would be
the happiest People in the World. As for their Food, it is notorious they seldom taste
Bread or Meat; their Diet, in Summer, is Potatoes and sour Milk; in Winter, when
something is required comfortable, they are still worse, living on the same Root,
made palatable only by a little Salt, and accompanied with Water: Their Cloaths so
ragged, that they rather publish than conceal the Wretchedness it was meant to
hide; nay, it is no uncommon Sight to see half a dozen Children run quite naked out
of a Cabin, scarcely distinguishable from the Dunghill, to the great Disgrace of our
Country with Foreigners, who would doubtless report them Savages, imputing that
to choice which only proceeds from their irremediable Poverty. Let any one take a
Survey of their Cabins, and then say, whether such a Residence be worthy any thing
that challenges the Title of a human Creature. You enter, or rather creep in, at a
Door of Hurdles plaistered with Dirt, of which the Inhabitant is generally the
Fabricator; within-side you see (if the Smoke will permit you) the Men, Women,
Children, Dogs, and Swine lying promiscuously; for their Opulence is such that they
cannot have a separate House for their Cattle, as it would take too much from the
Garden, whose produce is their only Support. Their Furniture is much fitter to be
lamented than described, such as a Pot, a Stool, a few wooden Vessels, and a broken
bottle: In this manner all the Peasantry, to a Man, live: and I Appeal to any one, who
knows the Country, for the Justness of the Picture.[43]

As surprising as this chronicle of poverty may seem from the pen of
Burke, it could still be rendered compatible with the conventional Burke.
Aristocratic writers, after all, especially in the nineteenth century, often
wrote of the misery of the poor and placed its blame at the door of the
avaricious middle class, but not Burke in 1748. He dwelled on poverty as
part of a vicious assault on the great. It is with the stinging rage of the radical sansculottes that he asked:

Who, after having seen this, comes to town and beholds the sumptuous and expensive Equipages, their Treats and Diversions, can contain the highest indignation?
Such Follies considered in themselves, are but ridiculous; but when we see the bitter
consequences of them, 'twere Inhumanity to laugh. . . . I fancy, many of our fine

Gentlemen's Pageantry would be greatly tarnished, were their gilded coaches to be preceded and followed by the miserable Wretches, whose labour supports them . . . that among creatures of the same kind there should be such a Disproportion in their manner of living, is a kind of Blasphemy on Providence. . . . If we consider the natural Equality of Mankind is it not natural for a man who rides in his Coach on a bitter day, or lies on his velvet couch, secured from all the Inclemencies of the Weather, to reflect with Pity on those who suffer calamities equal to his enjoyments? [44]

Burke turned next to what could be done. "The evil is easier seen than remedied," he noted, but he did have a way out. The solution was the classic bourgeois alternative—industry, sobriety, hard work, improvements, and manufacture. This was made clear in the article by Burke's invocation, by way of example, of "a gentleman of fortune, whom I know." He told of a certain gentleman who had inherited a vast estate gone to seed, with tenants poor and land wasted and fallow. Through proper management he revived the estate and made it into a flourishing enterprise. The lesson for society writ large was obvious. He did this not by turning out his poor tenants and raising rents; on the contrary, "he retained all those to whose honest industry he had been witness." He lowered his rents and required his tenants "to make other improvements." In a few years "his rent was well paid, his tenants grew rich, and his estate increased daily in Beauty and Value." The good and wise gentleman also had a solution for a nearby village, equally in ruins:

When he designed the improvement of this, he did not take the ordinary Method of establishing *Horse-races* and *Assemblies,* which do but encourage Drinking and Idleness but at a much smaller expense he introduced a Manufacture which, though not very considerable, employed the whole town, and in time made it opulent. [45]

Burke's model philanthropist was pleased with all he had done. Though his estate and the nearby town flourished he refused to live an ostentatious or luxurious life. The reader is told that he saw no need to buy a new carriage each month, nor keep a French cook. He wore simple clothes to save unnecessary expenses. No bourgeois ideologue would better express the new world view that the middle class was offering aristocratic England than Burke did in this article written when he was nineteen. The ideal was summarized in the triumphant words of Burke's fictional gentleman: "I am satisfied I am making numbers happy, without expense to myself, doing my country service without ostentation, and leaving my son a better estate without oppressing any one." [46]

This was neither parody, satire, nor argument *reductio ad absurdum.* [47] *The Reformer's* aim was as obvious to the Dublin reader of 1748 as it is to the reader today, albeit the latter is somewhat surprised to find these sentiments written by Edmund Burke. The vehemence of the attack on the great is, however, entirely consistent with the Burke that emerges from the pages of his early correspondence. Intensely ambitious, young Burke shared the restless drive for upward mobility that characterized the progressive circles in his day. But the radical bourgeois ideals expressed in *The Reformer* would soon be forgotten and buried in Burke's past. This was easy enough, after all. When he arrived in England no one knew of this obscure periodical that existed for thirteen weeks in the winter of 1748. Moreover, its articles had been written anonymously and signed with cryptic letters. That Burke was their author would be known only years later when his letters to Shackleton became available. Even then, the world of scholarship has seldom noted them. No wonder that Burke's early radicalism was successfully overlooked. But these early principles would not be buried forever. This bourgeois dimension of Burke would surface often in his long career. His romance with the aristocracy would be a stormy one, moving by fits of love and hate. When hate was dominant, the youthful Burke of 1748 would emerge and echoes would be heard of his self-confident call in that year to topple the great and privileged.

This love-hate ambivalence toward his betters, so evident in the later Burke, stemmed, in part, from his ambivalence to his father, an ambivalence which also helps explain his complicated sense of self in these early years reflected in the alternating moods of self-pride and self-deprecation found in his early letters. His realistic sense of his emerging abilities vied with a sense of uselessness implanted in his childhood. Surely he was unworthy if his father preferred his siblings and saw fit to desert him for five years. In his mind this was part of the explanation of his father's activities. But much more important was the legacy of these attitudes toward his father in shaping Burke's feelings about authority in general. His resentment and anger inform that part of him that would be pushy and assertive, and generally rebellious. It helps explain the ease with which he would question and criticize the aristocracy and assert himself while seeking, indeed, to displace the traditional ruling class. On the other hand his search for love and affection, his idealization of what a proper father should be, inform that side of him that will glorify traditional authority, that will defer to his betters and superiors. This search for a loving father, this desire for the proper relationship to superiors, will also help explain Burke's future strategy of entering into dependent political relationships with great and older men. Hamilton and Rockingham will provide, as we shall see, opportunities for submissive and deferential Burke to deal with his need for a father figure. Equally important though, the hatred and resentment of the father for abandoning the child, for frustrating and thwarting his wishes through adolescence, will express itself in a rebelliousness that allowed Burke to challenge and ultimately leave Hamilton and on many occasions to criticize Rockingham. This can be transferred into ideological terms. The bourgeois Burke traced in this study is the rebellious son repudiating the traditional authority of the father; the aristo-cratic Burke is the dutiful son worshipping the father or longing for a father to worship. When Burke identified with the Jacobins or the dissenters, as we shall see, he expressed his and their hatred for paternal authority; when he turned on them he showed his other face, his never-ending quest for the secu-rity provided by loving superiors.[48]

In the metaphorical flourishes of his later writing Burke often referred to rebellious sons and dutiful sons, sons killing their fathers, and sons caring for their fathers. It would seem to be the ambivalence of his own filial atti-tude at work. In 1782 when Burke opposed radical efforts to reform the House of Commons he attacked the radicals by linking them with patricide. He ended his speech to the House of Commons by commenting:

I look with filial reverence on the constitution of my country, and never will cut it in pieces, and put it into the kettle of any magician, in order to boil it, with the puddle of their compounds, into youth and vigor. On the contrary, I will drive away such pretenders; I will nurse its venerable age, and with lenient arts extend a parent's breath.[49]

Burke fancied this image, or perhaps the relationship between rebellion, sons, authority, and fathers preoccupied him, for nearly ten years later he reused virtually the same words in condemning the Jacobin. Among their many sins was pitting children against parents. The Jacobins commit "impious parricide"; they "cut the throats of their parents."[50] The imagery in 1790 was more specific and more brutal, but radicalism still symbolized aggression toward the father. Burke might well have sensed the relationship between his own radical streak and his enduring hatred towards his father. Guiltily, however, he recoiled from the bloody horror and emphasized the loving and caring son. The good subject, he insisted,

should approach to the faults of the State as to the wounds of a father, with pious awe and trembling solicitude. By this wise prejudice we are taught to look with horror on those children of their country who are prompt rashly to hack that aged parent in pieces and put him into the kettle of magicians, in hopes that by their poisonous weeds and wild incantations they may regenerate the paternal constitution and renovate their father's life.[51]

Like Freud in *Totem and Taboo* Burke linked political rebellion and filial discontent. The temptation is there and Burke had much in his own experi-ence that inclined him to such considerations, but he resisted and with hor-ror condemned the very thoughts that could well have lurked within him. In these passages Burke touched certain primordial bases that awaited Freud's further explication. Even Freud's description of how the sons disposed of the father was anticipated by the fertile imagination of Burke. Boswell has writ-ten of Burke's telling Dr. Johnson, for example, that

It was not so necessary that there should be affection from children to parents, as from parents to children; nay, there would be no harm in that view though children should at a certain age eat their parents.[52]

The casual reference to such frightening and usually repressed fantasies is important in itself. But even more significant is its coming after Burke's disclaimer about filial responsibilities and his call for greater demonstration of parental love and concern. It leaped to mind in the very context of anger at the withholding of such affection.

ADOLESCENCE: BURKE AND DICK SHACKLETON

Burke's orientation to parents, to self, and to social issues were very much interwoven. Equally significant in shaping his sense of self and his attitudes to social questions were his relationships to his peers. In this light it is important to turn once again, before leaving Burke the student, to his correspondence with Dick Shackleton. These adolescent letters, which make up so much of volume one of Burke's correspondence, are important, not only in terms of what they reveal about Burke's ambition and sense of academic self, but also because of their relevance to Burke's developing sense of sexual self.

Among his many feelings of inadequacy, Burke at fifteen listed being "quite dumb in mixt company." It was no mere aside, for his letters in 1744 show Burke continually wrestling with problems of sexuality, love, and passion. He wrote Shackleton once of someone he had heard of, a lad slightly older than himself, who had fallen in love with a young servant girl. The lad proposed marriage and was refused. When his beloved married a Frenchman instead, the young man killed himself by taking arsenic. Burke was shaken by this tale; his letter was serious and deliberate. His comments about the suicide were revealing, both for what they indicate about the psychodynamics of his adolescence as well as for their suggestion of a potential strategy for dealing with sexuality. The suicide, he wrote, convinced him that there, indeed, was such a thing as love, and that, in fact, "it may very probably be the source of as many misfortunes as are usually ascribed to it." "Unrestrained passion," he wrote, led inevitably to self-destruction; passion was best repressed, lest, like the unfortunate youth, one be carried away by it. Burke's phraseology is fascinating. Passion was the work of an internal "Enemy" seeking "by all means to work our destruction." It's weapons were "craft and snobbery." One had to resist this internal evil, passion, and the snares it lay in the most innocent encounters.[53] He and Dick must take care "lest he make too sure of us, as is the case of that unfortunate youth." Young Burke set himself against passion and firmly on the side of repression.

Burke's intellectual resolve to repress passion occurred in the context of an evolving adolescent attachment to Dick Shackleton. Their extensive correspondence reveals a younger Burke seemingly infatuated with and dependent on Shackleton. In one letter Burke described himself as a prisoner to Dick, punished for his "breach of the laws of friendship." "Repeal the sentence," he pleaded, promising to be an ever more faithful friend.[54] Burke was mindful of competitors for Dick's attentions, and he did not hesitate to express his concern. In that same letter he wrote, "I am glad to hear that you have parted with the noble Chevalier—Aimé." Again in 1745 Burke reacted with pleasure when Shackleton informed him of falling out with a friend. "He wasn't worthy of you," Burke noted.[55]

The most serious threat to Burke's monopoly of Dick Shackleton came in 1745. Shackleton, three years Burke's senior, had fallen in love with his future wife, Elizabeth Fuller.[56] Shackleton wrote fewer letters to Burke and when he did he made no mention of his love. Burke's response was jealous pique. Shackleton, he mused, had tired of worthless Burke and sought correspondence with another.

I am at a very Great Loss to Account for your long Continued Silence, I did not Think my Dear Dick would so soon forget his friend in whose Company and whose Correspondence he used to express some pleasure in those happier times; Sickness could not have been the Occasion, I should have heard that from my Brother, what then should be the Occasion? I believe I have discovered it at length, palld with the long and insipid Converse of a person with all whose inmost thoughts you are acquainted, the Depth of whose notions you have tried, the fund of whose knowledge you have exhausted, with whom had you Corresponded any Longer you must have heard nothing but tedious repetitions of the same threadbare stuff which has exercis'd your Patients so often before, you have resolved to make yourself Amends by entering into a Correspondence with some one who will have something new to divert you something solid to improve you in whom at once you may find an agreeable friend and wise instructor . . . I have not the confidence to expect you would often write to me all I shall desire will be a line once in a twelve month perhaps to let me see that tho I am unworthy your Correspondence that I still retain a place in your friendship this shall be enough for me who am still.[57]

All was not easy in Shackleton's romance, however. Elizabeth turned down his first request for her hand. In the few letters he wrote to Burke during this period Dick shared his general unhappiness but gave no explanation for it. Burke pleaded with him to confide in his old friend. "Why may I not be a partaker of your sorrows? I am sure if you had any secrets they are with none safer." [58] Several months later Burke wrote: "Are you really still in sorrow? Pray answer; pray keep me not any longer in this perplexing uncertainty. What misfortune can be so strong, so lasting?" [59] Despite Burke's entreaties, and perhaps sensing the pain it would bring Edmund, Shackleton refused to tell Burke of his love.

Burke's letters to Shackleton throughout 1746 persisted in their pleas for some explanation of the change in their relationship. In May Burke wrote:

I cannot conceive what can be the reason that our correspondence is become so slack of late. If our friendship was to be judged by it, I believe very few would have any great opinion of it. I answer for myself, there is not the least decay of it on my side— absence and time only rivet my affections more strongly. I could wish to see things established on their former foundations.[60]

A week later, still hearing nothing from Dick, Burke wrote again. The long silence from Shackleton, he conjectured, meant that he was sick or that "you have forgot me." If the former, Burke wished his recovery; if the latter, which he could "hardly believe, notwithstanding appearances," Burke pledged to "acquiesce and trouble you no more." [61] But trouble him he did. In February 1747 he wrote of the "very great uneasiness" caused by "your long silence," of the "many melancholy suspicions" he had during that "horrid interval," when no letters came.[62] Two weeks later he wrote "all I desire is that we may continue as we are, and that you will love me while you live as well as you do now and as I do you." [63] Still no answer. Burke wrote again, lamenting: "seriously if you knew how much trouble your silence gives me after a long letter from me, you would never disappoint me." [64] Several months later Shackleton seems to have finally told Burke the details of his amorous adventure. In a letter of October 1747 Burke congratulated Shackleton. Humor and bravado characterize most of the letter, but a poignant tone of sadness intrudes with Burke's reflections on his own apparent immunity to the charms of Eros.

I don't know whether I shall congratulate or lament with you on your falling in love, for I see . . . you are overhead and ears . . . I am insensible to charms, when I tell you I do but perceive them and not feel them. . . . Man delights not me, nor woman neither . . . I believe my friend will soon be a paterfamilias, and then we shall in some measure lose Dick Shackleton who will look with contempt on us bachelors.[65]

Edmund did lose Dick Shackleton. From 1744 to 1747 Burke wrote several letters a month to Dick, often several in one week, but only five letters survive from the period October 1747 to 1749, when Edmund left for London. These five are also very different in tone from the earlier letters. They are more impersonal, free of pleading, filled with neutral details of Trinity or Burke's journal *The Reformer*. In fact, it is immediately after the break with Dick Shackleton that Burke plunged into his time- and energy-consuming journalistic enterprise.

It may well have been not simply bachelors that Burke feared would arouse Shackleton's contempt, a rather strong term of disapproval for such a normal difference of status. Burke may have feared that once a father and family man Shackleton would look on Burke's intense attachment to him with disgust. There is, alas, no way of knowing how Shackleton did feel about his friendship with Burke, about Burke's dependence on him, or about Burke's effort to maintain an exclusive relationship with him. There is, on the other hand, no indication that he looked on Burke with contempt. Years later, to be sure, after Burke had spectacularly launched his parliamentary career, a letter was circulated in London and later published, telling about Burke's family, religious affiliations, and upbringing. Its author was Burke's old friend, Dick Shackleton. Burke, as already noted, was furious. He saw it as a gratuitous provision of ammunition to his enemies. Convention has it that Burke was too harsh on his old friend who had "undoubtedly intended the letter as an assistance to his friend's fame." [66] But Shackleton could not have been that naive. Given English sensibilities, to write publicly of Edmund's Catholic roots and family background was an overtly aggressive act. Perhaps Burke was right. It took nearly twenty years, but Shackleton may have finally revealed his contempt.

CHAPTER 3

Burke's "Missing Years"

(1750–1756)

❖

 URKE arrived in London in the Spring of 1750 at the age of twenty-
one, ushering in what his biographers refer to as the "missing years" in his
life. The *Dictionary of National Biography* notes that "we scarcely know anything of this period of his life." Lord Morley, the great Victorian biographer
of Burke, referred to these years as "enveloped in nearly complete obscurity."
More recently Thomas Copeland, the editor of volume one of Burke's *Correspondence,* wrote in his preface "these are the missing years indeed." [1] A mere
half-dozen or so letters survive from these years. This "dark period" (again
Copeland's phrase) ended in late 1756 with Burke's marriage to Jane
Nugent, the publication of his two essays, *On The Sublime and Beautiful* and the *Vindication of Natural Society,* the resumption of his voluminous
correspondence and the beginning of his political career. One's curiosity is
drawn to these missing six years partly because Burke "was afterwards always
exceedingly unwilling to refer to them," [2] but also because they produced a
new Burke. The youthful law student was transformed into an adult writer
and public figure. Filling in this glaring gap in the Burke biography is
crucial for any understanding of the ambivalent and seemingly contradictory
adult Burke described in the chapters to follow.

"COUSIN WILL" AND THE NEW BURKE

During these "missing years" Burke experienced an "identity crisis" and a "moratorium" that correspond perfectly with the Eriksonian paradigm. He forged a central perspective, a new direction and working unity, out of the residue of his childhood and the aspirations of his anticipated adulthood. The phraseology is Erikson's, describing the general features of the identity crisis and it is singularly apt in Burke's particular case. This crisis for Burke was clearly set apart as a critical period, a kind of "second birth." Playing a central role in Burke's identity crisis, moreover, was the problem of "occupational identity." The choice of careers was at its very heart, raising as it did the issues of father, continuity, coming to terms with the past, and setting out in new directions. Complicating the episode for Burke, was also "strong previous doubt as to one's sexual identity," based, as we will note shortly, on unresolved oedipal issues.

These six years were a "self-decreed moratorium" in Burke's life, and, according to Erik Erikson, such withdrawal is an essential prelude to the "breaking loose," the "change of direction" which he discerns in the careers of large numbers of creative figures.[3] It is perfectly exemplified in Burke's career. Physically separated from family and former friends, experiencing a new and somewhat questionable life-style, Burke withdrew for six years. At its end Burke, aged twenty-seven, embarked on a new and distinguished career. Like Shaw, whom Erikson describes, Burke sensed the transformation his ego was undergoing. "I am but just beginning to know something of what I am about, which till very lately I did not," Burke wrote in 1751.[4] The crisis would pass, but Burke would be permanently shaped by this experience.

Before turning to the details of Burke's crisis and moratorium, an aside on sources is in order: this interpretation of Burke's missing years is not based upon the discovery of totally new materials. Most of the material used has been available at least since the late 1950s. It has seldom if ever been used as it will be here, however. Of critical importance for this reading of Burke are the few letters of those years which were made generally available in 1958 in volume one of the correspondence and a notebook kept by Burke in the 1750s published for the first time in England in 1957.[5] It also rests very heavily on two long poems published in both places. This poetry of Burke has never before been taken seriously. Copeland, who reprinted two of the crucial poems in volume one of the *Correspondence,* for example, has dismissed them as "highly uninformative poetic epistles." [6]

These poems, the other essays and poetry found in the notebook, and the few letters of these years when joined with the earlier speculation on Burke's childhood produce a picture of these six years that render them among the most fascinating and informative of Burke's entire life. They reveal that the crisis of these self-imposed years of moratorium centered around three themes: career, sexuality, and status. It was a period of utter role confusion when questions of Burke's being a lawyer or writer, of having a feminine or masculine identity, of knowing his place or being ambitious, all merged and overlapped. The crisis and the confusion was in turn complicated by the extent to which these questions touched sensitive and unresolved parental problems. All that remains to complete a simplified overview of Burke's identity crisis is to single out the other individual whose presence made his crisis possible. He was Will Burke, the "cousin" and alter ego of Edmund. So much by way of overview, now to the details of these years.

For most of these six years Edmund withdrew from the world not alone but with his newly acquired friend Will Burke. Immediately upon his arrival in London in May 1750, Edmund seems to have met and befriended Will, one year his elder, graduate of Westminister and Christchurch and fellow law student at the Middle Temple. Edmund always referred to Will as "my kinsman, my cousin," but there is no evidence that the Irish Burke was even distantly related to the well-to-do English Anglican Burke.[7] They soon began sharing rooms at the Middle Temple and became fast and constant companions, virtually inseparable. When they left their studies they vacationed together in the English countryside. Their friendship was to be a lasting one. After Edmund's marriage in 1757, Will, who never married, moved in and became a member of the household. They shared a "common purse" and along with Edmund's older brother Richard and eventually Richard Jr. (Edmund's son born in 1758) the four Burkes made up the formidable group that seemed to London wags to constitute its own social connection. Their finances were the finances of the Burke extended family. Edmund and Will were to be separated only during the many years Will spent in India. When Will lived in England it was under Edmund's roof.

During the early years of the 1750s when they were just the two unknown Burkes, theirs was an unstructured and bohemian existence. When they tired of working together on the law, they often wrote poetry to one another, or frequented London literary coffee houses, or traveled together in the country. The sojourns of such inseparable comrades among the less enlightened provincials seem to have produced a good deal of curiosity at least as Burke would tell it. He recorded this reaction in a letter of 1752. The good people didn't know what to make of this strange pair. "My companion and I puzzle them as much as we did in Monmouth." They were different, they were inseparable, and they read books. The unsophisticated rustics were confused. Burke contrasted the two of them with another stranger.

What makes the thing still better; about the same time we came hither arrived a little parson equally a Stranger, but he spent a good part of his hours in shooting and other country amusements, got drunk at Night, got drunk in the morning and became intimate with every body in the Village, he surprised no body, no questions were askd about him because he lived like the rest of the world, but that two men should come into a strange country, and partake none of the Country diversions, seek no Acquaintance and live entirely recluse is something so inexplicable as to puzzle the wisest heads even that of the parish Clerk himself.[8]

Apparent throughout the letter is Edmund's sense of being different and set apart as well as his suspicious vision of a critical chastising world.

Edmund and Will remained close to one another long after these intense early years of their friendship. When they parted in 1777 with Will going to India, Edmund wrote ahead to Philip Francis, then an officer of the East India Company, praying that he take good care of Will. In his letter Burke referred to those tender years in the early 1750s.

These thoughts occur to me too naturally, as my only comforts in parting with a friend, whom I have tenderly loved, highly valued, and continually lived with, in an union not to be expressed, quite since our boyish years. Indemnify me, my dear Sir, as well as you can, for such a loss, by contributing to the fortune of my friend.[9]

Dick Shackleton was forgotten, a thing of the past, dead and buried, as Edmund wrote to Will in 1782 "Oh! my dearest, oldest, best friend, you are far off indeed. . . . May God in his infinite Mercy return you to us."[10] Edmund would think of Will in the same breath as himself. When it appeared he could find no other parliamentary seat to replace Bristol in 1780 Burke wrote to the Duke of Portland, "the news of my being totally shut out of Parliament might kill Will Burke." In 1785 an effort was made to remove Will from his office of Deputy Paymaster in India. Burke saw this as a personal attack upon himself, "in the part in which I am most vulnerable."[11] Will, in turn, thought no less of Edmund. In 1750 he put it in verse:

> Your word Dear friend has been my guiding line
> Your conduct was and is the rule of mine.[12]

Sir James Prior's Victorian life of Burke, based in great part upon oral sources, depicts Will quite defensive about his closeness to Edmund:

Though no relation of Edmund, this gentleman was so much attached to him from boyhood, and so proud of the connexion, that, in the language of a friend of the family, "he would have knocked any man down who had dared to dispute the relationship."[13]

No doubt as they grew older it was clear to Will how advantageous their connection was. In 1780 he wrote frankly of Edmund's possible retirement from Parliament: "His retreat is unquestionably prejudicial enough to my little endeavors; which were aided, and as I may say sustained by the rank of Edmund's estimation in the world."[14] But it was more than mere opportunism that initially bound the two. In the early 1750s when neither of them was famous they were as one; they lived and traveled together, wrote pamphlets and poetry together, deserted law together. It was Will who would give up a parliamentary seat in 1765 so that Edmund could begin his career. In 1780 Will again would seek to find Edmund a seat. He genuinely thought of Edmund as "the only man capable of retrieving her [that ill-fated country] from ruin." [15] He could be carried away about Edmund and write: "Perhaps I think too much of my dear Edmund; but that, if it is a fault, is one I dont wish to mend." Edmund appreciated the devotion of Will. He would write Archbishop Markham in 1771:

Looking back to the course of my life, I remember no one considerable benefit in the whole of it which I did not mediately or immediately derive from him. To him I owe my connexion with Lord Rockingham. To him I am indebted for my seat in Parliament. . . . To encourage me he gave his own interest the first stab . . . This my Lord was true friendship, and if I act an honorable part in life, the first of all benefits, it is in great measure due to him.[16]

There is no doubt, then, that the friendship of Edmund and Will would be lasting and heartfelt; yet no two people would seem to have been more unlike one another. The letter to Markham in 1771 was, in fact, part of Edmund's response to Markham's criticism of his association with such an unsavory character. His contemporaries were struck by the contrast between Burke and his closest friend. Sir Gilbert Elliot said of Edmund, "the society in which Burke lives is less like himself than that of any other man." [17] Will's personality seemed the very antithesis of Edmund's, especially of Burke as conventionally rendered. It was principally Will who earned the Burkes the characterization of "Irish Adventurers." [18] While Edmund's image would be the man of highest principle aloof from material gain, Will's was the very quintessence of the speculative gambler by no means above chicanery and double-dealing. He gravitated to public positions with potential for big money. In 1759 he got himself appointed secretary and registrar of the island of Guadeloupe, and he turned out government pamphlets in these years stressing the great profit to be had from trade with the West Indies. Through this service it was William who developed the connection with Lord Verney which would lead to even more significant ties with Lord Rockingham. Verney secured a seat in Parliament for Will, which he in turn gave over to Edmund. Will was himself given a seat several years later. He made fortunes in stock and India speculations in the '60s and he lost his fortunes in the '70s. He also lost his Parliamentary seat in 1774 and turned his attention to recouping his fortune in India. After an early visit in the late 1770s he would spend nearly a decade in India from 1782 to 1792. Even with the influence of Edmund on his side Will never was able to undo the financial disaster of his earlier failures that had indebted him to Verney and Verney's heirs. Will was the very embodiment of the commercial and entreprenurial spirit. He once wrote, "I never yet had a quarter of an hours conversation with a stranger, before I knew whether he had a fortune or not." [19] Ever scheming, ever calculating, Will is captured best in a letter from India to young Richard:

Now of all things on earth a man must fight up against the regret of not finding his fortunes answered to his just hope . . . on every ground a man must wait the event of the coming hour, without any fond regard of the irretrievable Past . . . not to recur again, to what my letters to your father now, & formerly to yourself mentioned of vast fortunes from the remittance of the public debt of near 600,000 which would without risk or the possibility of failure put 6 times 25000£ in my pocket. But not to hope that Event too eagerly I can scarcely fail of the whole remittance from hence, of the whole of the M's troops, to Madras—about 160,000£ a year. & my profit can not be less than 5000£ a year—of course I do not draw on England for my Subsistence.—it will cost me near 3000—but the pay at home will with the remittance of two—give 4000£ a year clear in London,—to be used of course for our common benefit,—if Good can buy in the Bonds, this fund, with what I have, may clear me, and clear Beaconsfield.[20]

As one might expect, Will has fared poorly at the hands of those who have written on Edmund. He is something of an embarrassment. To Magnus he was "sinister and disreputable"; to Dixon Wecter he was a "sharp and self-assertive adventurer"; to Thomas Copeland he was "an aggressive, not-over-scrupulous person." [21] When the question is raised as to why the two Burkes first became and then remained such close friends the explanations vary from Edmund's need for "intense friendship," to citations of Edmund's humanity, his loyalty to family and kin. But it may well be that what appealed to Edmund about Will throughout his life was in fact the latter's very personification of aggressive self-assertion, i.e., of the bourgeois spirit. Will became for Edmund a projection of part of his own ambivalent self. In Will he could play that role with no disguises. In the political arena his other side, the aristocratic, would dominate. To understand how this bifurcation of Edmund's private self worked itself out through the relationship with Will requires looking more closely at those critical years of crisis and moratorium when their bond was forged.

The reconstruction of these years is based in part on a notebook inscribed "found among Mr. Wm. Burke's papers by W. Cuppage." (Cuppage was William's executor.) The notebook contains twenty-four pieces—poems, essays, and character sketches—partly in the hand of Edmund and partly in the hand of William. Some pieces are clearly labelled as to author, others are not. Some are dated, others are not; the dates given span the six years 1750–1756.[22] The first and most interesting item in the notebook is a long poem, "The Muse Divorced," "An Epistle from Mr. E. Burke to his friend Mr. W. Burke," dated November 1750. It reveals a tortured young Edmund at war with himself. While his ambivalence on the question of career is ostensibly the central theme, the poem deals equally as much with his anguish over the two other issues raised by the question of career—status and sexuality. The poem articulates Edmund's concern over whether he should pursue the law and thus follow his father's wishes or whether he should become a writer and public figure, a taste of which he had already had in Dublin. This dilemma was depicted as a choice between keeping to his assigned place, the lower middle-class status of his origins, or seeking the fame and acclaim of a higher public status. These categories were very much in his head at this time. We know, for example, that in August 1751 he wrote to Shackleton about the possibility of his becoming a "middling lawyer." [23] Law versus writing and public life became in his mind a choice between the status quo and rebellion, between dependence and striving for mastery and rank:

> Whate'er the stars determine at our Birth,
> Whether to conquer, or to Plough the Earth;
> Whether to wear the Ribband, or the Rope,
> Whether to be, or whether burn a Pope,
> Whether in gouty Pride on down to loll,
> Or Range with midnight whores the cold patrol,
> This rules our days; in vain the wretch would fly
> His stars o'erlook him with a conscious eye,
> Drag back the Rebel to his destined Fate.
> Een I while arming for the wordy war
> Neglect the spoils and trophies of the Bar,
> Drawn by th' attraction of my natal Ray.
> Against my Reason often quit my way.
> Yet preach to others in the same distress,
> Dissuade with words, and then dissuade no less,
> By sad Example of my own success. [24]

The career ambivalence and its association with a choice between ambition and the social status quo was linked to the dichotomy of Protestantism (dissenters burn popes) and Catholicism, which looks back to the polarity represented by his own parents. The aristocracy is contrasted with the sexually promiscuous, which anticipates a dichotomy we will encounter later in his letters. What dominates the poetry, as it dominated his youthful mind, was the concern that linked his personal being and public concerns:

> His stars o'erlook him with a conscious eye,
> Drag back the Rebel to his destined fate.

Edmund described the temptations of fame, "All the vain hopes of profit and of praise." It required abandoning law:

> The idle learning, which I wish forgot,
> The high romantick flights, the mad designs,
> Th' unnumbered number of neglected lines,

> The Itch, that first to scribbling turn'd my quill
> The fatal itch, that makes me scribble still.

But the Law is what one of his station ought to choose; only the privileged and powerful could indulge the luxury of a literary and public career. He tells the muse who sought to turn him from the law:

> Go! And may better fate thy steps attend
> Go! And learn better how to chuse a friend;
> Some Fop whose pride and vast Estate admit,
> The weighty charge of Idleness and wit.

The temptress muse is also Will! Will is the restless active spirit of assertion, of bourgeois mobility and improvement of status, and he is also the intimate friend who confronts Edmund with another anguished problem of identity. Edmund's sexual ambivalence is merged with career ambivalence, and social role with sexual role. The words take on subtler shadings as nuances of homosexual love parallel the theme of rebellion and conventionality.

> Thus whilst I spoke, my better Genius led;
> And yet anon I wish'd it all unsaid.
> The poets ail no remedies can ease,
> Because we cherish still our own disease;
> What e'er the turn of mind still verse presents,
> Here all the Passions have their Proper vents. . . .
> If the soft impulse of Desire we prove
> What so ally'd as Poetry and love?
> If wiser grown, we would Redeem our time,
> 'Tis but good manners to take leave in Rhime.
> If we succeed, success gives cause t'indite
> If we should fail, Despair provokes to write.
> The strong and weak consume in the same fire,
> The force unequaled, equal the Desire.

The paranoid fancies of Burke's letters describing their provincial holidays are evoked again as he asks:

> What Whips! What stings! What furies drive us on?
> Why all this mighty rage to be undone?
> Why still persist when ruin and Disgrace,
> When want and shame present their hideous face?
> When scornful silence loudly cries, Abstain,
> Our friends advise, our parents preach in Vain.

Occasionally the homosexual theme dominates, but the social theme is always there.

> Rous'd with these thoughts I lash my lazy side,
> And all my strength collect and all my Pride

All boyish dreams forever disavow
Then dream, and trifle, play, and rhime as now,
This of myself I know, and more amiss
But should Will Burke presume to tell me this,
The fool! The coxcomb! The ill mannered *elf!*
Who dares to think me—what I think myself.
   Can we, my friend, with any conscience bear
To shew our minds sheer naked as they are,
Remove each veil of custom, pride or Art,
Nor stretch a hand to hide one shameful part?
An equal share of Scorn and Danger find,
A Naked body, and an open mind
Both sights unusual, sights which never fail
To make the Witty laugh, the Pious Rail,
The children fly for fear, the women scream
And sages cry the world has lost its shame.
   And even some friends (that sacred name) we have
Whom so to keep, tis proper to deceive—
Who lofty notions build on Plato's plan—
And grow quite angry when they find you *man;* [25]

Once again outsiders look and fear "sights unusual." Indeed, when Edmund uses a clergyman to describe a conventional alternative to social ambition and search for gain, rather obvious attention is paid to the clergyman's conventional sexuality.

The hopeful parson new arriv'd in town,
Who just has got a wife, and just a gown,
Tho' young, yet rev'rend; warm yet nice in love,
Enjoys chast raptures with his Turtle Dove,
What pretty Chat! What soft endearing Arts!
What blinding souls! What Sympathy of Hearts!
This Swain, if nature to the test we bring
Tastes more true joy and nearer to the Spring
Than we, who vainly wise consume our years,
Ills to prevent, that only mock our cares,
Or tho' our fortunes our desires should shape,
Gain all we wish, and all we fear escape;

All is not one-sided; this is still ambivalence. The law, keeping to one's rank, and conventional sexuality still tempt and taste of joy.

Two years later in another poem found in the notebook Edmund returned to these same themes. Once again the dominant note is his ambivalent feelings on asserting his ambitious self or accepting his assigned place. The setting for the poem is a stay in the country home of Dr. Nugent, an Irish Catholic whose daughter Burke would ultimately marry. Nugent had brought Edmund back to health from what must certainly have been a breakdown.

> Tis now two autums, since he chanc'd to find,
> A Youth of Body broke, infirm of mind.[26]

If, as the editor of the correspondence suggests, this poem to Nugent was written in the fall of 1752, the breakdown would have occurred around the time Burke wrote the earlier poem to William. Two years may have passed, but the concerns were the same. Burke contrasted the peaceful calm of the countryside—"the sweet oblivion of a life of care"—with the "Busy bustle of the town." These are merely metaphorical renderings of his divided self—the countryside is deference to order and tradition, the town is striving and ambition.

> For solitude is neither here nor there,
> Turley's no more retired than Westminster,
> In vain we fly from place to place to find
> What not in place consists, but in the mind.

The sexual and social themes were still interwoven. Ambition and homosexuality weave their pattern between the lines. Both are tempting and both are forbidden. A part of oneself seeks both, a part resists both.

> Heav'n bless those folks, who seeming to be wise
> With specious names their faults would canonize—
> Yet under Planets so perverse are born,
> They wish to be the very things they scorn,
> That sage who calls a fop mankinds disgrace,
> Envies that fop, his figure and his face.
> That Dame, who rails at whores from morn till night
> Repines that infamy can buy delight;
> And I, who think it is the times reproach,
> To see a scoundrel Gamester in his coach,
> Think modestly 'twould have a better air,
> To see my humble self exalted there.

Nowhere is Burke more self-revealing than in this poem. The very depths of his divided self are stripped bare.

> Mean time ten thousand cares distract my life,
> And keep me always with myself at strife.

This strife is both social and sexual. His sense of driving ambition held out great promise, but not only was it balanced by countertendencies, the promise itself left him fearful.

> Too indolent on flying wealth to seize,
> Of wealth too covetous to be at ease.
> I look at Wisdom, wonder, and Adore
> I look, I wonder, but I do no more.
> Timrous the Heights of everything I fear,

> Perhaps even Wisdom may be bought too Dear,
> The Tortoise snatch'd aloft, to highest Air,
> Was high 'tis true, but was not happy there.
> Shall I then vapour in a stoic strain,
> Who, while I boast, must writhe myself for pain;
> Shall I who grope my way with purblind Eyes,
> Shall such as I, pretend to dogmatise?
> Better in one low path secure to crawl,
> To Doubt of all things, and to learn from all.

Was it better to seek the heights or to crawl on the lower path? Years later, as we have seen, he would write to Richmond, expressing one part of his divided identity, that such as he, Burke, were but crawling vines compared to the great oaks of the likes of Richmond which reached "to highest air."

The strife within, as it referred to Edmund's sexual identity, was now further complicated by his affection for Jane Nugent. Was he to be the assertive male and thus a fit suitor for Jane, or was he to be the passive idle female drawn to and dependent on Will's masculinity? The poem ends with what appears to be a resolve on the former. He would soar, not creep; but this was not done without its sense of William's hurt.

> But Providence has more than made amends
> And given what fortune cannot give us—friends.
> This pleasing thought yet further to pursue
> I want the aid of such a friend as you
> And hers no less, in whom just heaven has joined,
> The weakest body, with the firmest mind,
> We'll give you such good Humour as we have,
> Nay I will laugh, William shall be grave,
> Our fair and absent friend we'll toast the while.
> (I Will not wrong her in this creeping stile.)

OF MARRIAGE AND AMBITION

Burke's marriage to Jane in 1756 marked the end of his six-year moratorium. During these six years he also abandoned the study of law. It would seem, then, that he emerged from his years of self-discovery by resolving his crisis and fixing on his identity, choosing the masculine alternative in both cases. But it was by no means so simple, for he did not abandon Will. He, in fact, chose both. He would spend much of his private adult life with both Jane and Will under his roof. The resolution of his ambivalence took the unique form of perpetuation in the components of his immediate household. Jane, as we shall see, was the embodiment of the traditional, feminine, and passive—Catholic as well. Will was the embodiment of bourgeois man on the make. In Will's enterprise Edmund could vicariously satisfy the ambitious bourgeois longings within himself, while actively pursuing a public career notable for its aristocratic sympathies—reflective of the other side of his social ambivalence. Meanwhile, Edmund could express his male identity vis-à-vis Jane and his lingering female identity could be gratified by the relationship (latent or overt) with William which survived the marriage with Jane. Having both Jane and William in his household also brought into acceptable equilibrium the held over problem of the parental generation. Will provided Edmund the mirror of his father (Protestant, masculine, and assertive) and Jane his mother (Catholic, feminine, and passive). What ended the moratorium, then, was the common household of the three Burkes. Edmund's ambivalence was never totally resolved; it was made bearable. It would constantly resurface in later years in both its sexual and social dimensions. What Burke did with his basic ambivalences in these early years of the 1750s was to tame them by projecting and personifying his internal strife onto the members of his immediate household; he domesticated them.

When his moratorium was over, Burke would commit himself to an active and assertive public life, first in letters then in politics. The success of this depended, in turn, on the successful containment of his personal strife within the small circle of his household. Restricted to these limited boundaries it was manageable. At the same time, losing himself in public life turned his thoughts from whatever painful issues lurked at home, beneath the surface calm. This may account, in part, for Burke's obsessive fears at having the privacy of his household violated, having his private realm exposed and dragged into the public arena. His anger at Shackleton's letter to the London press a decade later thus takes on additional significance. His private life was no concern of others. But it could well be that he feared not only religious skeletons in the closet but others as well. When Shackleton's piece appeared, for example, Burke wrote his childhood friend:

It is evidently written by an intimate friend. It is full of anecdotes and particulars of my life. It therefore cuts deep; I am sure I have nothing in my family, my circumstances, or my conduct that an honest man ought to be ashamed of. But the more circumstances of all these that are brought out, the more materials are furnished for malice to work upon; and I assure you that it will manufacture them to the utmost. Hitherto much as I have been abused, my table and my bed were left sacred.[27]

Shackleton had, in fact, revealed absolutely nothing scandalous about Burke's private life. Burke was fearful, nevertheless, that any concern with his biography would "pursue me into the closest recesses of my life." [28] This could be read on one level as merely reflecting Burke's concern with his Irish and thus alien and Catholic roots; but his preoccupation with keeping his private life secret could also indicate that he saw Shackleton's article as merely the opening wedge of concerted efforts to find "some blot against me," perhaps a potentially more damaging blot than his Hibernian roots, a blot of a sexual nature. Burke was fearful lest his private life become a political issue and threaten his public career, but he was also fearful lest the personal pain of his earlier years so apparently settled in the household arrangement be brought forth once again front and center to his consciousness. In an important letter we have cited earlier Burke hinted at a maelstrom of deep-seated personal problems he would rather forget, indeed, that he fled from or worked out by the diversion of an active public life. The letter was, interestingly enough, to Shackleton, who just might have been expected to understand what Burke was alluding to. The letter was written in 1779 when Burke had suffered a series of political setbacks and contemplated retirement from political life. To do so, he wrote, might invite even more serious discomfort.

So little satisfaction have I that I should not hesitate a moment to retire from publick Business—if I was not in some doubt of the Duty a man has that goes a certain length in those things; and if it were not from an observation that there are often obscure vexations and contests in the most private life, which may as effectually destroy a man's peace as anything which happens in publick contentions.[29]

Burke's peace and the end of his moratorium were both very much wrapped up with his marriage to Jane Nugent in 1756. From Burke's notebook description of her we have a picture of all the stereotypical feminine virtues that hark back to Burke's sense of his mother, on the one hand, and which anticipate the language Burke would later use to describe the aristocracy, on the other. She possessed "delicacy" and "softness." Jane was "usually grave." Her voice was "low, soft musick; not formed to rule in publick assemblies,—but to charm those who can distinguish a company from a crowd." She did not do or say "striking things;" her skill consisted in her "avoiding such as she ought not to say or do." Her mind worked "not by reasoning but sagacity." There is in fact a striking similarity in the traits Burke attributed to Jane in his notebook in 1756 and his later visions of the aristocracy, as we shall see. "She has a true generosity of temper," a "natural disposition to oblige," and "everything violent is contrary to the gentleness of her disposition." [30] Years later Fanny Burney would describe Jane Burke in nearly identical terms. She was "soft, gentle, reasonable, and obliging." [31]

The notebook also contains a sketch of Will Burke written by Edmund.[32] While primarily trivial, e.g., describing Will's taste in books, there are some passages of interest, especially those in which Will appears very much like Edmund's violent and temperamental father. The sketch begins with Edmund suggesting that, while it may seem otherwise, knowing someone to "the last degree of intimacy" is not helpful in drawing his character. But this does not deter him. He proceeded to offer a prototypical masculine characterization of Will. His emotions, love, joy, hatred, are "sudden and violent," coming on "like fits." While they last, "nothing can oppose them." These violent fits then easily pass away and "leave him in a serenity which has not the least remains of the former passions." But passions return "with all their former violence, commit their former havoc, and pass away with the former facility." Edmund also saw Will as jealous and suspicious. His mind was like birds' feathers; "whilst you stroke them with the grain nothing can be more smooth, if you rub against it, nothing more rough and unpliable." Edmund ended the sketch by insisting that Will was not simply what he appeared to be. One might take him "for a man confident and assuming"; in reality, however, he was, according to Edmund, "timorous and diffident." Indeed, his violence, Edmund concluded, was "only a sort of clamour in which he would drown his own fears." Beneath self-confidence, ambition, and disruptive masculinity lurked fearful timidity. Will was very much Burke's alter ego.

The notebook has several other items which illustrate how preoccupied Edmund and Will were during these six years with concerns of ambition and success. There is, for example, a satiric letter dated May 1752 written by Edmund to Sir James Lowther, one of the richest men in England.[33] Edmund asked for a hundred pounds "with your advice how to use it. That will make me a fortune, and a fortune will make me happy." The letter is interesting for its evocation of Burke's avarice and its early linkage here to sexuality, a theme we will encounter often in Burke's later writings.

I have long had a great esteem for your character. If similitude of manners be a foundation for friendship, none can bid fairer for it than we do. The world says you love money; if I were of consequence enough it would say the same for me. In what then do we differ? In this only;—you enjoy your Desires; I still languish; you are worth a Million, I am not master of a single groat. How easy were it for you to make our resemblance, and consequently our friendship, quite complete? You may object that my want of money is proof that I don't love it as I ought; I might answer that I am an unpossessing lover, ten times more amourous, more passionate, more eager, than he that enjoys the height of all his wishes.

Just as in the earlier correspondence with Dick Shackleton, so here, too, in the notebook, there is a preoccupation with upward mobility, achievement, and the role of talent and merit. An item in the notebook labeled "The way to preferment" (not clearly attributable to either Edmund or Will), illustrates these concerns.[34] Many of those who possess the "highest offices and the greatest possessions," the essay holds, are men of no ability and no qualifications. This is patently unfair, since it is apparent that compared to the typical man of position:

How much better I deserved all this myself, and took comfort that my parts, my intrinsic merit, were a much better possession than his equipage.

But it is, in fact, the very lack of merit which explains the position of the great. "Their rise was owing to this very want of merit and nothing else." The sense that this was, indeed, the fundamental principle of aristocratic society would haunt Burke for the rest of his life. It would be the foundation of his bourgeois consciousness, however deeply it might be buried at any particular time. But, as we shall see, it would often be exposed, when he answered attacks on his being a "new man" in the '60s, for example, or when he penned his attack on Bedford just before his death. But this ambitious Burke always vied with self-effacing Burke, the Burke offering praise of the given social order, and his given place in it. This would be the meek Burke crawling along the secure lower path. This is the Burke who in 1782 would dismiss all talk of receiving a cabinet post by invoking the Chain of Being imagery he would utilize again so well in the *Reflections.* In 1782 he would apply it to his own place. It was by no means hypocritical. It would reflect the genuine ambivalence at his core.

God knew, Mr. Burke said, he had no such views, nor had he a right to have any such. The thing was not within probability. . . . He was neither a man who had pretentions to it from rank in the country, or from fortune, nor who had aspired to it from ambition. He was not a man so foolishly vain, or so blindly ignorant of his own state and condition, as to indulge for a moment the idea of his becoming a minister.[35]

Burke's moratorium, the quiet years between youth and adulthood ended in 1756. During these years in which he "broke loose" he alienated himself from family, friends, and homeland. He reoriented his life and radically changed its direction. With Burke during this crisis of identity, as he would be throughout most of the remainder of his life (but for interludes in India), was Will. Through his interaction with Will and what he represented Burke came to the precarious identity forged in these years. So intertwined were the sexual and social elements of identity that throughout Burke's career, as we shall see, the language of one would merge with the language of the other.

THE QUESTION OF HOMOSEXUALITY

Homosexuality, we know, was widespread in eighteenth-century England. In *Roderick Random* (1748) Strutwell proclams that it "gains ground apace and in all probability will become in a short time a more fashionable device than fornication." However prevalent it was, we also know that it never became fashionable. The genteel macaroni and dandy might be acceptable, but the fate of William Smith (see below) was much more common for ordinary sodomists. Social disdain and public disapproval forced many homosexuals to become recluses, or to flee abroad, often to Rome. The last three or four decades in the century saw a dramatic increase in the public prosecution of homosexuality, as well as an increase in cases of blackmail.[36] As one writer on the period has noted, "such a climate of opinion meant that men with any tendency towards homosexuality were forced at the very least into outward conformity, and often into concealing even from themselves what they felt." [37]

That Burke might have been a homosexual or showed homosexual tendencies was not an idea foreign to his contemporaries. Rumors to this effect circulated in opposition circles for years, often as part of the campaign depicting Burke as a Jesuit. Contemporary cartoons, for example, show him a particularly effeminate Jesuit. The ever-persistent rumors were given additional fuel by events in 1780, when Burke rose in the House of Commons to protest the treatment of two homosexuals, Theodosius Read and William Smith, who were sentenced, as part of their punishment for sodomy, to stand in the pillory for one hour. Smith died a victim of mob brutality. Burke spoke eloquently in the House against this barbarity and secured a pension for Smith's widow. While sodomy was, he insisted, in his speech, "a crime of all others the most detestable, because it tended to vitiate the morals of the whole community, and to defeat the first and chief end of society," the punishment of it should be tempered with mercy, inasmuch as it was a crime "of the most equivocal nature and the most difficult to prove." Better than cruelty and fury, he suggested, were "reproach and shame." [38] The *Morning Post* of 13 April responded to Burke.

Every *man* applauds the spirit of the spectators, and every *woman* thinks their conduct right. It remained only for the patriotic Mr. Burke to insinuate that the crime these men committed should not be held in the highest detestation.[39]

Burke brought suit for defamation of character against the newspaper, and he won his case.[40] His critics would not be silenced, however. Four years later the rumors surfaced again, this time in the *Public Advertiser*. Burke sued Henry Woodfall, its editor and publisher, for libelously suggesting that Burke was, if not himself homosexual, at least in sympathy with homosexuality. The case was tried before a special jury on 14 July 1784. Burke asked damages of £5,000 from Woodfall. The jury held in his favor by its verdict, but indicated its doubts by its award. They provided him with one hundred pounds in damages.[41]

In more recent years, while writers on Burke may have hinted at it they have never actually suggested that the relationship between Edmund and Will had any sexual dimension. Woodrow Wilson noted, for example, that Burke did have "some queer companions . . . questionable fellows, whose lives he shared, perhaps with a certain Bohemian relish, without sharing their morals or their works." [42] Thomas Copeland writes of the relationship in similar guarded but suggestive terms. The two young men, he notes, "lived together on the most intimate terms." [43] Sir Philip Magnus in his *Edmund Burke* cannot get himself to address the issue, skirting it with innuendo, but the implication is clear. Burke's letter telling of his having "tenderly loved" Will and having "continually lived with (him)" in a union not to be expressed" is Magnus' choice to depict the nature of their friendship. Magnus goes on to describe this "singular and inexpressible union." Will

was delighted with Edmund when he first set eyes on him. The two Burkes became intimate at once. . . . For several years Edmund and William led a Bohemian and somewhat aimless existence to which Edmund was exceedingly unwilling to refer. His reluctance may have sprung less from any false feeling of pride or shame than from an inborn stateliness of mind which rejected all sordid and uncongenial memories. [44]

While the issue of homosexuality, overt or latent, is far from certain, what little evidence there is does suggest that Burke did have problems in the area of sexual object choice. Psychoanalytic theory hypothesizes that such difficulty is rooted in oedipal and pre-oedipal experience and Burke's sexual ambivalence seems no exception. Successful resolution of the oedipal conflict requires an identification with the father. The fear of the father's angry rebuke of the young boy for his incestuous designs on the mother is resolved in this identification. It was just when such identification should have occurred that Burke's father was absent. Burke's separation from his father from age six to eleven thus looms as the critical experience in Burke's youth. His unresolved oedipal conflict becomes the intrapsychic, psychoanalytic issue which colors his entire life; it would be aspects of this irresolution which would recur in later neuroses.

According to Freud, oedipal strivings in normal circumstances are often themselves ambivalent, or in his own words, have a "double orientation, active and passive." Consistent with his bisexual makeup a young boy not only wants to replace the father as the mother's love object but also "wants to take his mother's place as the love object of his father." [45] He does this by identifying with her and assuming a passive feminine identity. Retaining this identification with the mother's sexuality and the passive homosexual wish for the father is often the source, according to Freud, of adult homosexuality.[46] There has to be a reason, however, to renounce the penis, as it were, and to identify with the mother. The triumph of the passive orientation, which represents an unsuccessful resolution of the oedipal conflict, requires, in other words, some unusual circumstances. These existed in Burke's case. To all outward appearances he was, in fact, successful in possessing his mother and having her to himself. She was with him a good deal more in those critical years than the absent father. Burke's mother, in addition, gratified his

oedipal desires by constantly appearing to love and worship him. Burke
seems, then, to have actually accomplished the parricidal fantasy which lurks
at the base of oedipal strivings. But having succeeded in the oedipal scenario
the youngster is subsumed with guilt and moved to a denial of his thrusting,
ambitious, father-toppling masculinity. He accomplishes this by identifying
with the mother's passive sexuality. The sick, weak, and delicate Burke
refusing to play with his mates could hardly be a father killer. This delicacy
is in turn reinforced by the mother's care and love, which thus caters to both
orientations of the oedipal ambition.

　　This identification with the mother's sexuality not only denied the
conquest of the mother, but it also would hopefully attract the father, a concern of great importance to young Burke. It pleads for his return to life by
denying any responsibility in violating the father's prerogative. Wanting to
be like his mother could win back the exiled or murdered father. In Burke's
case this was the father in Dublin who had left him with his mother's family.
The assumption of the passive feminine orientation would thus be at one and
the same time a statement of the child's innocence vis-à-vis the possession of
the mother and an enticement of the father by holding out the son's own
feminine sexuality as a repacement for mother. By winning his father's love
in this manner he would bring his father back.

　　When Burke's father returned, i.e., when he and his father were reunited, their relationship, we know, was a stormy one. The fragmentary evidence indicates that Burke saw his father as tyrannical and more favorably
disposed to the other children. Burke could easily have read this as oedipal
punishment and thus become quite literally and figuratively a runaway son
seeking to escape the castrating wrathful vengeance of the aggrieved father.
This would serve to have reinforced his residual feminine identity by once
again bringing it to bear to prove his innocence by an inability to possess his
mother in as much as he was really like her—a passive feminine object. Enter
in these years, then, Dick Shackleton who could play the active male foil to
the passive female strivings of adolescent Burke.

　　But it is an ambivalent sexuality we have here. The attraction to Dick
Shackleton need not have been homosexual; it could also have been the more
neutral homophilic. Burke could have, in fact, picked the older boy as a
masculine role model in an effort to free himself from the passive and regres-
sive strivings to remain attached to his mother. Identifying with Dick as an
ego ideal could have been part of Burke's effort to control or even put down
his feminine self. Similarly, in the psychological moratorium of his missing
years the ambivalent sexual dimension could be seen as central in the dilemma over career choice. Becoming a lawyer could be at one and the same
time a masculine substitution for the father and a passive feminine acceptance of the status quo. The attraction to Will could have, in turn, been
rooted in a passive feminine identification vis-à-vis Will's self-evident mas-

culinity, or it could also have been rooted in Burke's search for a strong masculine model. In this latter light, taking Will into his household could be interpreted as an act of restitution by which a masculine orientation was restored to Burke's life to still his fears of passive femininity. Having Will in the household might thus be seen as resolving Burke's guilt at having sequestered himself once again in sole possession of a woman—once his mother, now Jane—and thereby being identified with her.[47]

The manifest ambivalences of Burke's life reflect these latent intrapsychic tensions. In his youth and in his adult years he vacillated between ambitious putting forth of self and guilt-laden confessions of inadequacy. Aggressively assertive on some occasions, he would be painfully self-deprecating on others. It is, as Erikson notes, the classic issue of the oedipal experience. But, because of the unsuccessful dissolution of Burke's oedipal crisis, aspects of its irresolution would recur throughout his life. Initiative, ambition, and phallic intrusiveness would, as we shall see, constantly struggle with guilt, denial, shame and doubt. Moralism and the preservation of the natural order would confront a masculinity restlessly tampering with that which was perceived as given and just.

Neither Burke's defense of the homosexuals in 1780, nor the libel proceedings in 1784, nor the suspicions of those who write of him and Will make a conclusive case for the nature of Burke's sexuality. The same must be said, of course, for the oedipal hypothesis. Burke's moving defense of Smith and Read rebounds to his eternal credit. The attacks of the 1780s could well have been just as Burke described them, another example of the vicious depths to which his enemies would stoop in discrediting him. There is no solid evidence that can be produced here which would positively sustain the interpretation of Burke's sexual and psychic life offered in this book. What can be said, however, is that it is a reading of Burke which far from seeking to discredit him hopes to enhance and enrich our understanding and appreciation of his life and thought.

CHAPTER 4

The New Burke: Service and Ambition (1756–1768)

THE MORATORIUM ended with Burke's marriage and the inclusion of Will in the common household. His emergence into adulthood was also marked by his entrance into the public life of letters with two books in 1756 and 1757. The *Vindication of Natural Society* and the *Philosophical Inquiry into the Origin of Our Ideas on the Sublime and Beautiful* have always seemed the wayward children in Burke's family of writings. They seem unrelated to the central concerns of his later work, and are usually mentioned in passing as youthful ventures designed merely to secure Burke's entrance into the public world of London culture. These two works, are, however, very much related to Burke's concerns in the 1750s. They are, in fact, the direct fruits of the moratorium years, and ought to be read in light of the problems Burke had been struggling with during those six years.

VINDICATING BURKE'S *Vindication*

The *Vindication* was a seemingly radical indictment of political institutions, laying at their feet all the miseries of mankind. Burke wrote the volume anonymously and gave the impression its author was the "late noble writer," Bolingbroke. The essay appears to be a subversive assault on the traditional order. In the second edition (1757) Burke added a preface, however, and revealed to all the ironic intent of the book. By applying Bolingbroke's ideas on natural religion to society he had hoped to prove how ludicrous they were. The essay was no radical threat, he insisted, merely an ironic ploy with which to ridicule Bolingbroke's irreligion.

This has persisted through the centuries as the accepted interpretation of the *Vindication*. But was it purely irony? Is it, indeed, possible to write ironically without giving some weight to what is ridiculed? During these years Burke was wrestling with his own ambivalent social views. A part of him did detest the established order, as we have seen. He had displayed it in *The Reformer*. Moreover, in his letters and poetry he had time and again conceptualized himself in positions of prominence in any restructured natural and rational society. To be sure, another part of him sought to crawl the low path of his assigned place, to embrace the secure warmth of tradition. How better to express this anguished dilemma than via his *Vindication*. It was at one and the same time a radical manifesto and a conservative apologia. By claiming irony he could have his cake and eat it, too.

A compelling case can be made for the *Vindication* as more than mere irony, as in fact containing a good deal of the radicalism that was already part of Burke. This would, of course, fly in the face of conventional wisdom concerning Burke. Prior insists that the *Vindication*'s litany on the evils of government, the errors of statesmen, the injustice of aristocratic distinctions, the tyranny and uncertainty of laws, and the virtues of the poor over the rich is "advanced, of course, ironically." [1] So the reading has gone among Burke scholars to the present day. For Kirk it is a marvelous parody, an "ironic masterpiece," for Stanlis a skillful satire of those who praised natural society. For Thomas Copeland it is simply taken as given that it was no more than "as is well known, an ironic attack" on Bolingbroke's freethinking. [2]

This reading, suggested by Burke himself, has not always occurred to non-Burkean readers, however. William Godwin, for example, was terribly excited by what he read as Burke's youthful defense of anarchism in which "the evils of the existing political institutions are displayed with incomparable force of reasoning and lustre of eloquence." [3] No surprise then, that in 1958 the contemporary libertarian anarchist Murray Rothbard rediscovered the *Vindication* and claimed it for his cause "as perhaps the first modern expression of rationalistic and individualistic anarchism." No sooner had Rothbard dared to question the consistency of Burke's conservative credentials than orthodox Burkeans rose up to squash the heretical suggestion. John C. Weston Jr. offered a reply to Rothbard entitled, "The Ironic Purpose of Burke's *Vindication* Vindicated." [4]

Weston and Stanlis make the case for Burke not holding to the ideas as literally set forth in the *Vindication* by citing passages from Burke's other writings during these years which in their conservatism and skepticism seem utterly at odds with the apparent radical and rationalist views of the *Vindication*. The problem with this method is that it can cut both ways. An equally strong case can be made for Burke quite literally and seriously holding certain of the views dismissed here as ironic by finding them repeated in his other writings, writings not usually regarded as satiric.

Take, for example, what seems to be the most un-Burkean aspect of his *Vindication,* and thus surely of no serious intent, its moving description of the grinding poverty of the poor and its radical assault on the oppression by the great and powerful who are responsible for the wretchedness of nine-tenths of humanity who "drudge through life." The "natural equality" of the human condition is violated when the people "are considered as a mere herd of cattle." The aristocracy "consider their subjects as the farmer does the dog he keeps to feed upon." He keeps him in a stye, allowing him "to wallow as much as he pleases in his beloved filth . . ." The poor provide the wealth of the rich through their labor, and the rich in turn make laws "confirming the slavery and increasing the burdens of the poor." The poor, these "unhappy wretches," "subsist upon the coarsest and worst sort of fare," their health is miserably impaired and their lives short. Burke notes, allegedly in ironic banter, that

if any man informed us that . . . innocent persons were condemned to so intolerable slavery, how should we pity the unhappy sufferers, and how great would be our *just* indignation against those who inflicted so cruel and ignominious a punishment! [5]

Those responsible for this punishment, this oppression of nine-tenths of humanity, are the aristocracy, according to Burke in the *Vindication*. The aristocracy who oppress and feed on the poor are themselves enervated "by every sort of debauchery." They are "degenerate" and wallow in "effeminate luxury." The poor administer to their every "idleness and pleasure." In artificial society there are always the poor "those who labour most" and who "enjoy the fewest things," and their betters, "those who labour not at all," and who "have the greatest number of enjoyments." Among these unproductive enjoyments are "playing, fiddling, dancing, and singing." [6] So much for the heavy hand of Burke's irony, then, as read by generations of Burke scholars.

But have we not, in fact, met this Burke before? It is, of course, the Burke of *The Reformer,* his Dublin journal of 1748. The passion is the same, the themes the same, the language very often the same. In number seven of *The Reformer* he had written of the poor in their wretched filth, living like swine and cattle and eating their miserable food. He had written there of "the natural equality of mankind," and its degeneration into the rich in their gilded coaches and their velvet couches, "followed by the miserable wretches, whose labour supports them." He had written there that anyone who sees this great disparity would react with "the highest indignation." In another issue of *The Reformer* he had coveted for more useful expenditure one-tenth "of what is expended on fiddlers, singers, dancers, and players." [7] Is *The Reformer* to be written off, then, as mere irony, too? Some of these social themes in the *Vindication* are also found in Burke's early correspondence with Shackleton and in his private poetry and prose of the moratorium years. The imagery of a luxurious and idle aristocracy is not new, nor is the charge that real merit is overlooked in the aristocratic world. The *Vindication* includes this familiar, albeit predominantly private Burkean lament. He writes there that "a shining merit is ever hated or suspected." [8]

Moving on to other themes in the *Vindication* one is forcefully struck by Burke's "ironic" attack on the law and lawyers. They are in the forefront, he writes, of those institutions adept "in confounding the reason of man, and abridging his natural freedom." Lawyers argue not over right, but over words. They preside over "the mysteries of the blindfold goddess," mysteries foreign to ordinary mortals. The science of the law is wrapped in "darkness and uncertainty." It is so intricate that its practitioners have themselves lost their way. Its painful delays, its "false refinement," its "injustice" all flow from its mysterious forms and ceremonies, its incomprehensible jargon. In the "intricate recesses" of "the labyrinth of the law" all forms of iniquity are conceived, writes Burke in the *Vindication*. [9] This, too, must be irony, Burke scholarship tells us, otherwise we would indeed have Burke as Bentham or Burke as Godwin. Unfortunately, the evidence is quite the contrary. Burke happens to have repeated these views in a large number of "serious" contexts. Leaving aside the anonymous reviews in the *Annual Register* which Copeland attributes to Burke and which ridicule lawyers, there are numerous cases of such easily attributable criticism. [10] In the very serious *Abridgment of English History,* published after Burke's death in 1811 but conventionally dated as having been written in 1757, Burke offered an assessment of law and lawyers strikingly similar to that of the *Vindication.*

Thus the law has been confined, and drawn up into a narrow and inglorious study; and that which should be the leading science in every well-ordered Commonwealth, remained in all the barbarism of the rudest times, whilst every other advanced by rapid steps to the highest improvement both in solidity and elegance; insomuch that the study of our jurisprudence presented to liberal and well-educated minds, even in the best authors, hardly anything but barbarous terms, ill explained; a coarse but not a plain expression, an indigested method, and a species of reasoning, the very refuse of the schools; which deduced the spirit of the law, not from original justice or legal conformity, but from causes foreign to it, and altogether whimsical. [11]

The last thought is itself an interesting allusion to the premise of the *Vindication.* Onto the natural principles of justice operating in natural society have been grafted artificial, i.e. foreign and whimsical, additions.

Frequently when Burke took the floor in the Commons, it was to denounce lawyers. In 1771, for example, he asked why judges-lawyers "should

be thought exempted from the common lot of humanity." They were not in-
fallible. In fact, he suggested, the wisdom at large in the nation was generally more dependable than "the boasted discernment of all the bar." [12] In his
famous speech on American taxation, Burke noted that study of the law
was not apt "to open and liberalize the mind." [13] Two years later, he talked
to the House of low "petty-fogging attorneys." [14] In 1789 Burke sounded
like Bentham when he complained of "the penal laws in this country as radically defective." There were simply too many laws, and their confusion was
compounded as their number was multiplied daily. According to the parliamentary reporter, Burke "recommended a revision of the whole criminal
law." [15] Burke, it would seem, had rather serious reservations about the law
and lawyers. Perhaps we might, then, take more seriously yet another part
of the *Vindication.*

There is more to the attack on lawyers in the *Vindication* than its being,
as we now can insist, a serious textual and thematic interest. It also begs biographical comment. The essay also represents a symbolic end to Burke's career crisis, and a coming to terms with his father, and his father's profession,
issues central to the moratorium years. In his 1757 attack on the law in the
projected history of England, Burke wrote that "young men are sent away
(from the study of law) with an incurable, and . . . a very well-founded
disgust." [16] He was such a young man. The law and being a lawyer was very
much on his mind when he wrote the *Vindication.* He had himself just
rejected it and with it his father. The intrusion of his personal crises into the
essay helps explain the passion of his attack and also gives the issue a
seriousness of the highest order. The essay was in this small respect neither
irony nor ambivalence, but personal apologia.

One final piece of evidence exists crucial to the claim that its interpretation as pure satire must be revised and that it must be seen if not necessarily
as a radical tract at least as an important indication of Burke's ideological ambivalence. In his *Tracts Relative to the Laws Against Popery in Ireland,* written,
it is customarily assumed, around 1765, Burke would return to many of the
themes and radical arguments that were found in the *Vindication.* The tracts,
significantly enough, like his *Abridgement of English History* were not published till after his death, but their "seriousness" has never been questioned.
What is striking about *The Tracts* is its radical tone which, while it may seem
surprising in Burke, is in fact quite consistent with the Burke of the *Vindication.* These anti-Catholic laws, Burke insists, are unjust and in terms of natural law doctrine not binding. They are laws "against the majority of the people," and thus invalid laws against the people themselves. No one can
imagine that a free people would subject themselves to such laws which so
disqualify them. The laws are "null and void" because there is no right to
make laws which violate God's higher laws.[17] Burke insists here in *The
Tracts* in good Lockean language that "a conservative and secure enjoyment

of our natural rights is the great and ultimate purpose of civil society." It follows, he adds, that government is justified only to the extent that it achieves that purpose.[18] At the foundation of society, he writes, is "the great rule of equality," and what these laws do in Ireland is to "create an artificial difference between men." This is not only in terms of "a consequential inequality in the distribution of justice," but also an inequality in the distribution of economic and social rewards. They produce "many hundreds of thousands of human creatures rendered to a state of the most abject servitude." [19] This is a radicalism quite akin to that of the *Vindication,* which may well explain why Burke never published *The Tracts* in his lifetime. He is saying that men set up artificial institutions of government and law to protect the cherished rights of natural society. What happens, instead, at least in Ireland, is that the tendency of these artificial institutions is to demolish natural equality and obliterate natural rights. This is a far cry from the Burke we are used to. He is here the theorist if not of natural society than certainly of natural law. But it is not Burke the natural law theorist as perceived by today's Burkeans. It is Burke the radical theorist of natural law, using the theory just as Locke and the bourgeois radicals did.

Burke's *Vindication* reveals the basic ideological ambivalence which is at the core of his politics and his being. From this perspective the *Vindication of Natural Society* becomes a much more critical part of Burke's writings than hitherto realized. Turning to it as he did immediately after his years of moratorium he put much more of himself in it than meets the eye. He is fighting with himself in its pages and in its preface, as much as he is with "the philosophical works of Lord Bolingbroke." [20]

BURKE'S AESTHETICS REVISITED

The essay *On the Sublime and Beautiful* also bears the stamp of these moratorium years. Always recognized as a much more important book than the *Vindication,* it is traditionally regarded as a critical document in the emergence of the Romantic spirit, repudiating as it does the classical aesthetic of moderation, harmony, distaste for change and variety. Burke's essay on aesthetic theory was praised by a long list of distinguished writers that includes Johnson, Wordsworth, Blake, Hardy, Lessing, Diderot, and Kant.[21] On one level *On the Sublime and Beautiful* was intended to be a useful passport into the closed world of the intellectual and cultural elite, which indeed it became. But it seems to have had even stronger links to Burke's private concerns. If his *Vindication* is evidence of the deep ideological ambivalence that was a basic part of Burke as he emerged from his moratorium, then *On the Sublime and Beautiful* provides interesting indications of his sexual ambivalence, for the conceptualization in the essay is drawn along clearly discernible sexual lines. Hovering over every page is a dichotomy of male and female, and while, according to Burke, the feminine principle, the beautiful, is important in art as in life, the male, the sublime, he suggests, is even more critical. Even so, the best aesthetic materials as well as the best of virtues, are, according to Burke, a combination of both.

For Burke the source of the sublime is whatever excites the idea of pain or danger, "that is to say whatever is in any sort terrible." [22] The ideas of pain are much more powerful than those of pleasure, which is the domain of beauty and love. This is as it should be for the sublime passions of pain and terror are the passions which operate for the self-preservation of the individual and the species. The beautiful passion of love and pleasure is the generative principle. It sees not to the protection of the species, but to its multiplication, a function rooted in "gratification and pleasure." Self-preservation is more basic than multiplication; the latter presumes the former, but any viable society has both. So, too, any work of art contains both principles of terror, the sublime, and love, the beautiful. The sublime is an individualistic quality referring ultimately to fear and danger necessary for the preservation of the self. The beautiful is a social quality which "inspires us with sentiments of tenderness and affection towards their persons." [23] The sublime is egocentric and characterized by pain, fear, and terror. The beautiful is social and emanates pleasure, tenderness, and affection. One admires the sublime, one loves the beautiful.

Describing the sublime and its characteristic of terror, Burke emphasizes changeability, sudden and unexpected fits of passion and violence that were reminiscent of his recent description of the unpredictable, nearly demonic, moods of Will Burke.[24] The sublime is a package of masculine traits, the beautiful, feminine.

On closing this general view of beauty, it naturally occurs that we should compare it with the sublime; and in this comparison, there appears a remarkable contrast; for sublime objects are vast in their dimensions, beautiful ones comparatively small: beauty should be smooth and polished; the great, rugged and negligent: beauty should shun the right line, yet deviate from it insensibly: the great, in many cases, love the right line, and when it deviates it often makes a strong deviation; beauty should not be obscure; the great ought to be dark and gloomy: beauty should be light and delicate; the great ought to be solid and ever massive.[25]

The contrast is remarkable. In writing of the sublime Burke emphasizes the qualities of "power," "strength," "violence," "pain," and "terror." [26] Everything sublime must have some quality of power, and overtones of "rapine and destruction." The animal which Burke singles out to epitomize the sublime is the bull, with all the destructive strength and sublimity of its pent-up rage and terror.[27] Kings are sublime; their power and strength evoke fear and admiration. One dreads their majesty, one does not love and cherish their grace and delicacy. Similarly, Burke writes of the sublimity of God. Of all his attributes "his power is by far the most striking. Some reflection, some comparing, is necessary to satisfy us of his wisdom, his justice, and his goodness. To be struck with his power, it is only necessary that we should open our eyes. . . . If we rejoice, we rejoice with trembling." [28] Sublimity is inherent in overpowering size, as, for example, in "a tower one hundred yards high," [29] or in the oak, the ash, or the elm, or any of "the robust trees of the forest." No one considers them beautiful. "They are awful and majestic." They inspire fear and reverence. On the other hand, the jasmine, the orange, the almond, the myrtle, are considered mere vegetable beauties. These nurturing trees are delicate, beautiful, and elegant, which brings us to Burke's notion of the feminine aesthetic principle, the beautiful.

The beautiful is the realm of love, of diminutives and smallness. It is also the realm of submission. We admire and fear the great and terrible and submit to it, bulls, kings, lords, what have you. Small, tender things, on the other hand, submit to us, Burke writes, and "we love what submits to us." [30] Beauty is a quality in things which produce in the beholder a sense of "affection and tenderness." Beauty is smooth and devoid of sudden angularity; it is clean and fair, delicate and fragile, weak and timid, graceful, sweet, elegant, soft, relaxed, and enervated.[31] While sublime objects and actions are grand, lofty, noble and powerful, and leave one with feelings of awe and respect, Beauty tends to produce languor and melancholy, or at most affection and sympathy. If the tower and the robust forest elm are the representative symbols of the sublime, then that of the beautiful is "that part of a woman where she is perhaps the most beautiful, about the neck and breasts." [32]

A basic part of beauty is the repetition of form, the lack of sudden deviation. This is the principle of rhythm, as in the delicate smoothness and swells of the female body. This aesthetic principle has its social counterpart, according to Burke. Sympathy with others, a concern with what others feel, leads to a form of repetition, an imitation of what they do. Sympathy for the sufferings of others is thus a feminine social trait, related to tenderness and affection. The imitation of others leads to a repetitive rhythm in life, a smoothness and lack of deviation or abrupt change. In contrast to this Burke describes "ambition," a critical component of the masculine sublime which lifts man from the easy pleasures and delights of imitation to realms of danger and terror. Ambition is the creative foil to feminine imitation. If everyone imitated previous patterns there would be no change, Burke insists. The feminine beautiful thus becomes the embodiment of tradition through this principle of imitation and repetition. The masculine sublime as ambition breaks the pattern of continuity and raises, via the quest for personal fame, the level of species distinction and achievement. Sublime ambition must break the traditional hold of pleasurable imitation lest "if men gave themselves up to imitation entirely, and each followed the other, and so on in an eternal circle, it is easy to see that there never could be any improvement amongst them." To remedy this, "God has planted in man a sense of ambition, and a satisfaction arising from the contemplation of his excelling his fellows." [33] Ambition is thus masculine intrusion, breaking into the circle of imitation. It operates in the public sphere not in the household, and it is linked to the terror of the sublime.

Ambition "produces a sort of swelling and triumph." This swelling is most clearly apparent "when without danger we are conversant with terrible objects." Phallic masculinity is merged by Burke with ambition and striving. The swelling and triumph "raise a man in his own opinion," and leave him with a sense of "glorying" and "inward greatness." [34] This is part of the sublime.

The eternal circle of imitation, the realm of tradition, is feminine, and as such is appealing for its pleasure and its beauty. But there is no majesty or glory in beauty, only in the terror of the sublime, the tastes of which are sweet to the ambitious man who, while he may have substituted the market for the jungle, still fearfully but joyfully confronts other terrible objects—not with tenderness and affection, but with strength and power.

If there were any doubt that the discussion had specific gender referents for the categories of sublime and beautiful, the text makes it quite clear in Part III, Section X where Burke applies the aesthetic categories to qualities (virtues) of the mind. There are, Burke suggests, sublime virtues, which elicit admiration and produce terror. These are "fortitude, justice, wisdom and the like." There are also beautiful virtues, "softer virtues," which "engage our hearts" and which leave us "with a sense of loveliness." These are "compassion, kindness and liberality." These softer virtues are distinctly second-class virtues, of less immediate and of less momentous concern. They are amiable, but of less dignity. These "subordinate virtues" are emotive and affective, dealing with indulgences, gratification, and relief. They involve the social concerns of family, friendship, and lovers. "The great virtues," on the other hand, are concerned with the dangers of public life. They prevent mischief and do not give favors and kindness. They are venerable, not lovely.

The world, Burke suggests, is divided into people of great virtue and people of softer virtue, the sublime and the beautiful respectively. The former are people of shining qualities; they are glaring objects. The latter are companions of softer colors whom one turns to in relief from the dazzling great. One admires, reveres, and fears the former, and from a distance. One gets familiar with and loves the latter. When Burke ends the section by invoking the models of father and mother one could hardly be surprised. The sublime virtues are embodied in "the authority of a father," venerable, and distant. No one, Burke the "runaway son" suggests, has as much love for a father as for a mother. So it is, then, that the beautiful or lovely virtues are embodied in "the mother's fondness and indulgence," i.e., in "feminine partiality." [35] Mothers and women in general are creatures of "compassion," and the "amiable, social virtues." These are "lesser virtues" and "domestic virtues." Opposed to these are the "greater virtues," the sublime realm of "politic and military virtues," where fathers and men in general confront terror, honor, and fear and in the process satisfy their ambitious urges to excel.[36] In the family, then, according to Burke, there is an ambitious father whom children respect, admire, and fear, and there is a loving mother who is kind, tender, and indulgent. The masculine realm is authority associated with pain and terror; the feminine is affect—friendship and love, associated with pleasure and compassion. The fear and uncertainty of ambitious striving is part of the fatherly, masculine, and sublime; the warm, secure embrace of tradition is an aspect of the motherly, feminine, and beautiful. The life-style of the bourgeoisie is inherently masculine, that of the tasteful and elegant aristocracy is inherently feminine.[37]

The strife of the moratorium years lingers in *On the Sublime and Beautiful*. In its pages, Burke's sexual ambivalence (even to its ideological coloration) is transformed into a powerful conceptualization of aesthetic taste. As in his own strife the masculine principle seems to win out, and the issue is put to rest. The sublime is clearly the greater, the more important, the more fascinating quality; the beautiful, the lesser, the subordinate. But inherent in the sublime is Burke's sense of fear and dread, and the potential for destructiveness and rapine. Masculinity is not without its danger; like the bull it represents contained aggression. Unleashed it can become terrifying demonic horror. It is best tempered and softened, then, by the feminine beautiful which blunts ambition and turns individuals to the cooperative and amiable concerns of social life. For Burke the sublime is Will and the beautiful Jane, and both are essential to peace and well-being. To be sure, he seems to assert the masculine principle in the essay and subordinate the feminine, just as in these years he seemed to assert his masculine identity in his marriage to Jane and to repress his feminine identity and his attachment to Will. But the ambivalence is still present. While he is partial to the masculine principle he fears it. He fears its potential for destructive terror; he fears the pain it causes. He insists that in good art and in good communities some feminine love and social concern is essential.

On the Sublime and Beautiful looks forward in Burke's career as well as backward. Its concerns with the virtues of love and friendship as opposed to power and authority will be a basic theme in his *Thoughts on the Cause of the Present Discontent*. But its most important legacy is its discussions of the sublime, and the ambivalent attitude Burke takes toward it. It is terrible and horrible, yet it inspires awe, admiration, and respect. The ambivalence is even more fundamental. Burke suggests that there is pleasure in the pain that is sublimity. He describes it in the essay as "a sort of delightful horror, a sort of tranquility tinged with terror." Along with the bull, a recurring symbol of the sublime in the essay, is the huge, rampaging wave in a storm-driven sea.[38] Interestingly enough, the ambivalent experience of joy in terror was described by Burke some twelve years earlier in a letter to Shackleton describing the horror of the flood waters that menaced his father's house. "It gives me great pleasure," he wrote to Dick in 1745, "to see nature in those great tho' terrible scenes; it fills the mind with grand ideas." [39] We will encounter terrible scenes again in Burke's writings, first on India and then on the French Revolution and Jacobinism in general. He will retail description upon description of terror, fear, danger, and demonic horror. He will offer passages not unlike his comments on the sublime in this early essay.

The large and gigantic, though very compatible with the sublime is contrary to the beautiful. It is impossible to suppose a giant the object of love. When we let our imagination loose in romance, the ideas we naturally annex to that size are those of tyranny, cruelty, injustice, and everything horrid and abominable. We paint the giant ravaging the country, plundering the innocent traveller, and afterwards gorged with his half-living flesh.[40]

This giant will later be Hastings and the Jacobins; but the question is whether Burke's response to the sublime thirty years later will be the same as in his essay of 1757. Will he be so partial to the masculine principle? Will he still experience a certain delight in the horror, a certain joy and pleasure in the terror? Will he approve then of the bull unshackled, of masculine ambition unleashed and of awesome masculine terror inflicted on gentle and delicate beauties? One might want to reread these passages of the 1780s and 1790s with a new understanding, searching for the hidden approbation in the frenzied anger. Or perhaps Burke would rethink his attitudes to the lesser virtues of grace and beauty of affect and tenderness represented by such as Marie Antoinette, the humiliated queen of the *Reflections*. *On the Sublime and Beautiful* seems to represent a coming to terms with the questions of sexuality that troubled Burke in the preceding years. They would lie buried for some time as he went about his career, but the doubts and uncertainties would resurface. After the decades of seemingly successful resolution of Burke's crisis in his early twenties, after the modus vivendi of his marriage and years of intimate friendship with Will, his problems would reappear with the giants and bulls that were Hastings and the Jacobins.

On the Sublime and Beautiful deserves a more important place in the corpus of Burkeana than it now occupies. A fascinating essay with terrifying and fearful fathers and gentle loving mothers, with ambitious Wills and gentle Janes, it directs one's attention to Burke's earliest years, while at the same time its towering and terrifying monsters link it directly to the concerns of his last years.

PICKING A PATRON: HAMILTON AND ROCKINGHAM

The end of his moratorium signaled by these publications and his arrival on the London literary scene was mirrored in Burke's correspondence. For six years there are but a handful of letters. Now the flow returned to its normal pace. Having come to terms with himself, he reopened channels of communication with those in the outside world. The renewed correspondence reintroduces ambitious Burke nearly one decade later. He had acquired a modicum of fame from the publication of *On the Sublime and Beautiful* and the *Vindication of Natural Society,* but apparently not enough. During this period Burke also began editing the highly successful *Annual Register,* but, interestingly enough, since this smacked too much of low-level Grub Street, Burke never admitted that he was editor of the *Register.* This deception, probably not an easy one, was kept up for many years.

His writings guaranteed him access to and membership in the cultural establishment of England for the rest of his life. But membership in the intellectual elite could not still Burke's restless ambition. Conquering the clubs and the salons was no mean achievement, but flashy intellectuals, especially good talkers, generally had an easier time of it. It could not satisfy Burke. He was a typical intellectual in that sense, with aristocratic aspirations and a sense that with his qualities he had a passport to the even greater heights of the political and social elite. The assertive Burke felt no qualms in 1759 asking Mrs. Montagu, who was spreading his literary name and fame in her bluestocking circles, if she could intercede with the elder Pitt to get Burke appointed consul in Madrid. Putting himself forward in this way was a bold stroke. Burke had never even written to Mrs. Montagu before and it was a position of no mean value, £1,000 per annum. Yet Burke saw fit to belittle it and himself as well, to understate his overt display of ambition. "I presume however that it is not an object for a person who has any considerable pretensions by its having continued so long vacant, else I should never have thought of it." [41]

After this first abortive effort at advancement, Burke was more successful. Coleridge, always perceptive when it came to Burke, described him as "a great courtier." [42] What Coleridge drew attention to was Burke's natural pose of dependence, as the man who served and waited upon those greater and more powerful than himself. But what Coleridge, in fact, hit upon was Burke's constant quest for an older male figure who would provide both affection and authority. This would be a central dimension in Burke's future political attachments to Hamilton and Rockingham and it had already manifested itself years before in Burke's turning to the father of his friend Dick Shackleton.

Abraham Shackleton, the master of Burke's school, seems to have been an exceptional man. He took a fancy to Burke, then just entering his teens. He was a tolerant and kind man, who accepted the clever and witty pranks of Edmund and Dick, his two prize pupils. Moreover, he appeared to Burke as a man of singular principle and piety, in sharp contrast to the legal and business acquaintances of his father's circle in Dublin. Burke described his schoolmaster in some lines of poetry where the contrast with his father seems evident.

> And here as the fair land adorns the men,
> The men no less adorn the land again;
> Yet Shackleton mid these with such a light
> Shines as does Hesper amid the lamps of night;
> Whose hopes Ambition never taught to roam,
> Whose breast all virtues long have made their home,
> Where Courtesy's stream does with flattery flow;
> And the just use of wealth without the show;
> Who to man's vices tho' he ne'er was thrall,
> Pities as much as he had felt them all;
> And in a word such cares his hour engage
> As fits the planter of the future age. [43]

Burke's letters to Dick after he left school indicated how important Mr. Shackleton had been for the adolescent Burke. "Best respects to your father," he wrote to Dick in June 1744, "whose goodness and care to me was boundless." Only death would erase "the remembrance of all his favours." Writing from Trinity, Burke again conveyed respect to Dick's father citing "all whose favours" he would never forget. Burke, in turn, was eager to please his beloved teacher and win his approval. When in July 1745 he scored first in his exams at college he asked Dick "please to acquaint your father with this." He would, Burke added, derive great pleasure from hearing this news. [44] Shackleton appeared to Burke to be everything his own father was not. He keenly appreciated, for example, the impressive intellectual and literary achievements that Burke amassed while at Trinity. Burke saw himself in a very different light after graduating from college, already a journalist and scholar of note in Dublin. It was as if he were a new person. In producing this new person Shackleton was perceived as the new and supremely beloved father. Burke wrote of Shackleton in 1749:

> To whose kind care my better birth I owe,
> Who to fair Science did my youth entice,
> Won from the paths of ignorance and vice. [45]

Burke the courtier emerged full-blown, however, in his first important introduction to public life, his six-year service as private secretary to William Gerard Hamilton. Burke never received the consulship in Madrid but in that same year, 1759, he met the wealthy and powerful Hamilton, member of Parliament and Chief Secretary to Lord Halifax, Lord Lieutenant for Ireland. Until 1765 Hamilton and his protégé Burke spent most of their time either in Dublin with the Irish Parliament or in London handling Irish affairs. In these years of service Burke was introduced to and began to master the world of public men and public affairs. As a vehicle of mobility and visibility it was almost an uncanny realization of the strategy he had jokingly suggested as a fifteen-year-old—diligent service to the great eliciting munificence and recognition. Whether or not this was by now a self-conscious life strategy is unclear. One thing is clear, however: the strain of making his own mark while serving Hamilton, his superior, became unbearable, and led to an unpleasant break in their relationship. The signs of the impending rupture could be seen as early as March 1763. Hamilton had gotten his protégé a £300/year pension on the Irish establishment. A dutiful and subordinate Burke wrote him of his gratitude for this gift "much above my merits" and "above my reasonable expectations." But Burke indicated that he still wanted some time of his own to be his own man. He had his own literary reputation which he wanted to cultivate and keep alive. He would need time on his own "to study and consult proper books." Still when all was said and done, he recognized he was not his own man but Hamilton's servant, deferential and self-deprecating.

I am not so unreasonable and absurd enough to think I have any title to so considerable a share in your interest, as I have had, and hope still to have, without any or but an insignificant return on my side; especially as I am conscious that my best and most continued endeavors are of no very great value. I know that your business ought on all occasions to have the preference, to be the first and the last, and indeed in all respects the main concern. All I contend for is, that I may not be considered as absolutely excluded from all other thoughts in their proper time and due subordination:—the fixing, the time for them to be left entirely to yourself.[46]

By 1765, however, Burke had left Hamilton, the arrangement having broken down. The tension between the contradictory forces of Burke's ambition to make his own mark and the necessity of dependence and service to his superior was revealed in a remarkable set of letters which Burke wrote that year to Hamilton. Hamilton apparently had asked Burke to commit himself permanently to being his secretary, an arrangement Hamilton thought was implicit in the pension arrangement of 1763. Burke saw his ambitions stifled if he remained in Hamilton's service.

I made you and not myself the first object in every deliberation, I studied your advancement your fortune, and your reputation in every thing with zeal and earnestness, and sometimes with an anxiety which has made many of my hours miserable. . . . I acted in every respect with a fidelity which I trust cannot be impeached . . . what you blame is only this: that I will not consent to bind myself to you for no less a term than my whole life: in a sort of domestick situation, for a consideration to be taken out of your private fortune, that is to circumscribe my hopes, to give up even the possibility of liberty, and absolutely to annihilate myself for ever . . . what have I done . . . but to prefer my own liberty to the offers of advantage you are pleased to make me? [47]

In writing to a friend about the break several months later Burke asked: "Was ever a man before me expected to enter into formal direct, undisguised slavery?" No, he would not stay on with Hamilton; to do so would be "not to value myself (as a gentleman a freeman a man of education; and one pretending to literature)." [48] He constantly returned to this theme. To another friend he wrote that Hamilton "would fain have had a *slave.*" He refused to have Burke as a friend, "which is a creature of some rank." [49] In that same letter of May 1765 the ambitious Burke poured out the depths of anger he had harbored against the great man he had served. It would by no means be the last time he would lash out at his betters.

Six of the best years of my life he took me from every pursuit of literary reputation or of improvement of my fortune. In that time he made his own fortune (a very great one), and he has also taken to himself the very little one, which I had made. In all this time you may easily conceive, how much I felt at seeing myself left behind by almost all of my contemporaries. There never was a season more favorable for any man who chose to enter into the career of public life; and I think I am not guilty of ostentation, in supposing my own moral character and my industry, my friends and connections, when Mr. H first sought my acquaintance were not at all inferior to those of several, whose fortune is at this day upon a very different footing from mine. [50]

It bears remembering that as Burke entered the political world in the 1760s he was both the friend of Johnson, Goldsmith, and Garrick, and a darling of bluestocking society. He was a very successful intellectual, and he could, of course, never lose that aspect of his marginality. Just as he would forever be an Irishman in an English parliamentary club, so he would forever be the intellectual in a political world of Hamiltons, Rockinghams, Bedfords, and even Foxes. This was more food to feed Burke's basic sense of ambivalence. It means, as Coleridge noted, that Burke felt a "measureless superiority to those about him." Yet, "these coarser intellects," were for the most part his superiors. [51] So Burke vacillated from sycophantic moods of deference to explosive fits of resisting service and asserting his independence from and indeed superiority to the political elite. His is the painful ambivalence that would come to be the characteristic lot of the upwardly mobile bourgeois intellectual. He would endure all the pain and dislocation of upward mobility in order to escape the actuality of his middle-class origins and status. Part of this involved aping and serving the privileged aristocracy and their world. Alongside this, however, was a disdain for these betters and Burke's sense of his purer prestige based on talented intellect.

What made this entire incident so particularly painful for Burke, however, was the extent to which it raised issues he had hoped resolved, where once again, ambition, status, and sexuality merged. Questions of submission and superiority, dependence and independence were raised that had both social and sexual referents. Burke could well be saying in those impassioned letters that not only had Hamilton held back his career, but that he was uncomfortable playing the submissive role to Hamilton's dominance. Hamilton had denied or threatened his sense of manhood. Burke had made service to him "and not myself the first object." Burke was always faithful, but he would not "bind myself to you . . . in a sort of domestic situation." He would not "be a slave" to Hamilton.

Hamilton was furious at Burke. He poured his anger onto a page of rough notes. They indict Burke for breaking their agreement. His scrawled comments also suggest a deeper source of fury. "Said 1,000 times to Jeth: the Man of all others to live with. . . . All He wanted was his wife and child—Footing of mere Friendship, but denies Gratitude." The patron seems never to have forgiven the rebuke from his client. After the latter's death Hamilton wrote a scathing sketch of him. Burke's writings were "puerile and pitiable absurdities." Like Shackleton, Hamilton had his revenge.[52]

However much he was burned by this relationship, Burke's recovery was quick and unbelievably successful. Only a few months later he became private secretary to the First Lord of the Treasury, the Marquess of Rockingham. Despite the unfortunate denouement of the relationship with Hamilton, Burke reverted to the same pattern outlined in the adolescent letter to Shackleton. Social mobility would be achieved through dependent service to the great. And in Rockingham Burke had truly found the great! One of the largest landowners in England and Ireland, Rockingham had great power in the House of Commons derived from the extensive reaches of those immediately "attached" to his interest as well as from his influential position of leadership among the great Whig magnates. Burke's service to Rockingham over the next sixteen years would catapult middle-aged Burke to fame, power, and social position. But, as one might expect, it would also lead to tension, occasionally unbearable, between the demands of selfless service and self-serving ambition. That the relationship could last as long as it did, indeed until the death of Lord Rockingham in 1782, was made possible by Burke's election to Parliament in December of 1765. Will Burke had received a seat in Commons from his patron, Lord Verney, himself a member of Rockingham's aristocratic Whig set. Will gave the seat instead to Edmund. Verney and Rockingham agreed and Burke entered Parliament where he would remain for nearly thirty years. Membership in the House gave Burke the arena within which to make his own mark, to become his own man. Until 1782, however, he was never completely his own man; he was very much in the service of Rockingham, both in personal terms and also in the service of the "party" of high-minded, well-acred magnates who clustered around Rockingham. The pattern would be crucial for middle-aged Burke—as he served the great he himself became great. But, it was to be a life strategy fraught with psychic pitfalls.

Burke's success was immediate. The literary splash he had made in the middle 1750s paled beside the political sensation he became in 1766 and 1767. Dr. Johnson wrote of Burke's parliamentary debut that he had "gained more reputation than perhaps any man at his [first] appearance ever gained before. He made two speeches in the House for repealing the Stamp Act, which were publicly commended by Mr. Pitt and have filled the town with wonder." [53] Burke made no effort to hide his pride in this sudden fame. He wrote to his old friends in Ireland of how well he was received in the House, and of the "strong and favourable expressions" he received from the great Pitt and other luminaries.[54] There is good evidence that this early and satisfying political success was matched by an equally dramatic financial improvement—no more an uncommon connection in eighteenth-century politics than today. In 1766 William and Edmund Burke made a great deal of money in the stock market. By now friend William, Edmund, and brother Richard were operating a joint purse, with William clearly the principal financial operator. The financial success of 1766 fit perfectly into the Burke plans; being one's own man required the aid of independent financial resources. The letters indicate the extent to which this was part of their life strategy. Will wrote to Charles O'Hara, a Burke friend in Ireland: "If Ned [Edmund] gets to you . . . he will tell you that our fortunes are in a condition to second our views of Independency." [55] Edmund wrote himself two weeks later: "Will's news is indeed marvellous in the success, marvellous in the conduct, marvellous in the motives of action. . . . This certainly will leave one with some freedom of conduct." [56]

While William made the killing in stocks, Edmund was busily learning and mastering the new world of trade and commerce. Years later in his *Reflections on the Revolution in France* Burke would ridicule tradesmen and men of the counting house who replaced the gentlemen of the manor house in positions of power. But at the outset of his political career Burke made his own way as Rockingham's expert on commercial and trade policy. He, in fact, became one of the Whig Lord's major contacts with the commercial community. Out of this would grow Burke's involvement with American politics in the 1770s. Rockingham picked his man well. Perhaps he read Burke's character (or at least part of it) better than posterity has, for Will Burke wrote in March 1766:

As for ourselves, Richard eats, drinks, sleeps, and laughs his fill—Ned is full of business, intent upon doing real good to his country, as much as if he was to receive twenty per cent, from the commerce of the whole empire, which he labors to improve and extend.[57]

Burke was returned to Parliament in the general election of March 1768, through the generosity of his patrons, Verney and Rockingham, to be sure. But Burke had also arrived on his own right. To symbolize publicly his arrival, and to demonstrate his achievement, as Englishmen conventionally did, Burke purchased "an house, with an estate of about 600 acres of land in Buckinghamshire 24 miles from London; where now I am. It is a place exceedingly pleasant; and I propose, God willing, to become a farmer in good earnest." [58] All the Burkes moved in; Edmund, his wife, Jane, his son Richard, his brother Richard, and his friend William. They lived there for the rest of their lives, and Edmund farmed on his respites from Parliament and when he was not carrying out Rockingham's business in London. It was a singular success story. While, as he himself put it, he "gained prodigious applause from the public," he was able to purchase an estate that cost £20,000.[59] To this day its financing is shrouded in mystery—money from stock speculation, mortgages, friends—the exact details are unknown.[60] But to the eighteenth-century mind one thing was clear; it spelled success and a life-style befitting greatness.

Through the ambition and achievement, however, there lurked the anxiety of the man on the make. Immediately after his arrival in Parliament in December 1765 Burke wrote to a friend of his "success in a *New Walk of Life* for which I am little prepared, and about which I entertain so many anxious apprehensions, as greatly to abate the satisfaction I should otherwise find on making so considerable a Step in the World." [61] In almost classic manner his insecurity and anxiety led Burke to feverish activity, "full of business" as Will described it. No surprise then that in March 1766 Edmund wrote of a physical breakdown brought by round-the-clock efforts to master commercial details.[62] In the letter written in 1768 to his oldest friend Shackleton informing him of the purchase of the estate, Burke confided, "I am sorry to say it, I have never been quite correct and finished in my style of life; and I fear I never shall." [63] Burke has himself written the most fitting comment on this stage of his career in a letter to O'Hara in 1768. Things were never as simple as they appeared. It may have seemed a straightforward success story, but beneath this lay much more complex personal aspirations and fears. He affirmed and retreated from his ambition in the same paragraph.

Every body congratulated me on coming into the House of Commons, as being in the certain Road of a great and speedy fortune; and when I began to be heard with some little attention, every one of my friends was sanguine. But in truth I never was so myself. I came into Parliament not at all as a place of preferment, but of refuge; I was pushed into it; and I must have been a member, and that too with some Eclat, or be a little worse than nothing.[64]

CHAPTER 5

Present Discontents

(1768–1774)

✦

BURKE published his first major political essay in 1770. *Thoughts on the Cause of the Present Discontents* dealt with what many saw as the manifold crises in English politics at the turn of the decade. The Wilkes affair dragged on with the House of Commons continually locking horns with the radical constituents from Middlesex who were determined to have their man Wilkes seated. The House of Commons felt its own integrity threatened by the increasing domination of the executive under the management of George III. Over all of this there still loomed the unresolved crisis in the Empire as the thirteen colonies fresh from their victory over the Stamp Act (repealed by Rockingham's government in 1766) made new and ever more ominous noises against Parliament's commercial restrictions. Burke's essay offered a solution for all this discontent—party government under the leadership of Rockingham.

OF BOLD NEW MEN

The mood of public crisis that Burke forever captured in this memorable essay was paralleled by a sense of deep personal crisis in the career of Edmund Burke. The "present discontents" were both England's and Burke's. His newly won place in life, his new sense of self, suffered severe stress in this six-year period. His anxiety, the anxiety of the ambitious arrivé, persisted. His fear that perhaps he had overreached the position that was his natural due led him to avoid the country houses where Rockingham's social circle met. Nor did he attend their race meetings, or their watering spots. Ever sensitive, Burke noted in a letter that Lord Shelburne (not a political ally) "has been for many years very polite to me; and that is all." Burke described his patron and party leader Rockingham as neglectful and cold on occasion.[1] This may be no more than the sensitivity and trace of paranoia one expects from Burke, but in this period of life there were more than sufficient grounds to justify his anxiety. Two events in particular threatened the entire foundation of his recently acquired success.

The first was the bursting of the Burke financial bubble. Richard and Will's spiralling speculations backfired in 1769 and from the sense of security and optimism that prompted the purchase of his estate in 1768 Edmund was thrust to virtual financial ruin and despair. His letters of those years indicate constant borrowing of thousands of pounds.[2] The very months he wrote the *Present Discontents* saw him falling deeper and deeper into debt. He wrote to O'Hara of "the ruin of our situation," his own that is, not England's.[3] Will went off to India to recoup the family fortune, and Edmund was partially rescued by timely financial gifts from Rockingham. As Rockingham at the head of a new party government would rescue the country from its political crisis, according to Burke's essay, so he, in fact, helped rescue Burke from his personal financial crisis.

Like many an ambitious upstart Burke's anxiety over the vagaries of economic fortune focused on his offspring. Middle-class wealth had none of the generational certainty of a broad-acred fortune. Burke lamented to Rockingham in 1773 that he would have nothing to leave his son, no legacy, no fortune.[4] The financial reversal had dashed all hopes for that. This was all the more grievous for much of Burke's ambitions were by then already being transferred to the future achievements and success of his beloved son. Young Richard was sent first to Christchurch, the most lordly of Oxford's colleges, and then to Europe on the Grand Tour, as befitted a gentleman. Burke hoped he would be "doing something for himself in the world." [5] As he grew older Burke would become more and more intent that his son make an even greater mark than he had, but it is no mere accident that the introduction of this theme in his letters occurred in this period of personal discontent.

The second source of Burke's discontents was the unceasing criticism to which he was subjected by Parliamentary and journalistic critics of Rockingham's connection. They came down savagely on his social and political pretensions, ridiculing him as an outsider, overly ambitious to make it. They joked about his Irishness, his new estate, even his financial reversals. The *Public Advertiser* (21 September 1769) criticized "a display of eloquence by some Hibernian Orators, who have not great credit in a certain alley in the city." [6] The scene of perhaps the most vicious attack on Burke was a Parliamentary debate in April 1770. Sir William Bagot, a Tory M.P., "chose to harangue and pronounce a Philipick on Ned," as William Burke described it in a letter to a friend. Bagot decried the danger to good government from the presence of such "new men" like Burke in Commons. An angry Burke rose to defend himself, to defend his very sense of identity, to defend his right to the place he had worked so hard to achieve. He accepted and in fact reveled in the accusation. Will's letter described the response.

He took to himself the appellation of a *Novus Homo*. He knew the envy attending that character. *Novorum Hominum Industriam Odisti;* but as he knew the envy, he knew the duty of the *Novus Homo*. He then, valuing himself only on his industry . . . shewed he had performed that duty in endeavoring to know the commerce, the finances, and Constitution of his country. . . . He expatiated upon the Impropriety and danger of discouraging new men, this rising merit stamped with virtue would indeed seek to rise, but under the wings of established Greatness, and if their industry and their virtue was greater than etc. etc. etc. they must be equal, nay the superior to the lazy something that came by inheritance. If they are precluded the just and constitutional roads to ambition, they will seek others . . . it was the case in Ch. [Charles] Ist time, and those who value themselves on their vast property, and envy all merit that seeks to be useful may as they did then, be servants of Brewers, and low Mechanics. . . . All wise governments have encouraged rising merit, as useful and necessary. [7]

This is the bourgeois creed of careers and positions open to talent and merit. It invokes the Revolution of 1640 as not only legitimate but as motivated primarily by the dynamics of upward social mobility. Two weeks later writing to his Dick Shackleton, Edmund repeated this defense of himself against his critics. He had not sought to make it on the coattails of the great.

Whatever advantages I have had, have been from friends on my own level; as to those that are called great, I never paid them any court. [8]

This, of course, is not true, but what is more important than the exaggeration is Burke's insistence on his own worth, his own achievements. He saw himself as important to Rockingham and his circle because of his skill and talent, as they had been for him with their power. This is but one side of Burke's ambivalence, however, this praise of self-made men and their destiny to govern is balanced by Burke's equally strong and sycophantic attitudes about the destiny of the virtuous aristocracy. When his anxiety over his new position and his sense of inadequacy took the better of him, attitudes bound to surface occasionally in someone so recently arrived in an age still dominated by aristocratic assumptions, he would be the blatant apologist for aristocracy and the dutiful servant of his betters. It was in 1772, after all, that he wrote to Richmond of the aristocratic great oaks in contrast to his common vine that crept along the ground. The premise of the *Present Discontents* was that Rockingham and the great Whig magnates in his party should govern, while Burke behind the scenes might at most organize the party, be its propagandist and manager, but certainly not a leader.

This tension within Burke's own mind was projected onto a public vision of inevitable social conflict in society. Throughout his career Burke saw two great forces contending in the social order. The names of the contenders would differ from episode to episode but what would always remain the same was the nature of the struggle. The confrontation was always between bold and adventurous newcomers, who sought power or status, and those in power who were naturally entitled to such privileges. Wherever Burke turned he saw this social conflict at work. It was his genius to recognize in this way the ideological dynamic that lay behind the great confrontation of his age between aristocratic values and bourgeois values. What is intriguing, of course, is to speculate on the extent to which his own personality and divided self was in part the original source of his great historical insight. The very terms of its formulation here—upstart newcomers replacing the naturally privileged—evoke oedipal themes.

An early formulation of what we can call Burke's law of social conflict is found in a letter to Rockingham of December 1769. Burke wrote to complain that Rockingham's party was not responding creatively and quickly enough to the Wilkes crisis.

Bold men take the lead, to which others are entitled; and they soon come to a power, not natural to them, by the remissness of those who neither know how to be effectual friends or dangerous enemies, or active champions in a good cause. They complain of the unnatural growth of such people, and they are the cause of it.[9]

In another formulation of his law Burke attributed this social bifurcation between the bold and the slow, an ambitious middle class and honest plodding aristocracy, to givens in human nature and ultimately to God. He wrote in August 1769 to O'Hara:

But God has given different spirits to different men. The profligate and inconsiderate are bold, adventurous, and pushing. Honest men slow, backward and irresolute. In order to do Evil in the end, the dashers take noble steps; pretend good; and sometimes do it. The others are so fearful of doing ill, that they frequently fall short of doing the good that is in their power. The world is thus constituted: and it is jest to murmur at the course of human nature and affairs.[10]

What is unclear here and what would be unclear for much of Burke's life is what he really thought of those "bold men," or of those "others," the "honest and slow," for that matter. His career can, in fact, be charted conveniently in terms of which of these two inevitable contending forces he championed at any particular time, which itself represented whichever side of his own personal ambivalence was then dominant.

There is no doubt about one thing, however. At this time of crisis and discontent Burke's contemporaries read him as very much a "bold man." Indeed, the analysis offered here helps shed some new light on an enigmatic episode in the conventional Burke story. In 1771 Burke was thought by many to be "Junius," the anonymous writer whose brilliant, vitriolic, and radical letters attacking King George and demanding triennial Parliaments were very much part of the crisis atmosphere of these years of discontent. The rumors were widespread and hints were often found in the press that Burke was the real author of the *Letters of Junius.*[11] The conventional explanation for this attribution is that the brilliance of Burke's debut, his literary flourish as a writer, his cutting wit as orator drew attention to him as the possible author. Had he not written an essay of radical satire in 1756 to put down the ideas of Lord Bolingbroke? Burke referred to these grounds for the charge in a letter to Charles Townsend on 17 October 1771, complete with due modesty and self-deprecation. "You observe very rightly that no fair man can believe me to be author of *Junius.* Such a supposition might tend indeed to raise the estimation of my powers of writing above their just value."[12] But the basis for the allegations were more probably ideological, not literary. Burke was accused of being Junius because he was perceived by many in these years as just the kind of talented and bold person who could write such critical material.

This, then, was the setting for one of the most revealing of Burke's early defenses of himself as assertive self-made man. One of his oldest friends, Dr. William Markham, former Dean of Christchurch, Oxford and then Bishop of Chester, wrote Burke in November 1771 that the suspicions that he was Junius were based, in part, on the widespread impression that Burke and his kinsmen, Richard and William, were out to make their mark by repudiating and even perhaps replacing their natural superiors. Markham advised his friend Burke that he mind his place. Burke's reply to Markham is a central document in illustrating his ambivalence on the social issues brought to the surface in this attack upon him. This letter defending and justifying himself is the longest found in the nine volumes of his correspondence.[13] Burke rejected the charge that he was too ambitious, and that "I do not act a proper part in life." He denied that his actions were in any way unseemly. Why, he asked, should I "bring down the aims of my ambition to a lower level? You accuse me of maltreating the greatest men in the kingdom," Burke wrote, of being "a man capable of things dangerous and desperate." He answered the charges. "I am a respecter of authority. But my Lord I execute my share of an important magistracy, and I conceive that it may happen to be part of my office to accuse and even very ill treat the first men in the Kingdom." What Burke had done, he claimed, he had to do, and moreover it was merely responsive. In a comment revealing for its combination of defensiveness, insecurity, partial truth, and partial paranoia, Burke justified his career by asking: "Does your Lordship think it absolutely incredible, that attempts might be made to *pull me down;* and that I may have been necessitated to make some strong efforts to *keep myself up?*" [14]

Burke's response to his critics in these years was not simply a defense of himself as a "bold man," with no cause to recant. His attitudes were deeply ambivalent on this crucial identity-defining issue. No surprise, then, to discover that in this period of his discontent he also lashed out at the real radicals—the real bold men and women—on the scene, and he did this from the perspective of the aristocratic norms he served as embodied in his service to Rockingham and his advocacy of party government by the Whig magnates. Several letters written in late 1770 unusual for their harsh tone find Burke assailing the "Bill of Rights people," the Wilkes supporters, and city radicals, the likes of Horne Tooke and Catherine Macaulay. We have already noted these letters in which he assailed those who "expect perfect reformation," and who bring in "speculative questions" to politics. Contrasted with these philosophers were prudent men. "All that wise men ever aim at is to keep things from coming to the worst." [15] These letters illustrate what will become a recurring pattern in Burke's career, lashing out at radicals in terms of the very characteristics Burke often saw in himself and, indeed, of which he was just as often quite proud. The city radicals led by Mrs. Macaulay, "our Republican virago," as Burke described her, had been extremely critical of Burke's *Thoughts on the Cause of the Present Discontents.* Mrs. Macaulay saw it for what it was, propaganda to serve the cause of the aristocratic clique around Rockingham, and she criticized it and the clique as worthless and highly dispensable. [16]

Burke was upset by this criticism of his essay. But the tone of his response was so uncharacteristically harsh and vindictive for this stage in his career that there seems to have been more involved here than meets the eye. He condemned the "Bill of Rights people" for the "violence, rashness, and often wickedness of their measures." They were veritable traitors, and thus, "how well these villains deserve the gallows." Perhaps their real crime was the boldness of their political and social ambitions. [17] Was Burke turning upon part of himself through this attack on the radicals? Did it express his ambivalence over his own ambition and failure to play his natural part? Was he projecting onto the public realm and onto the party of bold, ambitious, middle-class radicals the problems he had with this dimension of his private self, which when externalized and opposed helped relieve the sense of guilt which had been brought to the surface by the attacks on him as a new man? By his own choice of words Burke may have provided an answer to these questions. When he turned in his letter to the radical "Bill of Rights people" he referred to them as "a rotten subdivision of a Faction amongst ourselves," which does, of course, accurately describe the historical situation. [18] These radicals were a part, the left flank, of the

broad-based opposition to the king and his ministers which had Rockingham as its titular leader. Still, the choice of words is revealing. They were a
part of ourselves, a part that needed to be exorcised. It could well be a part
of himself to which Burke referred.

PARTY AND THE IDEAL OF SERVICE

Burke's *Thoughts on the Cause of the Present Discontents* mirrored Burke's personal state of mind during these years. The public solution it suggested for
the nation's crisis also served as the basis for the private salvation of Burke's
crisis. As Rockingham helped bail out Burke from his financial woes he
would, Burke argued in his essay, bail out the country from its troubles.
More significantly, however, the solution offered by the essay was party, and
as it would solve England's discontents so a case can be made that it would
also resolve Burke's discontents.

The theoretical core of Burke's essay is the defense of party government,
a government of men united by common ideas, which would save England.
This was an important statement of principle. Parties and factions were customarily criticized by writers on politics in the eighteenth century, and to
the extent that party government has become an important aspect of modern
constitutional doctrine, Burke deserves recognition as perhaps the first major
theorist of party.[19] There is, to be sure, a great deal of debate in the world of
scholarship over how genuine or even how meaningful this commitment to
party was. It was most certainly a partisan statement directed against the
model of personal leadership offered by the elder Pitt and no doubt it pushed
the cause of one particular party "or body of men," the one associated with
Burke's patron Rockingham.[20] But this is beside the point. The more important issue at stake is the role that the party played in the working out of
Burke's personal crisis. What it did was to provide an extremely useful
mechanism for dealing with the tension inherent in Burke's servile relationship to the great, the tension between the dependency of the agent and
the independence of the ambitious man. That Burke could stay on with
Rockingham for sixteen years (until the latter's death) was due in no small
part to the fact that the situation that led to the break with Hamilton was
avoided because of party. How was this possible?

That the theme of service was a crucially significant one in understanding eighteenth-century English life has already been suggested in this
book. Aristocrats were unique in that they waited on no one, they served no
one. They were independent. While many English aristocrats in the eigh-

teenth century turned to entrepreneurial activity, canals, banks, etc., few entered the law, for example, for the very reason that attorneys were servants of their clients. No matter how successful and enterprising lower- or middle-class individuals might be, it was difficult for them to break out of the circle of dependence and service to the great. It is for this reason that themes of independence and being one's own man were so central in bourgeois and radical rhetoric. Burke faced this problem, not that atypical for the age, in his relationship with Rockingham. On the one hand he was making his own career, on the other he was in service to a social superior. There would be good reason to expect that at some point the two patterns would clash as they had with Hamilton, when the superior became infuriated with the threatening independence of the servant. This inherently difficult situation was made even more so for Burke because he was self-consciously aware that in part of his mind he perceived his drive for personal independence and fame as threatening to the aristocracy, as an effort of a bold man to throw off notions of service and indeed to covet replacing those entitled to rank and privilege.

The intricacies and intensities of this dilemma were eased for Burke via party. It was not for Rockingham that he worked, it was for a party, "a cause," the cause of a collectivity of high-minded men. Burke could abide by the imperatives of the aristocratic principle as energetic servant of a party, and indeed Burke was the real organizer and critical element in Rockingham's party for over sixteen years. While doing this he could still express the bourgeois principle, i.e., further his own ambitions and make his own mark, fortune, and fame. He could do this without threatening the aristocracy, or his social superior, without being a usurping leveller like the ambitious men and women who went wholeheartedly into radicalism. The critical feature of the principle of service was its personal quality. Allegiance to the party, however, rendered Burke's relations with Rockingham and the great easier and less problematic. By serving party and making his mark through it he did not threaten Rockingham with his independence nor violate the crucial principle of service so basic to the aristocratic culture. Because of party loyalty Burke could speak his own mind in the years to come, even criticize Rockingham, without appearing uppity or insulting to his superior. It was not for his own advancement that he did so, but from his service to the collective and impersonal superior—the party. Through party, then, Burke could, in fact, express both the bourgeois and the aristocratic aspects of his divided self. It was in the service of party that ambitious Burke could find his place, and while it by no means resolved all the tensions inherent in the relationship of his personality to his politics it certainly helped Burke deal with the discontents of these years without having the additional problems of what we might call the Hamilton syndrome. Party government was, thus, a critical discovery by Burke in 1770. Ironically enough, its greatest success was its personal usefulness to Burke. Rockingham's party would have an opportunity to resolve England's crisis for only a few short months in 1782. But as a principle and a reality for which Burke worked for so many years, party continued to serve the important function of easing inner conflicts. It represented an extremely successful and creative merger of private need and public principle.

Burke's essay on party government provides additional insights into the relationship between his political writings and his personal needs. A persistent theme in the essay, for example, is the need to place politics more firmly on an affective base. As the family is the heart of the Commonwealth, so, then, in politics the natural ties of "friendship and attachment" ought to be the organizing principle and not artificial ties of momentary interest.[21] While Burke suggests that it is the sharing of common ideals which unite a party there is also an effort in the essay to infuse public life via party with the private virtues of affection and friendship. Parts of the essay read as a demand that the beautiful virtues of *On the Sublime and Beautiful* replace the sublime virtues of Pitt's leadership, or of George III's for that matter. His objective is "to bring the dispositions that are lovely in private life into the service and conduct of the Commonwealth."[22] Burke sees in party a humanization of politics, a return to a genuine community as opposed to an artificial community where men combine but are unrelated to one another by friendship and tenderness.

Party is thus an idea riddled with paradox for Burke, i.e., expressive of his ambivalence. It is a platform for his sublime ambition, yet it glorifies the beautiful feminine social ideals of "friendship's holy ties," of "affection," and of "attachment."[23] Searching for the warm emotional embrace of party, of affectionate friends, is for Burke the resurrection of family at the center of politics. Yet "the dearest connexions" of party are all men.[24] The feminine principle of beauty, of love and pleasure, is carried on the strong shoulders of "a body of men united. . . ."[25] The affective male bonding that party represented for Burke in 1770 became a reality. It became, one could argue, the principal expression, on the surface and tolerable, for his homophilic instincts. No one who reads the details of the painful rupture with his "dearest connexions" like Fox, when Burke left the party two decades later, can but be struck with how powerful an arena of friendship and affect this all-male party had become for Burke. Fox cried openly like a boy on the floor of Commons when he and Burke fell out.[26] Burke's language in the Commons said as much as Fox's tears. Party seems to have had an emotional and psychological significance for Burke far transcending even what the most anti-Namierite traditionalists have argued. Disregarding what may be the conventional exaggerations of rhetoric, it is clear that this was no ordinary "party squabble," nor ideological falling-out.

Mr. Burke said, that although party connexions were extremely proper for mutual arrangement in private, and convenience of public business, they were seldom fit to become the subject of public debate . . . To talk of parties was, he remarked, a matter of particular delicacy, as the confidence of private friendship was often so much intermixed with public duty, that the transaction of parties required a sort of sanctity which precluded any disclosure. This delicacy was particularly increased, when friends, who loved and esteemed one another, were compelled, in consequence to a difference of opinion, to pull different ways and felt all the distraction natural to virtuous minds in such a situation.[27]

CHAPTER 6

Recovery: Burke and His Betters (1774–1782)

$$\maltese$$

$\mathbf{B}$URKE'S discontents persisted until the general election of 1774, when he was returned to The House of Commons from Bristol. Just before the election he wrote to Rockingham in a melancholic expression of his inadequacy. Perhaps "I ought not totally to abandon this public station for which I am so unfit, and have, of course, been so unfortunate." [1] His sense of worthlessness emerged again that same month in a letter to Richmond. It was vintage Burke, at least in terms of part of his ambivalence, the sycophantic aristocratic principle, that denigrated self before the obvious superiority of the great. "Your birth," he wrote to Richmond, "will not suffer you to be private. It requires as much struggle and violence to put yourself into private life as to put me into publick. Pardon a slight comparison but it is as hard to sink a cork as to buoy up a lump of lead." [2]

AMBITION AND AMERICA

Recovery, however, would be the major motif of the next eight years in Burke's career. It was introduced by his success in the polls at Bristol which, as he wrote to a friend, gave him "much more importance in the eyes of everyone else." [3] Burke no longer represented a pocket borough in the Rockingham connection, he was victorious in an open election in England's second-largest city. He had been invited to contest the seat by Bristol merchants impressed by his concern for the colonial cause in America, which he served so well, both as member of the opposition to Lord North, and as paid agent for New York. The victory provided Burke with a sense of importance and a degree of independence. He still served Rockingham as personal secretary, to be sure; but his base of power shifted to his own heavily populated constituency and out from under the umbrella of aristocratic patronage.

The feelings of inadequacy continued, surfacing from time to time. To the Marchioness of Rockingham he confided, for example, in 1779, that his ambition had been "to be suffered as the lowest among a select few." That same year he wrote to William Eden that he (Burke) was "too weak and obscure a person" to have any real impact on commercial policy.[4] By and large, however, this eight-year stretch was characterized by achievement and pride, the hegemony for the time being of his bourgeois self. In these years he acquired new fame as parliamentary champion of the Americans, seeking conciliation with the colonies and defending their commercial and political rights which he saw threatened by Government policy. He also emerged as the leading opponent of parliamentary reform in England during this period, as well as a major critic of George III, which culminated in his proposals of 1780 and 1782 to reduce the patronage power of the Crown and thus reduce its power to control the Commons. As this period ended Burke was in fact holding a government office—a very lucrative one if not that prestigious—as Paymaster of the Forces.

So much for the objective outline of Burke's career and its obvious successes from 1774 to 1782. His letters in these years point to developments not so obvious. One sees there patterns of private concern which relate directly to themes raised earlier. Of primary significance is Burke's further articulation during these years of his distinction between the principles of active ambitions and boldness on the one hand and slow and honest inactivity on the other. He refined the distinction into an overt one between what we have suggested was the bourgeois principle, on the one hand, and the aristocratic principle, on the other. This emerges most clearly in a long string of letters in which Burke needled and criticized the aristocratic leaders of his party. He had done this earlier over the Wilkes affair; now in the discussions among opposition politicians on how to deal with America Burke renewed his criticism of his betters. From his newly acquired parliamentary independence Burke became, at least in private correspondence, much more openly critical of Rockingham's circle, again revealing a side of himself not conventionally part of his image.

Burke's criticism of the aristocracy was muted in one sense. What he principally faulted them for was their failure to live up to their responsibilities and duties. He continually berated them for not acting, not leading, not shaping events, but merely responding. In 1769 it was around this feeling that he had initially articulated his law of social conflict based on the inevitable polarity of personality types. He wrote to O'Hara in that year contrasting the aristocratic party he served and its radical allies in the opposition.

We are diffident, scrupulous, timid and slow into coming into a resolution. . . . As for our allies their manner is quite different; they resolve early and with boldness; . . . I have lately seen enough both of the one and the other. You know how much I felt from the slowness and irresolution of some of our best friends. Even to this moment, there are some of them who cannot be prevailed upon to take the lead, which is natural to their situation, and necessary to their consequence.[5]

Burke constantly returned to this theme when discussing America. As servant and principal propagandist for Rockingham's party, he pleaded with his superiors to act in the crisis, to offer a bold policy alternative that would recommend itself to the Government and perhaps even keep the Empire intact. In January 1775 he wrote to Rockingham, "the question, then, is whether your Lordship chooses to lead or to be led; to lay down proper ground yourself, or stand in an awkward and distressing situation on the ground which will be prepared for you." [6] He wrote again in August to Rockingham making "no apology for urging again and again how necessary it is for your Lordship and your great friends most seriously to take under immediate deliberation, what you are to do in this crisis." With obvious irritation Burke suggested that it served no good for the great to be part-time statesmen dabbling in affairs of state between race meetings and watering spas.

This is no time for taking publick business in its course and order, and only as a part in the Scheme of Life, which comes and goes at its proper periods and is mixed in with other occupations and amusements. It calls for the whole of the best of us. . . . Indeed my Dear Lord you are called upon in a very peculiar manner. America is yours. You have saved it once; and you may very possibly save it again.[7]

Burke's criticism of Rockingham, made somewhat safer by his alleged service to the greater superior, party, is unusual and striking. In one letter he characterized the magnate's opposition as "weak, irregular, desultory, and peevish"; in another, he described Rockingham's opposition as characterized by "too much despondency." There was, he wrote, "too much languor, inactivity and remissness in the whole tenor of our character." [8] But Burke also knew that prodding Rockingham to activity was ultimately doomed to fail. There was little an opposition party could realistically do to influence policy, to be sure, but much more significant was Burke's sense that Rockingham's passivity was fated. It was, after all, only an inevitable expression of Burke's own law of the polarity of social personalities. How could Rockingham break from the character of his class? Aristocrats, were, after all, "in general somewhat lanquid, scrupulous and unsystematic." "Men of high Birth and great property," Burke contended, "are rarely as enterprising as others." [9] Being men of integrity they were too careful in the choice of means, and thus seldom engaged in adventuresome and bold activity. Writing in 1777 to a party friend, Burke characterized their leaders—Saville, Rockingham, the Cavendishes—as "minds too delicate for the rough and toilsome Business of our time." Burke was quite certain about what accounted for these personality traits. It was "their want of the stimulus of ambition." [10] In a letter to Fox that same week he noted "that some faults in the constitution of those whom we most love and trust are among the causes of this impracticability. One could hardly wish them cured of these faults," he added, for they are "intimately connected with honest disinterested intentions, plentiful fortunes, assured rank and quiet homes." It was inconceivable that such men would display "a great deal of activity and enterprize." They lacked ambition and the desire to improve themselves as motives to action. The only thing that jolted them from inactivity, Burke wrote, was "gross personal insult," which stimulated the great in the way ambition did the common man. [11]

The bifurcation of the social and political world into the ambitions of bold commoners and the inactivity of great aristocrats also informed Burke's reading of the relationship between the American Colonies and England, where it was given an even more specific ideological character. Writing to his old friend O'Hara in 1775 he noted with admiration the incredible active and assertive spirit of the Americans. He singled out two men for particular reference, the aide-de-camp to Washington, "a very grave and staunch Quaker of large fortune," and Washington himself, who "stakes a fortune of about 5,000 a year." They were, of course, "very inferior" to those with whom Burke associated, but he marveled at the spirit that animated them. These talented men were bold and their spirit adventuresome. They risked their hard-earned money and were tested by a "remote and difficult country." Contrasted to them Burke saw in England only ruin, despair and "the listlessness that has fallen upon almost all." [12] In a letter, written several days later to Rockingham, Burke again contrasted the upstart Americans with the English who had experienced "a great change in the national character." No longer an eager, inquisitive, fiery people, the English were "cold" and "languid," excited to no passion, prompted to no action. England, he wrote, had declined from its former grandeur to ruin and corruption. [13] In his *Letters to the Sheriffs of Bristol* Burke contrasted the "unwieldy haughtiness," of an England "pampered by enormous wealth," with "the high spirit of free dependencies." [14] Against the passive feminine English, the Americans seemed the quintessence of bold and youthful masculinity. Though they were still "in the gristle, and not yet hardened into the bone of manhood," there was about them something "savage" and "uncouth." [15] Moreover, they were "animated with the first glow and activity of juvenile heat." [16]

This was, of course, at least in its social terms, a common theme in English letters during this period, especially in radical and dissenter circles. It was, in fact, a theme basic to all opposition sentiment in the eighteenth century since its articulation in Bolingbroke's assault on Walpole's Robinocracy. Burke bridges the gap between its Tory formulation earlier in the century and its radical invocation in the age of the American and French Revolutions.[17] Decadent and corrupt aristocratic England wallowing in idle luxury is contrasted with vital, hard-working and prosperous America. In his *Speech on American Taxation* Burke claimed, sounding like many a bourgeois radical, that "nothing in the history of mankind is like their progress." And this is due to their not being "slow and languid" but instead being living proof of "successful industry."[18] The ideological theme was central for radicals in the later half of the century, as well as for Burke. America represented the bourgeois principle and England the aristocratic. It should be remembered, too, that Burke was at this time a member of Parliament from Bristol, a center of middle-class dissenting economic interests and that in a parliamentary speech of 1775 he insisted that it was the commercial half of the House who opposed the American policy while the landed part approved it.[19]

But there is much more to Burke's championship of the Americans than simply this. To be sure, as noted above, Burke was defending the lost rights of America against the break in continuity brought by innovative English commercial policy. In this sense he was offering a defense of the aristocratic principle, inactivity, and continuity, against innovation and action, service of the lesser America to the greater England. Bur Burke's ambivalence is at work here, too. On another level America means something completely different to Burke. Identification with America in the 1770s expressed that side of his personality that longed for the independence with which to be his own master, his own man. America, like that ambitious part of Burke, refused to keep its place, the rank and position assigned it by custom, history, or social convention. It represented the triumph of the bourgeois over the aristocratic principle. Burke often wrote of America in terms that were strikingly appropriate to himself. Like him they were outsiders, "a set of miserable outcasts, a few years ago." As he had left voluntarily to make his fortunes in a strange, inhospitable land, so they were "thrown out, on the bleak and barren shore of a desolate wilderness."[20] As an Irishman he identified with the colonial cause and, indeed, linked the two. In 1765 when Parliament was considering the repeal of the Stamp Act he wrote to his Irish friend Charles O'Hara, that "the liberties (or what shadows of liberty there are) of Ireland have been saved in America."[21] Like the Americans opposed to "the spirit of domination," the "relish of honest equality," the upstart Burke defended himself against those who accused him of opposing his betters. Like them he spoke out against "those habituated to command," and like them he could be accused of "assuming to themselves, as their birthright, some part of that very pride which oppresses them." [22] In a recently discovered fragment on America found among his papers in Sheffield, Burke points to this very personal significance of the American episode. To the Americans, he noted, "I owe eternal thanks for making me think better of my nature." [23]

There is a final theme that pervades Burke's writings and speeches on America that also speaks to the personal significance of the issue for him. He, like many observers, referred to America and England in familial terms. But he persisted in the metaphor with dogged insistence while drawing interesting lessons from it. Concern with the proper relations of parents and children would be, after all, a continuous thread woven through Burke's life and writings, which makes his comments on America all the more fascinating. His plea here was for a kind and good parent, understanding the natural rebellious urges of children. The response to American violence should be "fidelity and kindness." England should be a nonrepressive parent, and the child in turn would respond with love and affection.[24] "When children ask for bread we are not to give a stone," he cautions the Commons. England's child looks to its parent for warmth, assurance, and understanding, and all it gets is restraint, caprice, and arbitrary repression. Burke could sympathize with the colonial cause when rendered in these terms; it was a family situation not unlike his own. Lord Camarthen had asked in debate, if "the Americans are our children . . . how can they revolt against their parent." [25] Burke's reply was a stirring defense of the "present opposition of our children." Their rebellion is not shocking, it is a legitimate response to parental "abuses of authority" and "desire of domineering." Children will not suffer lightly the "rankness of servitude." What they want from their parents is "lenity, moderation, and tenderness." [26]

ON ACTIVITY AND PASSIVITY

In his disputes with Rockingham over the question of America Burke continued developing his distinctions between activity and passivity, which, it has been suggested, correspond to the basic division and ambivalence found in Burke's sense of himself, an ambivalence between assertive ambitious Burke and passive serving Burke knowing his place. The latter aristocratic principle, it should be noted, was itself two-sided; it could reflect the ideal of service which bound nonaristocrats to the aristocracy or the inactivity associated with a class or rank not moved to action by ambition. As a principle it could refer, then, both to serving the aristocratic ideal and to the characteristics of the aristocracy itself.

These distinctions entered into virtually every issue Burke dealt with in his long career and it would be wise at this point to note the gender implications of Burke's distinctions, for when Burke described the bourgeois principle in his letters and writings he repeatedly used stereotypical masculine adjectives. Fiery, hearty, bold, industrious, independent, enterprising, active, rough, spirited, pushy, ambitious, assertive, and adventuresome are some examples. When he described the aristocratic principle he used equally stereotypical feminine adjectives: listless, timid, diffident, idle, peevish, irresolute, precious, languid, indolent, passive, dependent, inactive, and supine. It is, of course, by no means certain that this patterning of words had conscious gender association for Burke, or, for that matter, particular linkage to social or class character. On the other hand, Burke was as susceptible as any one else to the pervasive generalizations found writ large in western culture, stereotyping women as passive and men as active, men as transcendent and women as immanent. What does seem important in Burke's case, however, is the patterning of language in light of our earlier psychosexual hypothesis about his childhood, adolescence, and early adulthood.

This antagonism between what Burke conceived of as the active/bourgeois/masculine principle and the passive/aristocratic/feminine principle also informed his thoughts on party during these years. In his elitist vision party was the active male principle leading the passive feminine people who were willing and waiting to be led. Burke called upon the aristocracy, who made up the party which he served, to become more manly and to stop playing the feminine role. They might never be able to transcend that role, as he had himself noted, but still he called on them to try. If they would not act, then the manly bourgeoisie would take charge and lead the inactive people. In doing this they would replace the natural leaders of the people, unless, that is, the aristocracy acted equally as boldly. If the aristocracy remained idle, he wrote O'Hara, the people would be led by those who are "by no means our wisest or perhaps our best men." [27] He wrote in 1775 to Richmond, "The people are not answerable for their present supine acquiescence . . . God and nature never made them to think or to act without guidance and direction." They look to their "natural leaders," the party of men of "rank and fortune in the country," that party which according to Burke was in the year of 1775 sadly inactive and lacking in boldness. The party was faulted for doing "so little to guide and direct the public opinion." Writing to the Duke of Portland, a leader in the Rockingham circle, Burke described "a real fault" with the party: "I mean a little dilatoriness; and a missing of opportunities for action, from the want of a spirit of adventure." [28]

That Burke should link the aristocracy to the people by a common characterization of passivity and idleness in these comments on party should not be that surprising for it reflects his basic social ambivalence. It allowed him to express and praise those middle-class traits he perceived in himself while demanding that the aristocracy be, in fact, more like himself. Lumping aristocrats and people in one class and gender basket highlighted the uniqueness and value of the bold, adventuresome, and masculine middle class with which Burke at times identified. Burke's thoughts on party did involve, then, and, to a certain extent, mask these private concerns. This is all the more apparent when it is noted how often and how easily in his calls for party action over America Burke personalized the issue and related it specifically to himself. He constantly apologized to Rockingham for his own boldness and assertiveness while demanding the very same from the aristocratic leaders of his party. In one letter he described the "imprudent officiousness of my zeal." In another he apologized for his "importunity" and "earnestness." By 1777 he was writing to Fox confiding that perhaps he (Burke) had been too bold, too pushy in his urgings over America.[29]

The personalization of these dichotomies is even more evident in Burke's development of his theory of representation. Here, too, the principles of activity and passivity can be seen at work. Burke's conception of the responsibility of the representative to his constitutents is, without doubt, one of his most important contributions to the history of political thought. As noted earlier, his is the classic repudiation of the radical theory which sets up the representative as no more than agent, a mere delegate for his constituents. According to Burke, the Member of Parliament was elected for his wisdom. Far from being the mouthpiece of his constituents, he expressed his own virtuous insights on matters of state, informed by his enlightened sense of national interest.[30]

Burke's correspondence in this period indicates that behind this theory of representation lay his preoccupation with issues of leading and being led, action and passivity, boldness and idleness, with the one difference that here it was manifestly Burke the member of Parliament from Bristol who was one half of the formulation. As the party was the active masculine principle vis-à-vis the nation and the people, so the representative was the active leader and his constituents the passive follower. Radical theory unfortunately had it reversed; it would have the constituents the active masculine principle and Burke, the member of Parliament, the passive idle servant. He, as representative, Burke argued, had to actively and boldly lead his constituents, "bring them" he wrote to Portland, "over to my principles." [31] His letters to his Bristol commercial constituents constantly enjoined them to follow his views and in turn gave short shrift to any suggestion that he should follow theirs.[32] It was his role to shape their opinions. Burke had no ostensible regrets over losing his parliamentary seat in 1780, he wrote to Rockingham. He had ignored Bristol's instructions, he insisted, because they were either foolish or unwise. But it was also a preoccupation with problems of leading and being led, of action and inaction, that emerges from his letters.

But as to leaving to the crowd, to choose for me, what principles I ought to hold, or what course I ought to pursue for their benefit—I had much rather, innocently and obscurely, mix with them, with the utter ruin of all my hopes, (which hopes are my all) than to betray them by learning lessons from them.[33]

His constituents posed a threat to Burke's bourgeois sense of independence, his sense of being his own man, in their demands for his passivity. They were calling upon him to express the aristocratic principle of service, inaction and dependence. The controversy raised once again the whole struggle and internal strife that was the enduring mark of his rise to prominence, and the resultant ambivalence it left with him. He dealt with it here by repudiating the aristocratic principle of service to others. He would lead and not serve! He was insisting once again on his manhood and putting to rest any feminine identification. Members of Parliament, he insisted in 1780, should have no taint of femininity.

Let us cast away from us, with a generous scorn, all the love-tokens and symbols that we have been vain and light enough to accept;—all the bracelets . . . and miniature pictures, and hair devices, and all other adulterous trinkets that are the pledges of our alienation, and the monuments of our shame.[34]

The touchstone of Burke's social attitudes was always ambivalence, however, and among the letters to his constituents in Bristol there is one which shows the other side of his ambivalence at work. His position on representation was elitist, to be sure, and smacked of an aristocratic notion of natural leaders and natural followers. But in terms of Burke's private division of the social world into the active and the passive it was, like his notion of party, also a statement of the bourgeois principle, and reflective of that side of his divided attitudes, just as it represented a bourgeois commitment to independence as opposed to the aristocratic principle of service. Occasionally, however, Burke reacted strongly against any overt display of his bourgeois proclivities. Just such an occasion occurred in November 1777, when Burke wrote a letter to a group of Bristol supporters. The letter itself is less important than a draft of it which Burke never sent. The draft, which he censored, was found years later among his manuscript papers and published in 1961 alongside the other in his *Correspondence*. The draft may never have been sent because it contains one of Burke's most explicit critiques of the aristocratic principle and defense of the middle classes in politics. Parliament, he wrote in the draft, cannot be reserved for a select few. In other countries office is restricted to "men whose office calls them to it." But, according to Burke's draft, the ability to serve the public "is extremely rare in any station of life," and the privileged have no monopoly on it. Indeed, "there is often found more real public wisdom and sagacity in shops and manufactures than in the Cabinets of Princes." [35]

This is not conventional Burke, defender of the doomed aristocratic age;

but, to be sure, Burke repressed the letter and never sent it. It was too extreme a statement of the bourgeois creed for his aristocratic-service side to tolerate. For conventional Burke to emerge fully, however, bourgeois Burke had to be deeply buried, and this would be very much the pattern that emerged in the last fifteen years of Burke's life. His aristocratic self would turn upon his bourgeois self and lash at it with vicious fury. The bourgeois self would emerge full-blown, as we shall see, only just before his death in the attack on Bedford, in his economic writings, and in his essays on Ireland. It is as if Burke stood back from himself and was horrified at what unleashed bourgeois inclinations could lead to in the external and objective universe, e.g., India and France. He responded to his guilt at harboring these very inclinations within himself by self-flagellation, at least of part of himself. He accomplished this by publicly championing the aristocracy, and thus asserting in his own identity the superiority of the aristocratic principle over the bourgeois.

He did not have to wait for developments in India or France to bring his aristocratic dimension to the fore. An opportunity provided itself in 1782, when native English radicals sought to reform the House of Commons. Burke was appalled at their demands and his response, given in his speeches to Commons, was a virtuoso rendition of self-deprecating, deferential Burke. He knew his place, lowly as it was. He defended both the existing and unreformed constitution and the meager rank he deserved within it.

In that constitution I know, and exultingly I feel, both that I am free, and that I am not free dangerously to myself or to others. I know, too, and I bless God for, my safe mediocrity: I know that, if I possessed all the talents of the gentlemen on the side of the House I sit, and on the other, I cannot, by royal favor, or by popular delusion, or by oligarchical cabal, elevate myself above a certain very limited point, so as to endanger my own fall, or the ruin of my country. I know there is an order that keeps things fast in their place: it is made to use, and we are made to it.[36]

CHAPTER 7

Obsession One: Indianism (1783–1795)

NO ONE could have predicted in 1782 that India would be Burke's principal concern in the 1780s. In that year ambitious Burke achieved the pinnacle of success. Rockingham had rescued him in 1780 with a parliamentary seat and when the Rockingham Whigs replaced Lord North in 1782 Burke was given the ministerial post of Paymaster General. With this position he became the Right Honourable Edmund Burke as well as a member of the Privy Council. A letter to Will Burke indicates Burke's state of mind on his elevation. Will was in Madras where he had gone to make his fortune in India service and knew nothing of the change in government. Edmund did not write of the final success of the party and "cause" which he had so highmindedly served since 1765. He did not write of the return of government to sober, broad-acred men of principle. He failed to comment on any of this; instead, he was carried away with personal and family success, ambition realized.

My dear, my ever dear friend, why were you not here to enjoy, and to partake in this great, and I trust, for the country, happy change. Be assured, that in the Indian arrangements, which I believe will take place, you will not be forgotten, at least I hope not. . . . I have kissed hands, and gone thro' all the ceremonies. The office is to be £4,000 certain. Young Richard is the Deputy with a salary of £500. The office to be reformed, according to the Bill. There is enough to Emoluments. In decency it could not be more. Something considerable is also to be secured for the life of young Richard [to] be a Security for him and his Mother. My Brother is deep on the Western Circuit where he has got full as much credit in one or two causes as he could, or any man could, get. It has been followed with no proportionable profit. He has now before him the option of the Secretaryship of the Treasury, with Precedence in the office.[1]

The optimism that pervades this tally sheet was dashed in July by the death of Rockingham and the falling apart of the alliance between Shelburne and the Rockinghamites. The younger Pitt emerged in 1783 as the king's first minister and Burke, thrown from the heights of accomplishment, stood alone. It was at this point in his career that the obsession with India and Warren Hastings began.

"WHETHER THE WHITE PEOPLE LIKE IT OR NOT"

The trial of Warren Hastings and purging India of his kind took on the character of a crusade for Burke; it transcended the particulars and became an assault on virtually all the corruptions of Burke's time. This was no petty proceeding; it was, he wrote to a friend, "my ten years' warfare against the most dangerous enemy to the justice, honour, laws, morals, and constitution of this country, by which they have ever been attacked."[2] Burke's near maniacal obsession with this "warfare" took its personal toll. Because of it his reputation and influence in Parliament declined. His colleagues shouted Burke down in 1785, protesting that he talked too often about India. They were appalled at his constant insistence in the Commons that Hastings "was the scourge of India," who had reduced the country to "a waste, a howling desert."[3] Samuel Parr noted sadly in 1787 that whereas formerly when Burke spoke, the "Senate listened in the stillest silence," now, "he cannot, but with difficulty, obtain attention." In 1789 he was, in fact, censured by the House for his alleged excesses in handling the case.

But Burke would not be deterred from his crusade. He was, he wrote, "not in the smallest degree affected" by the criticism of his colleagues.[4] Writing to a friend in 1789, he defended "this perseverance in us (which) may be called obstinacy." Advised by parliamentary leaders like Pitt and Fox to drop the matter, Burke refused, "bad as our chances are, and great as the discouragements under which we labor." He would stick to it with "the best executions of patience and perseverance." Nothing would stop him, "neither hope, nor fear, nor anger, nor weariness, nor discouragement of any kind, shall move me from this trust."[5]

Explaining Burke's obsession with Hastings and India has always puzzled his students. How does one, in fact, explain the extraordinary commitment of time, energy, and intense involvement that Burke brought to Hastings and India for nearly fifteen years? Surely it was more than party politics or even self-interest, as some have charged, noting that Will Burke's interests in India coincided with local opponents of Hastings' rule. Burke's motivation was, indeed, complex, a fascinating amalgam of lofty public principles poured out in speech after speech and private need deeply buried in the development of his personality.

In the realm of public principles, what emerges from Burke's speeches, writings, and letters on India is his critique of the excesses of colonialism. The English had foolishly lost much of their great empire in the West; only a wise policy would keep intact the empire in the East.[6] Burke was no advocate of freedom for India but he also had no truck with the inhuman and exploitive features of English rule. He ruthlessly exposed the suffering of India and he pulled no punches. In a letter of 1786 he wrote, "I know what I am doing; whether the white people like it or not." [7] Hastings, he wrote to Lord Loughborough in 1796, had "beggared and famished" the Indians. And how did the English punish him for such evil? They awarded him a lifetime pension.

You know that the whole revenue and the whole trade of India comes out of the vital substance of the unhappy nations of that country. We cry out against their oppression; and we end our process, by rewarding the person, whom we have fixed upon as the author of it. Oh! it is not a reward, but a compensation! Let this distinction be translated for them; and see how far it will go in filling their empty stomacks.[8]

India was a vast stage upon which Burke could parade his conservative defense of tradition and custom. "What havoc should we make," he wrote to a friend, "if we were to set about laws to prevent the further growth of Braminism, to destroy the castes." Hastings, on the other hand, showed no respect for such "prejudices" nor for prescriptive or aristocratic institutions. He had sold "the whole nobility, gentry, and freeholders, to the highest bidder. No preference was given to the ancient proprietors. . . . All the castles were, one after the other, plundered and destroyed. The native princes expelled." [9] His speeches on India provide a majestic display of Burke's conservatism, his respect for the past, his humane disdain for colonial innovators who would destroy local and immemorial custom.

But God forbid we should pass judgement upon people who framed their laws and institutions prior to our insect origins of yesterday. With all the faults of their nature, and errors of their institutions, the institutions, which act so powerfully on their natures, have two material characteristics which entitle them to respect:—first, great force and stability; next, excellent moral and civil effects . . . They have stood firm on their ancient base—they have cast their roots deep in their native soil.[10]

So much for the motives from public principle. What can be said about Burke and India from a more personal and private perspective? One might note, to begin with, that the intensification of Burke's concern with Hastings coincided with the sudden reversal in Burke's own career in 1783. After seventeen years of serving the cause of Rockingham, Burke was truly on his own. The passion he gave India reflected in part the extent to which it came to represent political emancipation for Burke. The long years of servitude to Rockingham and party were over. This was his issue, and only his. He wrote proudly to a friend in 1786 that there was no party position here; he knew what he was doing.[11] It was this independent act by which he would make his mark. But not surprisingly this also raised anxious concern about his ambitious drive for fame. At one and the same time, therefore, the Hastings trial represented making it on his own and also an occasion for criticizing and putting down that very ambitious striving. It was a singularly useful and appropriate expression of his fundamental ambivalence. Writing in 1785 to Philip Francis, Burke admitted in a moment of striking candor:

Speaking for myself, my business is not to consider what will convict Mr. Hastings (a thing we all know to be impracticable) but what will acquit and justify myself to those few persons and to those distant times, which may take a concern in these affairs and the actors in them.[12]

This passage could refer simply to Burke's acquisition of fame for posterity through his rigorous effort to get Hastings. It could also be read as Burke's acquitting himself in another sense, freeing himself from any identification with such aggressive, bold, ambitious types as Hastings. By attacking him, Burke disassociated himself from Hastings and thus acquitted himself from any charges that he was like him.

"THE AVARICE OF THE ENGLISH DOMINION"

Burke's crusade was directed against no ordinary mortal. Hastings loomed larger than life. His was a demonic presence that begged comparison with history's greatest despoilers. This "grand delinquent of all India," was, according to Burke, "the greatest criminal who ever lived," "successor of Tamerlane," and "emulator of Genghis Khan."[13] Burke's obsession was less with India than with Hastings. It was not the colonial system itself he attacked, he told the House of Lords in 1794, only Hastings. "He was the primary and sole cause of all the grievances, civil and military, to which the unhappy natives of that country were exposed."[14]

Behind Hastings and the East India Company's role in India stood a particular evil, the bourgeois spirit or, as Burke put it, "the avarice of the English dominion." Hastings and his agents had an "unbounded license to plunder." They built no schools, Burke told Parliament, no hospitals, no bridges; they were merely "a vehicle of tribute." The only concerns of Hastings and his men were "profit," and the "transmission of great wealth to this country." Their motives were "avarice" and the "extraction of wealth." What Hastings had done in India was the fruit of "golden dreams and speculations of avarice run mad," and nothing was compared to his corruption in all the records of all the ages.[15]

Hastings and his servants personified the bourgeois spirit in another important sense, too. They were ambitious upstarts restlessly tampering with the traditional order of power and status. They were young, for example. Theirs was "the desperate boldness of a few obscure young men," who "drink the intoxicating draught of authority and dominion before their heads are able to bear it." [16] Burke's preoccupation with these generational upstarts, unfit by dint of immaturity to rule in India, was paralleled by his feelings that even in England the likes of him, sober men of years and experience, were being pushed aside by what he called "juvenile statesmen." The youthful Pitt in power after 1784 was, of course, the prime offender. That same year saw large numbers of young M. P.'s elected to Parliament, many of whom had little tolerance for Burke and often laughed at the orator who had held the Commons spellbound in the previous decade. On one such occasion "Mr. Burke sat down saying, he little minded the ill treatment of a parcel of boys." [17] Burke was growing old himself and he was angry at inexperienced youth displacing him.

Hastings and his young upstarts threatened not only the established order in India, but even more horrifying was the threat these youth posed in England. "Today the Commons of Great Britain prosecute the delinquents of India," he pleaded in the impeachment trial, "tomorrow the delinquents of India may be the Commons of Great Britain." [18] Burke saw a conspiracy of new India money at work subverting the traditional order at home. Crucial in generating this fear, as well as for the timing of his turning on Hastings in general, was this election of 1784. In a landslide for the Pitt ministry, over a hundred supporters of the Fox-North coalition (the remnants of the former Rockingham-led opposition) were turned out of the Commons. Burke saw this as the work of "some politicians, for subverting not only the liberties of this country, but all steady and orderly government, by the money furnished by the devastation of India." [19] He dreaded what he called "the force of money" in English life. It would sweep away all the traditional manners and virtues of the English. The national character had to be preserved from "the operation of money." [20] Once again, as in his letters to Rockingham during the Wilkes years, Burke complained to the great of bold and ambitious upstarts, men of money who sought to dislodge power from those whose natural function it was to govern. Burke pleaded with Sir Henry Dundas, in a letter of 1787, to act, to crush the conspiracy of new monied men, which had at its center none other than Warren Hastings!

A body of men, united in a close connexion of common guilt and common apprehension of danger in the moment, with a strong and just confidence of future power if they escape it, and possessed of a measure of wealth and influence which perhaps you yourself have not calculated at anything like its just magnitude, is not forming, but actually formed in this country. This faction is at present ranged under Hastings as an Indian leader; and it will have very soon, if it has not already, an English leader of considerable enterprise and no contemptible influence. . . . Nothing can rescue the country out of their hands but our vigorous use of the present fortunate moment, which if once lost is never to be recovered, of effectually crushing the leader and principal members of the corps.[21]

The "English leader of considerable enterprise" seen in the wings ready to take the lead in this conspiracy was Lord Shelburne (by then Marquess of Landsdowne). He was regarded by Burke and his friends as the leading figure supporting Hastings. He was also, of course, the patron of Price and Priestley, the leading intellectual spokesmen for the bourgeois radicals in England. Burke lumped together as threats to the established order the native middle-class ambitions of the primarily dissenting radicals, whom he had already condemned in 1771 and whose demands for parliamentary reform in the 1780s he also rebuked, and the nabobs, the arrivistes of Indian wealth. This was no mean and penurious conspiracy. Hastings, according to Burke, had made vast sums in India. He was representative, he wrote to Dundas in 1792, "of a body of the greatest wealth, power and influence that has hitherto appeared in this country." [22] Burke was convinced that it was the influence of this vast wealth that ultimately acquitted Hastings, and which even earlier had turned opinion against him, the chief accuser.

On the vast stage that was India Hastings and his troop of young players were acting out the "selfish and mischievous ambition" which in his *Reflections* Burke would describe as the essence of bourgeois radicalism. Hastings and his company became the symbols for this transformation. They embodied the historical process by which untrained and unqualified understudies took over new roles, roles of importance, roles of station and rank. In India servants became masters and schemes flourished of the "most wild and desperate ambition." The natives were sacrificed "to the provocation of ambition, (and) avarice." [23] Burke was particularly interested in the phenomenon of the Indian banians, who, themselves ambitious upstarts, were essential to English rule. The banian, originally from the caste of banians or merchants, was primarily a dewan or steward. He functioned as steward in the household of the Indian privileged classes or the English gentlemen in India. He was himself a domestic servant who was also in charge of estate affairs and of the other servants. According to Burke, these men, born to serve, were taking over the mastery of Indian society under Hastings' patronage. These menial servants, whose fathers the traditional rulers of India "would have disdained to have sit with the dogs of their flock," were being set up by Hastings to govern India, and to own the patrimonial lands.[24] The banians were "the lowest," and "the basest" of the native rabble. In searching for a description more likely to move the peers sitting in judgment on Hastings' impeachment, Burke used the traditional English caricature of men of money, one he would use again in his *Reflections* to condemn the Jacobins. The banians were:

My Lords . . . a person a little lower, a little more penurious, a little more exacting, a little more cunning, a little more money-making, than a Jew. There is not a Jew in the meanest corner of Duke's Place in London that is so crafty, so much a usurer, so skillful how to turn money to profit, and so resolved not to give any money but for profit.[25]

Munny Begum was one such banian that Hastings elevated to ranks of power and influence far above her assigned platoon. Burke spoke often about Munny Begum in the years consumed by the trial in Commons and then again in pleading the case before the House of Lords. She haunted his nightmare vision of traditional society inverted on its base, of a world turned upside down. Hastings, Burke argued, took this slave, bred as a dancing girl, and raised her as the successor of Mahomed Reza Khan as principal minister to the Nabob of Bengal. She was a vile creature, whose "dances were not decent to be seen nor fit to be related." That Hastings could vest power in a woman, in a slave, in a "fantastic dancing-girl" instead of in "the men of the first rank" with rightful claim was indicative of the extent of his crimes.[26] As the Jacobins, according to Burke, made governors of dancing masters and hairdressers, Hastings chose dancing girls and prostitutes. As France would be governed by the lowly profiteer, so Hastings gave possession of an India plundered from the nobility to "usurers" and "bloodsuckers." Like the Jacobins, Hastings raised criminals to the government of a great kingdom and to the estates of the pure and natural chieftains of society.[27]

Hastings and India were the embodiment of the bourgeois nightmare that tormented not only Europe but also Burke. His fifteen-year "warfare" against Indianism also represented his aristocratic self at war with his own bourgeois inclinations. Projected outside of himself onto the person of Hastings it was easier for Burke to exorcise this part of himself. Burke was pushed toward stressing the aristocratic principle in India by the horrors the bourgeois principle had inflicted there, and his own guilt-ridden realization that he, too, harbored such aspirations within himself. A good deal of the intensity and passion of Burke's crusade against Hastings flows from Burke's sense that there was much of Hastings in himself. In condemning Hastings and exorcising this part of himself he could be free of the stigmata he bore as an ambitious upstart. His was at times a restless and unstable mind tampering with the traditional social order; he was not free from ambition, selfish and mischievous. Much of what he said of Hastings could be said of him. He, too, was a servant who insulted his masters. On occasion, he, too, showed little respect for rank and title. He, too, was a steward to the great who sought "high station, great rank, general applause, vast wealth," as Burke described Hastings' ambitions on 21 April 1784. When a fortnight later he said of Hastings that "he wishes to have affluence; he wishes to have dignity; he wishes to have consequence and rank," he could as easily have been speaking of himself.[28] The huge payment to Hastings was infuriating; it rewarded Hastings for living the life that Burke had sought so hard at times to express and at other times to repress in himself. It was truly ironic, and part of Burke was consumed with envy, if not great doubt, as to the life strategy he had adopted.

As a last minute effort to block Hastings' acquittal in 1794 Burke warned the Lords that to do so would be a great victory for Jacobonism, for like the Parisian philosophers Hastings stood "against property, rank and dignity," indeed, "against the very being of the society in which we live." Burke's last words before the peers on 16 June 1794 talked of the danger to the House of Lords from such as Hastings and conjured up images of their graces murdered, drawn and quartered.[29] This was not a new emphasis, for ever since 1790 Burke had added Hastings and India to France and Jacobinism as representative of the crisis that confronted England and Europe, indeed all civilization. Modern bourgeois man, restless, ambitious, and innovating, no longer stood in awe before hallowed traditions and customary institutions. Hastings and the French Jacobins were symptoms of the same disease. "Indianism and Jacobinism," he wrote in 1794 to the Earl Fitzwilliam, were "the two great evils of our time." In another letter to Fitzwilliam he linked Hastings, avarice, and the Jacobin spirit, referring with irony and sarcasm to "the late, just, honorable and decorous acquittal of citizen Warren Hastings from a charge of certain peculations, robberies, frauds, swindlings and various other exercises of the Rights of Man." [30] Of these two evils, Indianism and Jacobinism, Burke ranked that represented by Hastings as the more dangerous.[31]

Perhaps it was the immediacy of Indianism to Burke that made it the greater evil, the sense that while Burke's ambitions were only with difficulty projected onto the Parisian Jacobins, they could easily be transferred to India hands. Living under his own roof, after all, was Will, the mirror of one side of Burke's personality who, had things been different, might have himself become a Hastings in India and given the Burkes high station, great rank, general applause, and vast wealth. But it is primarily his aristocratic self that Burke puts forth in his speeches on India. Seldom, in fact, did Burke so starkly assert this part of himself as he did on the fifth day of his general reply to the House of Lords in 1794. It is vintage sycophantic Burke grovelling like the vines and insects along the low path. No soaring high here.

And here I must press one observation upon your Lordships: I do not know a greater insult that can be offered to a man born to command than to find himself made the tool of a set of obscure men, come from an unknown country, without anything to distinguish them but an usurped power. . . . Oppression and robbery are at all times evils; but they are more bearable, when exercised by persons whom we have been habituated to regard with awe, and to whom mankind for ages have been accustomed to bow.[32]

"UNBRIDLED DEBAUCHERY AND LICENTIOUS LEWDNESS"

Hastings signified more than just the bourgeois principle run wild for Burke; he also represented irresponsible, aggressive, and conquering masculinity. Hastings personified for Burke the consequences of unleashed and unrepressed sexuality. Any understanding of Burke's long vendetta against Hastings must deal, then, with this most striking feature of Burke's writings and speeches on India and Hastings, the extent to which they are permeated with issues of sexuality, and in turn the extent to which this public performance seems deeply influenced by the needs of Burke's private world.

Burke's language links avaricious Hastings to sexual Hastings. As he and his men rob they "ravage at pleasure." Freed from all restraint, they were "rapacious and lustful" seducers of the tender and soft Hindu.[33] When Hastings left India a "vast, oppressive weight," was "removed from its breast," and when he returned to London, Burke imagined him reporting to his superiors that he had been "preying and plundering for you; I have gone through every stage of licentiousness and lewdness. . . ."[34] Everything he did in India became "pander and bawd to the unbridled debauchery and licentious lewdness of usury and extortion." Hastings and his men played at extortion and "this prohibited, prolific sport soon produced a swarm of sons and daughters." In his *Speech on the Nabob of Arcot's Debts* Burke describes the principles of English rule in India in terms of conquering sexuality.

This was the green cup of abomination, this the chalice of the fornications of rapine usury, and oppression, which was held out by the gorgeous Eastern harlots; which so many of the people, so many of the nobles of this land had drained to the very dregs. Do you think that no reckoning was to follow this lewd debauch? That no payment was to be demanded for this riot of public drunkenness and national prostitution?[35]

The English were aggressive and rapacious invaders, violating and taking advantage of defenseless and passive India. The bold and adventuresome upstart men of the bourgeois principle were the strutting lustful young men of the masculine principle. Burke's continued references to Hastings as the "bullock contractor," link the upstart Hastings to the sexual Hastings, as his description of the Nabob's debt links the avarice of English rule to masculinity. The debt of the Nabob was an awesome phallus. Initially shapeless, it acquired "plumpness," and became a "gigantic phantom." "In short," proclaimed Burke, "when you pressed this sensitive plant, it always contracted its dimensions. When the rude hand of inquiry was withdrawn, it expanded in all the luxuriant vigor of its original vegetation." It was "such a prodigy" as to fill any "common man with superstitious fears." Everywhere Burke looked in India, he saw this combination of avarice and sexuality. One of Hastings' hand-picked lower officials in Mooreshedabad was one Debi Sing, who, according to Burke, learned from Hastings how to please his superiors on the Provincial Council. He found them to be "composed mostly of young men, dissipated and fond of pleasure," who were also eager "of making a great and speedy fortune." Sing opened a brothel to provide for the entertainment of his young superiors. Burke notes that he gave his women sweet and enticing names, like "Riches of my life," "Treasure of Perfection," "Diamond of Splendor," "Pearl of Price," and "Ruby of Pure Blood." These metaphorical names, Burke noted, "heightened the attractions of love with the allurements of avarice." Wherever Debi Sing went his women went and there amidst "the most delicious wines of France, and the voluptuous vapor of perfumed India smoke," he would carry on his business. He was not satisfied "with being pander to their pleasures"; he also "supplied them with a constant command of money." By such proxies as Sing and by means such as these Hastings governed India. "Our dominion has been a vulgar thing," Burke sighed on 16 February 1788.[36]

When Burke had first turned his attention to India in 1783 he warned his colleagues that the stories he would tell them of Hastings' crimes would shock "every man of the least sensibility." A year later he promised that his reports would make them and their children blush.[37] Burke was true to his word; his speeches and writings on India are filled with meticulously told stories of shocking brutality and humiliation. He took particular pains to describe sexual horrors inflicted on women by Hastings and the hordes of licentious men who worked under him. In the appendix to his published speeches of 1785, *Speech on the Nabob of Arcot's Debts,* he included, for example, a testimonial letter describing the tortures inflicted on native women by local officials appointed by and responsible to the East India Company. The letter describes jewels torn from the women's bodies, their buttocks whipped while their husbands watched, cords tied around their breasts, children "ripped from their mother's teats," and left to die in the scorching sun.[38] This graphic description was, to be sure, added after the speech. But Burke did not always show such tasteful restraint.

On the third day of his opening speech on the impeachment in 1788 he described "such a scene of cruelties and tortures" as he believed no one had ever "presented to the indignation of the world." The "scene" took place in Rungpore and Dinagepore, where Hastings' local agents, according to Burke, plundered the wealth and possessions of all the inhabitants, "nothing but the bodies remained." There were suspicions, however, that the natives had hidden grain and other possessions in secret caches in the desert. These "under-tyrants of Mr. Hastings," furious at the refusal of the natives to reveal these places, if they had in fact existed, proceeded to torture them systematically, and just as systematically Burke related the details in his speech. He moved quickly over the horrible tortures meted out to the men, the broken fingers, the beatings on the soles of the feet, the drownings, the whip's angry lashes on weak and innocent backs. He passed even more quickly over the scourging of children before their parents. But when it came to the torture of the village women he lingered over each and every excruciating detail. These are the fruits of unleashed masculinity and unrepressed sexuality.

. . . Virgins, who had never seen the sun, were dragged from the inmost sanctuaries of their houses, and in the open court of justice, . . . (but where no judge or lawful magistrate had long sat, but in their place the ruffians and hangmen of Warren Hastings occupied the bench), these virgins, vainly invoking heaven and earth, in the presence of their parents, and whilst their shrieks were mingled with the indignant cries and groans of all the people, publicly were violated by the lowest and wickedest of the human race. Wives were torn from the arms of their husbands, and suffered the same flagitious wrongs, which were indeed hid in the bottoms of the dungeons in which their honor and their liberty were buried together. Often they were taken out of the refuge of this consoling gloom, stripped naked, and thus exposed to the world, and then cruelly scourged; and in order that cruelty might riot in all the circumstances that melt into tenderness the fiercest natures, the nipples of their breasts were put between the sharp and elastic sides of cleft bamboos. . . . But it did not end there. Growing from crime to crime, ripened by cruelty for cruelty, these fiends, at length outraging sex, decency, nature, applied lighted torches and slow fire—(I cannot proceed for shame and horror!)—these infernal furies planted death in the source of life, and where that modesty, which, more than reason, distinguishes men from beasts, retires from the view, and even shrinks from the expression, there they exercised and glutted their unnatural, monstrous, and nefarious cruelty,—there, where the reverence of nature and the sanctity of justice dares not to pursue, nor venture to describe their practices.[39]

Hastings' men were "transformed into savage beasts." In this they followed their leader, for, according to Burke, Hastings also "acted like a wild, natural man, void of instruction, discipline, and art." [40] Beneath rational, civilized man was uncivilized man, whose mad and ferocious passions were unleashed in savage, brutal, and aggressive sexuality. The original sin that flawed mankind is transformed by Burke into a pre-Freudian vision of sexual conquest. Virtuous men venerate women; wild, unrestrained, and natural men violate women. Burke's charge in February 1788 against Hastings is the same he would make two years later against the Jacobins. "The tyranny of Mr. Hastings," he argued in the trial, "extinguished every sentiment of father, son, brother, and husband!" [41] The long-repressed oedipal conquest by the young Burke is relived, and in the attack on Hastings Burke reaffirms the denial of his own unnatural and masculine conquest. After describing the virgin torture Burke took ill and sat down, the parliamentary reporter noted. Some minutes later he again addressed the House, "noting that it was a subject with peculiar powers to agitate him. Even then he could not go on: too agitated, he sat down and the House adjourned."

Burke repeatedly charged Hastings with "destroying the honour of the whole female race" of India, of violating the "respect paid there to the female sex." In particular he was accused of having "undone women of the first rank." [42] The example Burke never tired of citing to substantiate this charge was the infamous treatment of the princesses of Oudi in the years of 1782 and 1783. Virtually every time Burke rose to speak on Hastings from 1784 through 1794, he spoke of the humiliation tendered the mother and grandmother of the Nabob of Oudi, "women of the greatest rank, family and distinction in Asia." [43] In his formal charges against Hastings in 1786, this incident receives fifty-six pages, far more than anything else cited against Hastings. It becomes, in fact, the emotional high point of the indictment. Some four years before the French Revolution Burke uses the degradation and humiliation of aristocratic women as the ultimate sin of his adversary. The attacks on Hastings and on the Jacobins have this striking parallelism, then. In his *Reflections* Burke would use the humiliation of the queen as the dramatic embodiment of Jacobin evil. At the rhetorical heart of his obsession with Hastings and the Jacobins is this same defiling of feminine rank by sexually aggressive upstarts. The treatment of these princesses becomes the grand metaphor for all that India represented for Burke just as the treatment of Marie Antoinette on the night of 6 October 1789 would symbolize the passing of chivalry and the old order.

It was the rapacity of Hastings and his licentious camp followers who plundered the vast landed estates, the jaghires, of the princesses of Oudi, which triggered the infamous incident. According to Burke, Hastings demanded all their wealth even to "plundering the mother of the reigning prince of her wearing apparel." The princesses, in turn, were forced to appeal to the people for support even to moving about in the public market "to beg their bread." How Burke laments this humiliation, their being pursued to "the extremity of exposing themselves to public view." There was no lower state of "disgrace and degradation" for women of rank in India. To avoid this many would have committed suicide, he notes. But this was not all. The officers of the company and their local forces attacked the women and their retainers by force. Orders were given to beat them. The troops were armed with bludgeons, the same weapon that Burke would give the unleashed masculinity of the Jacobins to turn on another innocent woman of rank. All the

while the women were "disgraced by being exposed to the view of the
rabble." [44] The princesses, he lamented,

were bereaved even of their jewels; their toilets, those altars of beauty, were sacrile-
giously invaded, and the very ornaments of the sex foully purloined! No place, no
presence, not even that of majesty, was proof against the severe inquisition of the
mercenary and the merciless. [45]

His colleagues in the Commons had obviously had their fill of Mr.
Burke's preoccupation with naked women for, on one occasion when he was
talking of the princesses, according to the parliamentary reporter, "the House
laughed." [46] But Burke constantly returned to this humiliation of the princesses of Oudi in his attacks on Hastings. In the speeches in reply to the
Lords in 1794 each day found some reference to "two of the first women in
India to be stripped of all they have." On another day it would be their
"disgrace and degradation, by exposing themselves to public view" or the attacks on them with bludgeons and their being "forced to give up even the
clothes from their backs." [47]

The riot and debauchery of Hastings and his under-tyrants filled Burke
with a disgust so powerful that he turned it on men in general. Men, he told
the House of Lords, were the inferior sex because they were closer to brute
creation. All human beings possess two qualities, the physical and the moral,
he argued; the former we share with the beasts, the latter is uniquely human.
Pain and suffering had usually a limited and temporary effect on our physical
nature. But the "unsatisfied cravings" of Hastings' men and "the blows of
the . . . bludgeons" were all the more acute, cutting to the very moral core
of humanity. This second moral nature of humanity is composed of prejudices, habits, and sentiments. It is the particular strength of women, Burke
insists, for in men the physical nature dominates. Hastings and his men,
these wild and savage beasts, deny the human potential of the species, which
according to Burke, is most realized in womankind. The actions of the
"bullock contractor" are loathsome and disgusting, an affront to the elevated
moral sensibility that women embody.

The sensibility of our moral nature is far more acute in that sex which, I say without
any compliment, forms the better and more virtuous part of mankind, and which is
at the same time the least protected from the results and outrages to which this sensibility exposes them. [48]

The disgust at Hastings' sexuality and at the suffering it inflicted on the
Indians moved Burke to affirm the superiority of the feminine principle.
Burke had always seen the English role in India in sexual terms, even before
Hastings had come to personify it for him. In 1772, for example, virtually
the first time he spoke on Indian affairs in Parliament, he offered a graphic,
albeit lurid, commentary on the English raj.

Sir, in the year 1767, administration discovered, that the East India Company were guardians to a very handsome and rich lady in Hindostan. Accordingly, they set parliament in motion: and parliament (whether from love to her person or fortune is, I believe, no problem), parliament directly became a suitor, and took the lady into its tender, fond, grasping arms, pretending all the while that it meant nothing but what was fair and honourable; that no rape or violence was intended; that its sole aim was to rescue her and her fortune out of the pilfering hands of a set of rapacious stewards, who had let her estate run to waste, and had committed various depredations.[49]

More interesting than the allegory was the disclaimer which Burke then added. He had himself resisted the temptation and was free of the evil that tainted his colleagues who had participated in the rape of India. He was, he told the House, proud of "my own virtue and self-denial." [50] He repressed his sexual passion, denied his conquering masculinity, while all about him men gratified themselves and in doing so inflicted pain and suffering. Hastings, then, comes to play a part in a lifelong personal concern which helps account for the overwhelming importance Hastings came to have for Burke. It was his embodiment of free and explosive satisfaction of sexual passion that infuriated Burke as much as anything else about Hastings. Here, too, Burke was also consumed with envy, envy so threatening that it could only express itself in terms of condemnation.

Long before Hastings, Burke had written of the power of untamed sexual drives, and even articulated a strategy for taming and subduing them. Writing in 1744 to Dick Shackleton, the fifteen-year-old Burke described love, the "unrestrained passion," as a great enemy working within men to destroy them, using all the craft and subtlety of the most insidious opponent. This enemy would "lay a bait in everything." It could be thwarted only by watchful care, "lest he make too sure of us." The only way to deal with this "source of . . . misfortune" was repression.[51] Two years later again in a letter to Shackleton Burke wrote fearfully of unrestrained sexuality, linking it, interestingly enough, to avarice. "The only passions which actuate the people high and low are those two—avarice and an abandoned love of sensual pleasure," he wrote. These were "sordid" pleasures which, if they took complete possession of an individual, "exclude everything else great and laudable." [52] To be successful and to do good an abandoned love of sensual pleasure, like unrestrained passion, had to be kept in its place. Repression of dangerous sexual passion becomes a conscious life strategy for Burke. It was severely tested, to be sure, after Dick by Will Burke; indeed, it was in part dealing with this that precipitated the crisis of Burke's "missing years." But he had come through that by what seemed a classic victory for repression and displacement. Its terms included the common household, losing himself in the business of public life, and ruling out any talk of the private world or background of Burke the public figure.

Throughout his career, as we have noted, issues of sexuality continued to emerge usually in the form of distinctions based on sexual identity which, it has been suggested, mirrored his personal preoccupation with the problem. This is certainly part of the sexual dimension in the discussions of India. The bold and adventuresome upstarts of the bourgeois principle were the assertive lustful men of the masculine principle. But sexuality itself becomes an overt theme for Burke in his reading of Hastings and India in a manner that it never had before in his writings, with the exception of his youthful letters to Shackleton and his poetry to Will and as they only would again in his discussion of the Jacobins. Hastings provided Burke with a perfect opportunity to vent his basic ambivalence on sexuality. Guilt over his own apparent oedipal conquest and the subsequent reactive identification with the mother led Burke to doubt his own sexual identity and to repress sexuality in general. The repressed sexual passion when projected outside and linked to Hastings allowed Burke to condemn publicly a part of himself that still aroused guilt. The private monster within Burke which he feared and with which he struggled could be more easily confronted when projected on some external object, in this case Hastings. By condemning publicly the sexuality of Hastings, Burke could put to rest the guilt-ridden private passions within himself. Moreover, condemning Hastings' sexuality allowed Burke, of course, to dwell on it. It was an effective neurotic compromise by which he could discharge his own sense of guilt in his condemnation of Hastings' sexuality yet gratify his preoccupation as he graphically spoke of the tortured nipples or the naked women. While he constantly condemned rapacious sexuality, he was permitting the repressed issue, sexuality, to remain in his consciousness.

There is ample evidence from Burke's performance in the House of Commons throughout his career to substantiate his preoccupation with sexuality. Here, too, the banter, the aside, the allegory kept the tabooed or repressed issue in his consciousness. In 1774, for example, he compared the Address from the Throne to a designing lover who, under the pretense of honorable intention, squeezes his mistress' hand, takes her to the park, "and so on, step by step, till at length he dishonors her." [53] Asides like this seemed to have played an important part in Burke's ability in these years before India to keep the House in gales of laughter. In a 1783 session the parliamentary reporter notes that "Mr. Burke displayed a great deal of humour in comparing this country and America to a woman courting." What is quite striking, however, about this particular interjection of Burke was that in commenting about this relationship he suggested that "the present Bill is somewhat like a courtship, if any were to take place between himself and a lady, where the natural order of things would be reversed, and the lady would have much to give, he little or nothing to return." The American-Great Britain analogy is irrelevent for our purposes; what is intriguing about this "debate on the American Intercourse Bill" in 1783 is the extent to which Burke could find harmless and yet quite conscious outlets for the expression in this case of the most tabooed and repressed issue of sexuality, his own ambivalence.[54] In that same session, speaking of the strength required for a certain task, Burke told an anecdote about a rather boastful lover who upon getting married was asked after his bridal night by an intimate friend, "how often?" He replied, "about fifty." "Then I am certain," says the other, "there was none!" [55] In a debate in 1784 Burke rose to criticize his colleagues in the House whose conduct reminded him of the caprice of a prostitute who gave her favors to different gentlemen throughout the night and forgot in the morning whom she had slept with.[56] Three years later in the debate on the trade treaty with France he likened France to a debauched women, caressed and coveted but still ruined, because she had lost her reputation.[57] This was the way with debauchery and licentiousness, they never paid off. In pointing this out Burke could, of course, derive some basic gratification: his own repressed sexuality could surface for that moment when his joking sexual banter would break up the House, and he could, in the spotlight for the moment, be very much one of the boys.

Wrestling with his own sexuality Burke was able, however, in turning on Hastings, to transcend the problems of his own immediate and private consciousness and subconscious. He gave to the western world one of its earliest and most perceptive insights into the linkage between sexuality and capitalism, and their common modalities of aggression and exploitation. Western culture has linked the two in its language. "On the make," "making it," or "to screw" have interchangable sexual and bourgeois meanings. Being on the make is asserting onself, enjoying competition, seeking conquest.[58] Burke was one of the first to note that the social characteristics of bourgeois society matched the sexual patterns of assertive masculinity. Hastings was "on the make"; he combined avarice, upward mobility, and sexual conquest in a manner that perfectly defines the notion as it would later be used. That Burke was able to perceive these connections in Hastings, so critical for the future culture of the bourgeois West, is in no small part a result of the arena Hastings afforded Burke for projection and displacement of various aspects of his own social and sexual self.

Burke's attack on Hastings deserves more attention than it usually receives. Seldom has the linkage of avarice and sexuality been better drawn than by Burke, the spellbinding orator, as he pleaded with the Lords in 1794 to put down Hastings as he, Burke, had put down his own avarice and sexuality. It was once again the story of the princesses of Oudi that Burke used, now told with Hastings in the role of aggressive, conquering lover out to possess these women and their fortunes.

It is said that nothing is proof against Gold,—that the strongest tower will not be impregnable, if Jupiter makes love in a golden shower. This Jupiter commences making love; but he does not come to the ladies with gold for their persons, he comes to their persons for their gold. This impetuous lover, Mr. Hastings who is not to be stayed from the objects of his passion, would annihilate space and time between him and his beloved object, the jaghires of these ladies, had now, first, their treasure's affection.[59]

The invasion of the fort and the possession of the treasure is described in terms that carry on the theme of the lover on the make. The troops, in Burke's words, "had to break through all the guards which we see lovers sometimes breaking through, when they want to get to their ladies." The thirst for gold is the same as the hunger for sex. The soldiers shout, "We have got to the secret hoards" of the ladies, and Burke adds that "hardly ever did the beauty of a young lady excite such rapture." No other charms could produce the same effect as produced by the secret hoards of these women. But this is not quite enough; one more theme must be introduced by Burke to have the complete notion of "making it," and Burke obliges. These impetuous lovers and conquerors were "persons who the other day would have licked the dust under the lowest servants of these ladies." [60] In Burke's mind social and political pushiness were intimately bound up with sexual pushiness. India and Hastings proved the seventeen-year-old Burke right. Everything "great and laudable" would be destroyed in the wake of unchecked "avarice and an abandoned love of sensual pleasure."

CHAPTER 8

Obsession Two:

Jacobinism (1789–1797)

✦

SIX MONTHS before he died Burke wrote to a friend that "we hate Jacobinism as we hate the Gates of Hell." [1] Because of this hatred Burke is read today. It was by no means evident to his contemporaries, however, that Burke would oppose the revolution, let alone mount and lead a crusade against it. His correspondence, for example, includes a letter from Tom Paine in January 1790, in which Paine, who had known Burke for some three years, simply assumed that since they had taken rather similar positions on events in America, Burke would share Paine's enthusiasm for events in France. Paine wrote excitedly to his friend that "the Revolution in France is certainly a forerunner to other Revolutions in Europe." [2] Two years later the great literary debate of these former friends and correspondents would become the principal symbols of clashing ideologies—bourgeois and aristocratic—as they have remained to this day.

OF "OVERBEARING AND DESPERATE AMBITION"

To his credit Burke read the revolution more accurately than most; he saw it for what it really was, the victory of the bourgeois principle. His ability to see Jacobinism in this proper perspective was in part derived from its evocation in him of personal themes with which he had been wrestling since his youth. He understood it better than most because in a very specific sense it meant more to him than it did to others. Its dramatic and metahistorical significance played out on the vast public stage of Europe was matched in him by its personal significance for the fragile and ever vulnerable private identity he had created for himself. While his deceived contemporaries, the poets and politicians, Wordsworths and Foxes, saw it as a political event marking the end of monarchical tyranny or ushering in a blissful dawn of kings overthrown, Burke perceived its true ideological nature. Referring to Jacobin aims in a letter to Fitzwilliam in 1791, Burke wrote, "its great object is not . . . the destruction of all absolute Monarchies, but totally to root out that thing called the *Aristocrate* or Nobleman and Gentleman." [3] A year later, writing to friends, he was still trying to convince them that what they saw as merely political "as nothing but the subversion of the monarchy" was, in fact, a crusade against a way of life. "They have waged inexpiable war against the nobility and the gentry." [4]

"They" were the men of money, the calculators and economists, who used the abstract, speculative, and metaphysical principles of the philosophical men of words to bring an end to "the age of chivalry." This, the central message of Burke's *Reflections,* would be repeated and amplified in everything Burke wrote after 1790. The highest power of the state has been given to petty lawyers, constables, Jew brokers, "keepers of hotels, taverns, and brothels," and to "pert apprentices . . . clerks, shop boys, hairdressers, fiddlers, and dancers." [5] Aristocratic principles of glory, honor, and national reputation meant nothing to such newcomers. That such men should govern was "an inversion of all natural sentiment," Burke wrote to his parliamentary friend William Weddel. [6]

The battleground for these competing ideological principles was also within Burke. The obsessive passion with which for the last eight years of his life he lashed out at the Jacobins without, as he had at Hastings, suggests once again the personal purpose served, the lashing out and putting down of the bourgeois spirit within. Such were the horrors of unleashed ambition and avarice. France was where it all led, even unto the gates of Hell. Guilt-ridden at the Jacobinism within himself, Burke in excoriating it in France was at one and the same time coming to terms with part of himself. He had to speak out against these upstarts and their ambitions to dominate public life. In his mind he knew that this was how he had often been described. When Fitzwilliam wrote Burke ridiculing the "audacious usurpation, the elevation of Tom Paine, from a staymaker to a fine Gentleman, from an excise man to a sovereign," Burke could well have wondered if similar thoughts were not in the good Earl's mind about his ambitious Irish middle-class correspondent. [7]

The Jacobins exemplified for Burke the bourgeois spirit of boldness and action. In the *Reflections* Burke dwelt on the dichotomy he saw as the central dynamic of his age. The Jacobins were the "vigorous and active principle," the propertied and privileged were the "sluggish, inert, and timid." The revolutionaries were "bold, presuming young persons." [8] Burke's *Remarks on the Policy of the Allies* (1793) repeats this theme. In this essay Burke carefully listed all the features that made the Jacobins vile and disgusting. They were wild, savage men, arrogant and presumptuous, lacking in morals and prudence. If they were so full of defects, what, he then asked, do they have to compensate for these shortcomings, what accounts for their success? *"One* thing, and *one* thing only," Burke answers, "but that one thing is worth a thousand—they have *energy.*" The Jacobin is driven by "a spirit of enterprise and the vigour of his mind." Against this energy, Burke adds, it is ridiculous to respond "with a languid uncertain hesitation." [9]

The boldness and action of the Jacobins was linked in Burke's mind to their obvious ability. His correspondence abounds with this appreciation of the Jacobins. Jacobinism, he wrote Fitzwilliam in 1795, was the peculiar vice of "all the energies and all the active talents of that country." To his Irish friend Sir Hercules Langrishe he wrote that "talents naturally gravitate to Jacobinism." [10] In his published writings there is the same emphasis. *The Preface to M. Brissot's Address* notes that the Jacobins are "by no means ordinary men." They are men "of considerable talents and resources." In his *Letters on a Regicide Peace,* Burke described Jacobinism as the revolt of "the enterprising talents of a country," and as "talents which assert their pretensions, and are impatient of the place which settled society prescribes to them." [11]

This emphasis on the talent and ability of the Jacobins is a critical link between the public issue and the private ambivalence. These, as we have seen, were important ideological themes for Burke as well as for the bourgeoisie of his day. The repudiation of the aristocratic principle and its assumptions of ascribed status by dint of birth involved at bottom the notion that status should be achieved through the play of innate differences and abilities, of talent, energy, hard work and merit. By dwelling on these themes in his characterization of the Jacobins, Burke is both condemning that critical and ever-present component of his own sense of importance and worth, and also parading it. The ambivalence is often right on the surface, as in this same *Letters on a Regicide Peace,* where Burke notes that he has "a good opinion of the general abilities of the Jacobins," of their "spirit of enterprise," their "native energies." His *Observations on the Conduct of the Minority* even more strikingly reveals Burke's ambivalence. Writing of English sympathizers with the Jacobins, he notes that "it is not in my power to despise," these men "of very great talents . . . of much boldness, and of the greatest possible spirit of . . . enterprise." Part of Burke is projected writ large in the Jacobin spirit, which helps account for his obsession with it in his declining years.[12]

The *Reflections on the Revolution in France* catapulted Burke to the fame and recognition that his ambitious self had always sought. But even in this moment of spectacular achievement and success there still lurked the other Burke, the Burke wracked with guilt that this very achievement, this realization of a life's ambition reflected within himself symptoms of the dreaded disease, Jacobinism. His comments on the Jacobins constantly draw attention to himself and beg the comparison. In his *Thoughts on French Affairs,* for example, he wrote that it appeared clear to him, from his own observation, that "envy and ambition" could play as upsetting a role in England as it did in other countries. In *Remarks on the Policy of the Allies* Burke justified England's war aims against France in a revealing discussion of ambition. Ambition is natural to men, he wrote. It could well be a part of himself that he dreads and defends here.

Among precautions against ambition, it may not be amiss to take one precaution against our *own*. I must fairly say, I dread our *own* power, and our *own* ambition; I dread our being too much dreaded. It is ridiculous to say we are not men; and that as men, we shall never wish to aggrandize ourselves in some way or other.[13]

His writings on the war against France have Burke defining the terms of the conflict with Jacobinism in language that speaks directly to his own war with his Jacobin self. No one, he writes in 1793, can take the middle position; he is either the firm friend or the declared enemy of France.[14] In 1794 he writes again that there is no neutrality. Those who are not actively opposed to Jacobinism are its partisans. "They who do not dread it, love it." Jacobinism returns us to the world of the sublime and the beautiful. No one can view it with indifference. It must be regarded with either "enthusiastic admiration" or with "the highest degree of detestation, resentment and horror." [15] But in that essay written nearly forty years earlier Burke had not contrasted admiration and horror, they were in fact both part of the strange fascination of the demonic sublime. Jacobinism also possesses this strange quality. It evokes in Burke both dread and fascination. It is as if he is lecturing himself in this passage, I cannot both hate the Jacobins and admire them. By telling others, he is telling himself, telling himself that lest he be seen as a partisan of Jacobinism he must declare his dread and detestation of it. Burke assumed, in fact, that he was uniquely equipped to lead the anti-Jacobin crusade. To defeat the enemy one had to be familiar with it. To destroy Jacobinism, he wrote in the *Letters on a Regicide Peace,* "the force opposed to it should . . . bear some analogy and resemblance to the force and spirit which that system exerts." [16] The Portlands, Bedfords, and Lauderdales were useless for this mission. Edmund Burke was a natural.

Burke never tired of describing himself as born in obscurity, a "poor outcast of the plebeian race," in contrast to "the chosen few, who are born to the hereditary representation" of the entire realm.[17] But he also never tired of describing Revolutionary France as governed by a "set of obscure adventurers," a phrase that had come to the lips of many an establishment observer in contemplating the tribe of Irish Burkes. Nor did Burke tire of reminding his betters, like Portland or Bedford, that unlike them he had, given his background, "a very small interest in opposing the modern system of morality and policy" that was Jacobinism.[18]

Burke's *Letter to a Noble Lord,* written during these years, represents his most direct linkage of the personal and the ideological. It reveals most poignantly the deeply ambivalent feelings of love and hate that Burke had harbored toward the aristocracy throughout his career. At the same time the extent of his ambivalence over his own bourgeois self is exposed more openly and publicly than it had been since he had entered public life. As Coleridge and other contemporaries noted, the essay was both an attack on the aristocratic principle and a profound defense of the bourgeois creed. Burke sensed that his assertiveness, his claim to a pension which he had "laboured hard to earn," had offended the chosen few. But he would not budge. He deserves his reward. He has a right to boast over a long life of toil in the service of his country. He compares his "long and laborious life" to Bedford's "few and idle years." [19] He wants his career to be judged by his peers, and Bedford does not qualify. He is no equal to Burke in either wisdom or experience in either achievement or merit. This essay finds Burke at his most assertive; Bedford is but a weak comparison in worth and virtue put next to Burke. While Burke has devoted a life to "public industry," Bedford is simply a "poor rich man." And what is the source of Bedford's wealth, prestige, and power? Bedford has done nothing more than inherit the status and rank of his ancestors who themselves had done nothing except help in the confiscation of noble estates and church property. Burke could not have made a more serious charge if the context be remembered. Burke writes this after his *Reflections* in which, after all, one of the most damning charges hurled at the Jacobins was their theft of aristocratic and church lands. Seen in that light the intensity of Burke's attack is all the more apparent and was obviously not lost on the contemporary reader. Burke attacks the original Russells and by implication Bedford in the identical language he had used against the Jacobins (and the English in India).

The lion having sucked the blood of his prey, threw the offal carcass to the jackal in waiting. Having tasted once the food of confiscation, the favourites became fierce and ravenous. The worthy favourites' first grant was from the lay nobilities. The second, infinitely improving on the enormity of the first, was from the plunder of the church.[20]

The point is unmistakable. Bedford's wealth, writes Burke, is derived from "a levelling tyrant . . . who fell on everything that was *great and noble.*" But Burke's point is not only to condemn Bedford, the "overgrown Duke of Bedford," as a descendent of an earlier Jacobin. He is even more concerned with depicting Bedford's "inglorious sloth" and his efforts "to oppress the industry of humble men" like Burke.[21] He who has had to show his passport wherever he has gone is maligned by a Duke who has no merit but his name. This is strong stuff from Burke. To contemporaries like Coleridge and the editors of the *Monthly Review* it read like Godwin, Paine, and Barlow. Well might they draw this conclusion, for Paine had written just the year before:

It is very well known that in England the great landed estates now held in descent were plundered from the quiet inhabitants at the conquest. The possibility did not exist of acquiring such estates honestly. If it be asked how they could have been acquired, no answer but that of robbery can be given. That they were not acquired by trade, by commerce, by manufactures, by agriculture, or by any reputable employment is certain. How then were they acquired? Blush aristocracy to hear your origins for your progenitors were thieves. They were the Robespierres and the Jacobins of that day.[22]

Burke's *Letter to a Noble Lord,* which contains Burke's most outspoken criticism of the aristocratic principle, also contains Burke's most open declaration of affinity with the Jacobins. He has close connections to the dreaded enemy, he writes. He knew them well, much better than the sluggish duke, because he, Burke, was so much like them. The aging Burke treated with utter integrity problems over which he had agonized since his youth.

I am better able to enter into the character of this description of men (the Jacobins) than the noble Duke can be. I have lived long and variously in the world. . . . I have lived for a great many years in habitudes with those who professed them. I can form a tolerable estimate of what is likely to happen from a character chiefly dependent for fame and fortune on knowledge and talent. . . . Naturally, men so formed and finished are the first gifts of Providence to the world.[23]

They remained this gift until they lost sight of God and threw off the instinctive fear of Him, and also the fear of man. When they did this and combined their efforts "to act in corps," they became the scourge of Providence, the anti-Christ, the devil incarnate. Burke walked a thin line. He was himself the worthy and virtuous man of talent and intellect because he still feared God and his social superiors, and because he strove alone, or at best for his family's sake, certainly not for a cabal of self-made men. He was ambitious but not intoxicated with ambition as were the Jacobins. It was perhaps his most self-conscious effort of comparing and contrasting himself with the Jacobins. But he was no Jacobin, whatever the duke may have thought of him. The irony was not lost on Burke that Bedford should fear him and not his proper enemy. What is not lost on the reader of Burke is the revelation of Burke's own tortured self, his simultaneous respect for and hatred of Bedford.

Bedford was not the only Englishman that Burke turned upon in the

1790s. There were others. If Burke were on Figaro's side in his *Letter to a Noble Lord,* then he was in Almaviva's camp in his passionate attacks on the dissenters. It is this assault which gives his general obsession with Jacobinism its particular English cast. It is fair to suggest that just as Burke wept over the violated Indians while his real concern was the effect of Indianism on English political and social life, so here, too, while he lamented the sad fate of the fair queen of France, his greater fear was the threat Jacobinism posed at home. Writing the French émigré de Calonne in 1790 of his *Reflections on the Revolution in France* Burke insisted that "in reality, my object was not France, in the first instance, but this country." [24] The book was written, as we know, in response to the Reverend Richard Price's sermon praising the principles of the French. It was Price and his fellow English dissenters, then, who were the real threat and against whom Burke penned his *Reflections.* In a letter to Philip Francis in February 1790 describing his forthcoming book, Burke pledged "to set in a full view the danger from their wicked principles and their black hearts." In response to the subversive dissenters he would "state the true principles of our constitution." His mission was to "expose them to the hatred, ridicule, and contempt of the whole world." [25]

As far as Burke was concerned, the English dissenters under the intellectual leadership of Price and Priestley were the domestic agents of the world-wide Jacobin conspiracy. Burke's obsession with Jacobinism in England and its threat to aristocratic principles, indeed to all civilization, came to rest after 1789 principally on his fear and loathing of English dissent. This preoccupation of his last ten years is one of the most significant aspects of Burke's long career, for in it are brought together many of the themes, private and public, that have been traced in this study.

Burke's ambivalence is evident here, too, for he had not always hated the dissenters. In Bristol it had been leading dissenters with commercial links to the American colonies who first approached Burke to represent them. His advocacy of the colonial cause endeared him to the dissenting community whose brethren peopled America. Moreover, Burke's eloquent pleas for religious toleration, while intended principally for Catholics in Ireland, were usually broad enough to embrace Catholic and dissenter alike in England. In the 1770s and 1780s Burke could usually be counted on to support any parliamentary move to ease or lift the civil disabilities that weighed down the dissenters. They were not, he told his parliamentary colleagues in 1772, "the whining, canting, snivelling" opponents of establishments as were their seventeenth-century ancestors. The next year he praised them as a bulwark against atheism.[26] But in 1789 he turned upon his former friends and allies. In that year he was asked to support Fox's effort to repeal the onerous Test and Corporation Acts which prevented dissenters from holding government or municipal positions. This became the occasion for Burke's shift. He opposed the repeal. In letters written in 1789 and 1790 to

Richard Bright, a Bristol merchant and prominent dissenter, Burke explained why he had chosen to oppose these whom he used to regard with such "esteem and affection." [27] He listed several reasons: they had abandoned his party for Pitt in the electoral debacle of 1784; their leaders, Price and Priestley, had been too close to Shelburne, the great rival for so many years to Rockingham; their demands for repeal of the Test and Corporation Acts were phrased in the abstract and metaphysical language of natural rights; and finally, they were too zealous in their approval of the events in France and of revolutionary principles.

Burke never returned to their side. As the decade wore on his hatred grew for these "insect reptiles who whilst they go on only caballing and toasting fill us with disgust." [28] One reason for his about-face and for the hardening of his hatred was omitted from the list in his letters to Bright. In turning on the dissenters he was also repudiating a part of himself that they more than any other force in English life embodied. As the horrors wrought in France and to traditional society in general by the unleashed bourgeois principle came home to Burke and forced him in guilt to repress that aspect of his personality, he was obliged to repudiate England's most obvious symbol of this bourgeois principle, the dissenters, his former friends.

Conor Cruise O'Brien makes much of the fact that Burke's *Reflections* were written in response to Richard Price and the other dissenters. It is crucial, for the general thesis he has recently developed insists that Burke's Irishness and his Catholic sympathies are at the center of his hatred of the Jacobins. The dissenters, radical Protestant enemies of the Catholic Church, thus become, according to O'Brien, the catalyst for Burke's defense of western Christianity and the values of the past.[29] O'Brien is quite right, I think, in stressing Burke's Irishness. It is central to his personality and the problems it created within him were immense. But to interpret the *Reflections* as directed principally against the dissenters because of their anti-Catholicism is something of an exaggeration and also overlooks a much more likely basis for Burke's hatred of the dissenters. The dissenters, in general, and certainly Richard Price, in particular, were by no means papist baiters in 1790. Some dissenters, to be sure, had been behind the Gordon Riots in 1780 which had, in fact, endangered Burke's life. But, by and large, dissenters were quiet on Catholicism, or, like Priestley, actively befriended by leading Catholic writers, like Joseph Berrington of Birmingham, who joined them in the campaign to repeal the Test and Corporation Acts as a prelude to universal toleration.[30] The dissenters are of critical importance to any interpretation of Burke's *Reflections;* on that point there can be no doubt. But this is due less to their dislike of Catholicism than to their embodiment of the bourgeois spirit. Their central role in the bourgeois revolution, their incredible achievement, is what lies behind Burke's attacks on them from 1789 to his death. They served him as the purest expression of the bourgeois principle and as such suffered the public wrath he was also directing at part of himself.

His comments reveal the extent to which Burke saw in the dissenters qualities over which he agonized internally. They, too, were ambitious upstarts seeking to make their mark, to achieve public place through their self-evident talent and merit. His comments about his old acquaintance Priestley bear this out. When he told the House of Commons that he would prefer George III or IV to Dr. Priestley, he added that dissenters like "Gunpowder Joe" "load the tyrannous power by the poisoned talents of a vulgar low bred insolence." [31] Like himself, the dissenters were upstarts seeking to "get above their natural size," i.e., to change their station. They were a small minority, but "awakened, active, vigorous, and courageous," while the rest of the nation was generally composed of men of sluggish tempers, slow to act." [32]

The dissenters evoked some of the more vivd horrors conjured up in Burke's writings. He wrote to Windham in 1793 of their "burning down of London, after the massacre of half of its inhabitants." [33] Earlier in May 1792 Burke had pleaded with his colleagues that they not let their king and the Houses of Parliament be made slaves to the Unitarian Society. He feared even worse, warning the House of Commons that it should not wait till the dissenters

met to commemorate the 14th of July, shall seize the tower of London and the magazines it contains, murder the governor and the mayor of London, seize upon the King's person, drive out the House of Lords, occupy your gallaries and thence as from a high tribunal, dictate to you. [34]

These nightmarish visions are now understandable. Though projected into the future they are consistent with all the guilt produced by the horrors of India and France. The triumph of the dissenters represented the total victory in England and in Burke of the bourgeois principle, unchecked and unbalanced by the aristocratic principle. It was an unacceptable resolution of Burke's inner ambivalence and as such he was moved to right the balance again by vigorous defense of the aristocratic principle.

"AN ABANDONED LOVE OF SENSUAL PLEASURE"

The Jacobins, like Hastings, represented for Burke more than just bourgeois avarice unleashed. Here, too, as with Indianism, the bourgeois principle was closely identified in Burke's mind with intrusive masculinity, and the aristocratic principle with violated femininity. And here, too, he seemed to recoil from the horror inflicted by unleashed masculinity and to plead the feminine cause. The extent to which Burke described the Jacobins in sexual language is striking, and always in terms of aggressive masculine conquerors bent on violating and possessing defenseless passive women. Just as the sexual role of Hastings was most vividly depicted and deplored in graphic descriptions of the humiliation of aristocratic women, so the *Reflections on the Revolution in France* reaches its emotional and ideological climax in vivid passages of the Jacobin assault on and violation of the exalted and defenseless queen of France. In his obsession with the Jacobins this incident parallels the story of the princesses of Oudi which Burke compulsively returned to in his attacks on Hastings.

In a letter to Phillip Francis describing the writing of the *Reflections* Burke confessed that the very poignancy of that scene drew tears from him as he penned the words.[35] In the text he apologizes to the reader for dwelling too long "on the atrocious spectacle." [36] But as in his speeches on India he had to dwell on sexuality in order to condemn it, thus enabling the neurotic compromise to work, so Burke described the queen of France lying down in her bed the night of 6 October 1789, "to indulge nature in a few hours of respite." This sleep was interrupted by a cruel band of Jacobin "ruffians and assassins" who, having just killed her guard rushed into the chamber of the queen and "pierced with a hundred strokes of bayonets and poniards the bed," from which the Queen, "this persecuted woman had but just time to fly almost naked." [37] She managed to escape the lustful ravaging mob, but she and her exalted mate are "forced to abandon the sanctuary of the most splendid palace in the world." She, like the palace, has been defiled, "polluted by massacre, and strewed with scattered limbs and mutilated carcasses." Her ravagers who had moved on to slaughter two of the king's bodyguards, marched in boastful phallic pride through the city bearing high their victims heads "struck upon spears." [38]

The eyewitness account of that night by Madame de la Tour du Pin, an aristocratic Irish lady-in-aid to the queen, is at variance with Burke's account. The queen's guard seems not to have been killed, and the incident seemed to most courtiers to have been the product less of Jacobin frenzy than of the incompetence of the guards whom it is suggested were part of an internal plot orchestrated by the Duc D'Orleans. Madame du Pin also notes that the women in the court had been forewarned of potential danger and had not undressed that evening. She makes no reference to the queen's lack of clothing when fleeing, a fact one might expect to be of some importance for an eyewitness chronicler. It would seem that no one even saw the queen flee by the little passage which linked her bedchamber to the king's.[39] Yet Burke is quite insistent that this humiliating violation was inflicted on the nearly naked queen.

Uncovering and exposing nakedness is, however, essential both for intensifying the sense of sexual violation and as a crucial link to Burke's central ideological argument. The humiliation of nakedness becomes an important theme in the *Reflections*. As the invading Jacobins viciously uncover a naked queen, so their athiesm does the same for society. We would, he wrote, "uncover our nakedness by throwing off that Christian religion." [40] Nakedness becomes symbolic in the *Reflections* for the end of the traditional order. "Our naked, shivering nature," is weak, inadequate, inclined to evil, and much too limited in rational capacity to allow one to cope without external crutches. [41] Mankind needs ancient ideas, prejudices, and ancient prescriptive institutions, like monarchy, aristocracy, and the Church to clothe and cover its nakedness. In the Jacobin effort to destroy aristocracy and hierarchy "all the decent drapery of life is to be rudely torn off." Old prejudices, reverence for ancient customs, are assailed by the Jacobins. In doing this they "leave nothing but the naked reason." [42] The ruffian Jacobins destroy all these features of the aristocratic age, rip off all the layers of clothing that represent the illusions of the past. They sever humanity from all the warmth and security provided by the corporate aristocratic world, leaving isolated, free, fearful, and shivering individuals "stripped of every relation in all the nakedness and solitude of metaphysical abstraction." [43] When the Jacobins uncover the particular nakedness of the queen, they discover the principle of equality. They destroy all rank and privilege, for in her nakedness without her regal robes, it is obvious that Marie is no different from any other woman. Contemplating the naked queen is to penetrate all the mystery of the aristocratic principle. In discovering that in her nakedness Marie is but a mere woman, Burke joins Jacobin ideology to the crudity of an obscene joke.

On this scheme of things, a king is but a man, a queen is but a woman; a woman is but an animal, and an animal not of the highest order. [44]

It is the bourgeois Jacobin as aggressive conquering masculinity that has wrought the "revolution in sentiments, manners, and moral opinions." [45] The aristocratic and chivalric ideal of the ancien régime was quintessentially feminine, as described by Burke. Its hegemony was the triumph of womanly guile. It subdued "the fierceness of pride and power," "without force" but through its "soft collar of social esteem." "Stern authority" was compelled "to submit to elegance," and "dominating vanquisher(s) of laws" were "subdued by manners." [46] But this reign of feminine virtue was doomed. The aristocratic principle stood threatened like Marie by the "bayonettes and poniards" of the Jacobins.

Throughout the *Reflections* Burke suggestively links the Jacobins with sexuality. To question a nation's constitution, to indulge in resistance and revolution, is described as "taking periodical doses of mercury sublimate and swallowing down repeated provocatives of cantharides to our love of liberty." The former is an eighteenth-century cure for venereal disease, the latter is the well-known aphrodisiac, Spanish fly. The Jacobins aroused the passions of freedom to unnatural excess. These artificial stimuli led to "orgies" and "enthusiastic ejaculation." The Jacobins "empty themselves of all the lust of selfish will." Their spirit is "renovated in its new organs with a fresh vigour of a juvenile activity. It walks abroad; it continues its ravages." [47] In Paris, instead of building and repairing the churches, the Jacobins, according to Burke, work on "the painted booths and sordid sties of vice and luxury." They renovate and remodel brothels, "the momentary receptacles of transient voluptuousness." Instead of spending money on temples, they waste it on "petit maisons, and petit soupers," the little houses designed as places for amourous affairs and the meal served at these assignations. [48]

As Hastings personally symbolized for Burke all the vices of Indianism, so here, too, Burke had his evil personified. The symbol of Jacobinism as masculine sexuality unleashed was Jean-Jacques Rousseau. Innovation, lack of reverence for traditional arrangements, destruction of hierarchy were all, to be sure, embodied in this one man, but above all else Burke regarded Rousseau as the hedonist professor of a new immorality. Burke viciously attacked Rousseau in his *Letter to a Member of the National Assembly* (1791).

The assembly recommends to its youth a study of the bold experimenters of morality. Everyone knows that there is a great dispute among their leaders which of them is the best resemblance of Rousseau. In truth, they all resemble him. His blood they transfuse into their minds and into their manners. Him they study; him, they meditate; him they turn over in all the time they can spare from the laborious mischief of the day or the debauches of the night. Rousseau is their canon of holy writ. . . . He is their standard figure of perfection. [49]

In Rousseau Burke saw the apotheosis of a new principle of love. He represented the victory of Jacobin masculine principles of love over what Burke described as aristocratic and feminine ideals of love. "Through Rousseau," he charged, "your masters are resolved to destroy these aristocratic prejudices." The aristocratic ideal involved "docility" and "modesty," "grace," "manners," "subtlety," "taste," and "elegance." The Rousseauean ideal was a "ferocious medley of pedantry and lewdness; of metaphysical speculations blended with the coarsest sensuality." [50] Under the old ideal, women were adored and worshipped; under the new they were objects to gratify the sexual appetites of men. "Is it absurd in me," Burke wrote his friend Francis in a letter of 1790, "to think that the chivalrous spirit which dictated a veneration of women of condition and beauty, without any consideration whatsoever of enjoying them, was the great source of those manners which have been the pride and ornament of Europe for so many ages?" [51] How very different, then, Burke is, compared to this vile Rousseau, he is suggesting. And yet the French "erect statues to a wild, ferocious, low-minded, hard-hearted father." Burke took Rousseau's abandonment of his bastard children as well as his "disgustful amours" as symbolic of the imminent destruction under the Jacobin-masculine principle of that most critical institution of hierarchy and continuity, the family. Rousseau's teachings would "destroy all the tranquility and security of domestic life." [52]

Burke had not always thought so ill of Rousseau. Like the dissenters, Rousseau had once found favor in his eyes. Writing in the *Annual Register* years earlier, for example, Burke had described *Emile* as containing "a thousand noble hints relative to his subject, grounded on a profound knowledge of the human mind." The book contains "strokes of the most solid sense, and instructions of the most useful nature." [53] But that was 1762; three decades later Rousseau was the great corrupter whose morals taught teachers of the Jacobin faith "to betray the most awful family trusts, and vitiate their female pupils." [54] Rousseau's *La Nouvelle Eloïse* praises the "debauchers of virgins," and it is only a short jump from this to the morality of the Jacobins, according to Burke. His attack on Rousseau reaches its conclusion in a brilliant rhetorical blend of the themes of upward economic and social mobility, destruction of the traditional order, and the sexual aggression of violating masculinity. All are placed at the feet of the statues erected by the Jacobins to Rousseau.

When the fence from the gallantry of preceptors is broken down, and your families are no longer protected by decent pride, and salutary domestic prejudices, there is but one step to a frightful corruption. The rulers in the National Assembly are in good hopes that the females of the first families in France may become an easy prey to dancing-masters, fiddlers, pattern-drawers, friseurs, and valets de chambre, and other active citizens of that class, who having the entry into your houses, and being half domesticated by their situation, may be blended with you by regular and irregular relations. By a law they have made these people your equals. By adopting the sentiments of Rousseau, they have made them your rivals. In this manner these great legislators complete their plan of levelling, and establish their rights of men on a sure foundation.[55]

The specter of Jacobinism hovering over Christendom was for Burke in part the nightmare of sexuality unleashed and unchecked. Rousseau may have in his own words suggested himself to Burke for this symbolic role. He had written, after all, in his *Confessions* that he, Jean-Jacques Rousseau, had "dared to strip man's nature naked." [56]

By 1796 Burke was convinced that everything he had predicted in his diatribe against Rousseau had come to pass. His *Letters on a Regicide Peace* describe a Paris not unlike a Hieronymus Bosch painting. The French legislators have produced a people "the most licentious, prostitute and abandoned" with no peers for their coarseness, rudeness, savagery, and ferocity. The Jacobins have produced "all sorts of shows and exhibitions, calculated to vitiate the imagination, and pervert the moral sense." Drunken women call for the blood of their own children. Fathers demand the murder of their sons. Paris is a "lewd tavern for the revels and debauches of banditti . . . and their more desperate paramours . . . puffing out . . . licentious and blasphemous songs." "Everything prepares the body to debauch" in France.

There is no invention of seduction, never wholly wanting in that place, that has not been increased: brothels, gaming-houses, everything. And there is no doubt but when they are settled in a triumphant peace they will carry all these arts to their utmost perfection . . . joined to that of a gang of strolling players, expelled from theaters, with their prostitutes in a brothel, at their debauches and bacchanals.[57]

Peace with the Jacobins was no better than defeat by the Jacobins. In either case sexual abandon would spread to England. Burke sees the Jacobin threat to England in sexual terms, too. In his *Appeal from the New to the Old Whigs* he angrily replies to those who caution England not to use force against the Jacobins. This is what they suggest, he writes. "Let the lady be passive, lest the ravisher should be driven to force. Resistance will only increase his desires." The proper response is on the contrary, to "drive such seducers from the house on the first appearance of their love letters and offered assignations." [58] These romantic correspondents and seducers were not only foreign, they included, of course, the "declarations of Priestley and Price—declarations . . . of *hot* men." [59] Should French principles be introduced into England, Burke warned the Commons in 1792, they would lose everything dear and sacred to them. "King, Lords and Commons . . . property, our wives." That same year he was charged with bad taste by Sheridan for holding up a dagger in the Commons and pointing to it stating, "it is my object, to keep the French infection from this country, their principles from our minds, and their daggers from our hearts." [60] The Jacobins were phallic violators who would ravish England as they had France, and as Hastings had India.

Burke could not escape the linkage of social and political aggression with sexual energy. In 1778, for example, in a debate on the use of Indians and slaves in the American war, he hypothesized that all Negroes and servants planning insurrection against their masters had as their principal objects "murders, rapes, and horrid enormities of every kind." [61] The inversion of the Chain of Being seemed to involve for him unleashing and fulfilling forbidden sexual desires. So it was that for Burke the Jacobins, like Hastings, were "men on the make," who combined avarice and sexual conquest. As such, they, too, were a projection onto external reality of issues deeply troubling to Burke. In maligning the sexuality of the Jacobins, Burke justified the policy of repression and denial that had given meaning to his own life. He reaffirmed it while at the same time providing an opportunity for the issues so deeply repressed in his psyche to have exposure. The ultimate horror of the Jacobins was their potential to utterly destroy civility and order in

orgiastic sexual license and abandon. It was a danger that justified marshall-
ing all the resources of the Christian world to defeat. This was not an impossible task, however. Had not Burke himself marshalled his own internal
resources to meet and defeat the urgings of sexual passion in order to keep
them in their proper subordinate place?

BOURGEOIS BURKE

Burke's rage-filled indictment of bourgeois radicalism in his *Reflections*
should not obscure the very real extent to which he was himself a spokesman
for bourgeois interests in these years. Once again, it is an ambivalent Burke
we are dealing with. Take, for example, his attitude to property. To be sure,
preoccupation with property was by no means the exclusive invention of the
bourgeoisie. What was new was their insistence that property rights were the
foundation of free government. The ideology of the old order saw private
property as a sacred right, too, but it did not make it the pivotal ideal around
which all social and political theory centered. The bourgeoisie did this. In
the aristocratic conception of government and society property rights shared
importance with other ideals, such as honor, justice, duty, glory, paternalism, and hierarchy. The sacredness of property rights was not elevated as the
sine qua non of the free and just polity. Middle-class liberal theory would do
this. In Burke's writings the defense of property far exceeded the modest importance aristocratic thought gave it. He sang its praises in enthusiastic
tunes second to no self-proclaimed bourgeois theorist.

    Almost immediately after the revolution began Burke's letters reveal
that what he thought most critical in France was what the revolutionaries did
to private and Church property, not the king, not the estates, and not to any
other sacred political principle. In November 1789 he asked of Dupont, the
Frenchman to whom the *Reflections* are addressed, what has happened to "internal freedom, security and good order?" If it were still the case that "the citizen . . . is in a perfect state of legal security, with regard to his life, to his
property, to the uncontrolled disposal of his person, to the free use of his industry and his faculties," or if "he is protected in the beneficial enjoyment of
the estates to which he was born," then Burke pledged that he, too, would
join the chorus approving events in France.[62] Of "the benefits of civil society," Burke wrote later, "property is the first origin; the continued bond,
and the ultimate end." To the Vicomte de Rivarol, Burke wrote that "the
fury which arises in the minds of men on being stripped of their goods" was
"implanted in them by our creator." [63] To an English critic who questioned

his assault on the "glorious revolution in France" Burke singled out the revolutionary assault on property as his justification. He offered a passionate defense of property and its differential distribution influencing industry and labor that could have been written by a Locke or a Priestley.

I never will suffer you, if I can help it, to be deprived of the well-earned fruits of your industry, because others may want your fortune more than you do, and may have labored, and now labor in vain, to acquire even a subsistence. . . . I am in trust religiously to maintain the rights and properties of all descriptions of people in the possession which legally they hold; and in the rule by which alone they can be secure in any possession. I do not find myself at liberty, either as a man, or as a trustee for men, to take a vested property from one man, and to give it to another because I think that the portion of one's too great, and that of another too small.[64]

By far the most important statement by Burke of the basic bourgeois principles of a laissez-faire state and economic order is found in his essay *Thoughts and Details on Scarcity* of 1795. Writing in response to the famine and scarcities of goods that hit England at war, Burke cautioned Pitt against using government to solve the crisis; to do so, Burke suggested, would violate the natural laws of the market.

To provide for us in our necessities is not in the power of government. It would be a vain presumption in statesmen to think they can do it. The people maintain them, and not they the people. It is in the power of government to prevent much evil; it can do very little good in this, or perhaps in anything else.[65]

Burke went on to lecture Pitt on the principles of the marketplace. "Labor," he wrote, "is a commodity like every other, and rises or falls according to the demand. This is in the nature of things." If a man cannot support his family, he asked rhetorically, "ought it not to be raised by authority?" No, to do this would be a "blundering interposition." Labor was subject to its own laws; the state should not regulate it. The natural laws of commerce could not be ignored. "The producer should be permitted and even expected, to look to all possible profit which without fraud or violence he can make; to turn plenty or scarcity to the best advantage he can . . . to account to no one for his stock or his gain." So much for what E. P. Thompson has called "the moral economy" of precapitalistic England. There is nothing that could be done in the season of famine, Burke advised Pitt. The Prime Minister should especially resist the notion, Burke wrote, "that it is within the competence of government . . . to supply to the poor those necessaries, which it has pleased the Divine Providence for a while to withhold from them." For the government to intervene would be an act "breaking the laws of commerce which are the laws of nature, and consequently the laws of God."[66] It was the creed of Adam Smith as stated by one of his earliest and most articulate disciples. Smith is, indeed, alleged to have once said, "Burke is the only man I ever knew who thinks on economic subjects exactly as I do."[67] With good reason, for seldom has the bourgeois theory of the relationship of state and society, government and economy, been so succinctly put as Burke put it.

> What ought the state to take upon itself to direct by the public wisdom, and what ought it to leave with as little interference as possible, to individual discretion . . . The clearest line of distinction which I could draw . . . was this: that the state ought to confine itself to what regards the state or the creatures of that state: namely the exterior establishment of its religion; its magistracy; its revenue; its military force by sea and land; the corporations that owe their existence to its fiat; in a word, to everything that is truly and properly public—to the public peace, to the public safety, to the public prosperity. . . .[68]

Shortly before his death in May 1797 Burke returned to these themes in a letter to his old friend Arthur Young, then Secretary to the Board of Agriculture. Burke was distressed at talk that the government might pass legislation regulating the employment of day laborers in agriculture. All such matters, he wrote Young, "ought to be left to the conventions of the parties." Any kind of regulations "against free trade in provisions" is "senseless, barbarous and, in fact, wicked." The great danger, he concluded, "is in Governments intermeddling too much." [69] Here, indeed, is the link between Burke's bourgeois economics and his general obsession with Jacobinism. Burke perceived (astutely) that despite their rhetoric about simplifying government, the most radical Jacobins would, in implementing their Utopias, be required to call upon government to exercise power, to augment its power, in short to intermeddle more. He saw this in France where as property was threatened the state allegedly reaped the benefits and advantages. Burke saw this also in store for England, sensing that Paine's vision of a simple self-regulating society with no government (or at best one governing least) could be achieved only through an initial expansion of governmental power. Burke realized that the social welfare objectives outlined in Part II of Paine's *Rights of Man* required an interfering state. Whatever one may think of Burke's values, credit is certainly due him on this score, for being perhaps the first "liberal" to perceive the initial incompatibility of limited government and radical reform. It may be of this that the real nature of his "conservatism" consists.

Bourgeois Burke is further revealed in this period by his attitude to the poor and destitute. During these early years of the Industrial Revolution bourgeois radicals like Priestley were developing a position on the poor.[70] It was a critical issue, for these radicals self-consciously considered themselves a "middle" class. This required that there exist a group above, an aristocracy, as well as a group below, the poor, both of which were depicted as morally inferior to the more virtuous middle. Much of this book has dealt with the bourgeoisie's contempt for those above them. Their views of those below were strikingly similar. The poor were also depicted as idle and lacking in industry and real merit. They drank, spent what they had, had no self-control, no discipline. The poor would always be, according to bourgeois theory. They never could be eliminated, nor for that matter should they be. The same could be said for the aristocracy. Both classes were despised but their continued existence was essential if the crucial defining superiority of the middle class as the middle, a moderate and virtuous mean, was to persist. It followed, then, for many bourgeois radicals that since it could not be eliminated there were only two ways to deal with poverty. First, stop government from dealing with the poor. Radicals like Tom Paine and Joseph Priestley became vigorous opponents of the Poor Laws; not only did they tax the industrious and interfere with the market, but they perpetuated widespread poverty by discouraging incentives to productive work.[71] The second approach was moral invocation, the two-pronged argument which either said that poverty was no blight in the eyes of God or encouraged greater practice of those traits that have become associated with the Protestant ethic. Burke's attitudes to poverty reflect both of these stock bourgeois themes.

In his *Thoughts and Details on Scarcity* Burke reflected with some resignation that the poor were poor only because they were so numerous. He cautioned the poor against direct action. "The throats of the rich ought not to be cut," nor their stores and warehouses looted, for they "are the trustees for those who labor, and their hoards are the banking-houses of these latter." [72] To turn on the rich made as much sense, wrote Burke, as destroying mills and throwing grain into the river to bring down the price of bread. If England experienced famine and this effected some more than others, it was because of "divine displeasure." Tampering with His economic laws, His laws of nature, by passing laws to aid the poor would merely aggravate God's displeasure. It was also unjust, Burke insisted, to aid the poor. People received their just deserts in proportion to their work and industry—"the more, the better, according to every man's ability." It was foolish and wrong to promise the poor governmental action that could aid them. "Patience, labor, sobriety, frugality, and religion should be recommended to them; all the rest is downright fraud," he concluded.[73] Burke reads here like any bourgeois manufacturer schooled in the principles of Manchester and the Protestant ethic. Moreover, in this lecture to the poor below there is heard the echo of the bourgeois attack on those above that the young Burke had made a half-century earlier in his Dublin *Reformer*.

Mary Wollstonecraft once wrote of Burke (more perceptively than perhaps she realized), that "misery to reach your heart" had to deal with "the downfall of queens." The sufferings of the vulgar and ordinary "could not move your commiseration" [74] We know now that this is not completely true. Burke could summon up the wrath of the Gods in defending ordinary people against aristocratic oppression as he did in Ireland. But this same bourgeois reflex could, indeed, leave him with little patience for the truly miserable. There is, for example, Burke's level-headed business attitude to his own few poor tenants as revealed in a letter written some twenty years earlier. Burke's kinsman Garrett Nagle had called Burke's attention to some problems with his tenants. Burke wrote back:

I cannot conceive why the tenants should be so very much behind. I know that the markets are not only reasonably good, but extremely high. . . . . I think it, therefore, not unreasonable, that they should be compelled to pay, and the sooner the better; for if persons so poor as they are, should be suffered to run long in arrears, nothing will be got from them.[75]

Burke was, thus, in many respects a man of the new bourgeois age. However eloquently he might defend the age of chivalry and rail against the age of calculators and economists, a part of him was firmly at home with the assumptions and mental set of a capitalist society. Parts of Burke's writings are indistinguishable from parts of Smith's or Bentham's. His famous *Speech on Economical Reform* (1780) is a case in point. The tone of the speech is obsessive in its efforts to eliminate waste in the king's household, and to replace it with public frugality. The board of trade had to be abolished because it was "useless, idle and expensive." [76] The terms with which he proposed reforming the king's household are characterized by the same bourgeois cum sexual zeal he would attribute to Hastings and his cohorts. The king's offices were "the stronghold of prodigality, the virgin fortress which was never before attacked." These useless offices were "the fine paid by industry and merit, for an indemnity to the idle and the worthless." There is nothing wrong, he told his colleagues, with ambition, "the improvement of one's circumstances." It is a principle basic to human nature, he adds, sounding very much like Smith. "It belongs," he insists, personalizing it, "to us all." But, like Smith, he would have ambitious men look elsewhere for their fortunes than to "the intrigue of a court." The suggestions proposed by Burke would render the king's offices compatible with the principles of capitalist enterprise. Unprofitable public estates of the crown were to be put on the private property market where they would be acquired and improved by the beneficial principles of competition. The whole financial operation of the king's office would be rationalized; all government expenditures would be planned and records kept.[77] Too much of the king's household, Burke insists, is based upon useless and outdated feudal principles. Bourgeois utilitarian and efficient Burke sheds no tears over prescriptive and traditional institutions here. It is as a cold-hearted, cost-accounting calculator, economist par excellence that Burke spoke to the Commons in his famous speech of 1780. No mysterious reverence of the past here, no embattled defense of the age of chivalry. Waste and superfluity must be rooted out, the relics of the past swept away.

But when the reason of old establishments is gone, it is absurd to preserve nothing but the burden of them. This is superstitiously to embalm a carcass not worth an ounce of the gums that are used to preserve it. It is to burn precious oils in the tomb;

it is to offer meat and drink to the dead—not so much an honour to the deceased, as a disgrace to the survivors. Our palaces are vast inhospitable halls. There the bleak winds . . . howling through the vacant lobbies, and clattering the doors of deserted guardrooms, appall the imagination, and conjure up the grim spectres of departed tyrants.[78]

Burke carries his bourgeois assault even to the king's table with a criticism of the wasteful and luxurious gorging of food in the royal kitchens. Royal contracts, he also suggests, should be let out to the lowest bidder. Efficiency and utility is the new ideal. That an office performs "no use at all," is grounds for its elimination. Pensions, on the other hand, are justified only if they encourage "virtuous ambition" and "merit." [79] The careful reader of this speech (Bedford was not) would have difficulty accusing Burke of inconsistency when he later accepted a pension upon retiring from the Commons. But much more significant, this speech reveals the glaring bourgeois face of Burke.

Another, even more important, glimpse of that face is found in Burke's *Letters on a Regicide Peace,* a much more unlikely place, to be sure. This most unrestrained of Burke's attacks on the Jacobins as grave-diggers of the glory that was Europe is at the same time an apology for the spirit of bourgeois capitalism; as such, it is perhaps the most telling evidence of Burke's ambivalence. No more than fifty pages after his attack on the bourgeoisie and their "spirit of ambition" as impatient subverters of the settled place society has given them, Burke defends the ethics of ambitious money men. Usury is justified, indeed, essential, Burke writes, in recommending the financing of continued war against the French. "The monied men have a right to look to advantage in the investment of their property." They take risks, and that risk is justly included in their price. It would be "unjust and impolitic" not to allow their interest. Having recited his Bentham, Burke moves on to Smith. There is no shame that government creditors who finance the war derive financial gain. "There must be," Burke writes, "some impulse besides public spirit, to put private interest into motion along with it." The love of money is essential for progress and improvement!

This desire of accumulation is a principle without which the means of their service to the state could not exist. The love of lucre, though sometimes carried to a ridiculous, sometimes to a vicious, excess, is the grand cause of prosperity to all states. In this natural, this reasonable, this powerful, this prolific principle, it is for the satirist to expose the ridiculous: it is for the moralist to censure the vicious; it is for the sympathetic heart to reprobate the hard and cruel; it is for the judge to animadvert on the fraud, the extortion, and the oppression; but it is for the statesman to employ it as he finds it, with all its concomitant excellencies, with all its imperfections on its head. It is his part, in this case, as it is in all other cases, where he is to make use of the general energies of nature, to take them as he finds them.[80]

The similarities with Smith continue. Burke urges that taxation be directed at the unproductive, those who "cease to augment the common stock," who no longer "enrich it by their industry or their self-denial." Those who are idle and wallow in luxury and ease should be taxed, Burke insists, "not because they are vicious principles, but because they are unproductive." [81] Like the bourgeois radicals, Burke divides the world into heroic industrious producers who deny themselves immediate gratification, and profligate men of idleness and luxury. Marx does not seem that far from the mark in his characterization of Burke in *Capital* as "an out-and-out vulgar bourgeois." [82] This bourgeois division of the world between the productive self-deniers and the luxurious idle even breathes through Burke's proposed *Sketch of the Negro Code,* his suggestion for an orderly and gradual freeing of the slaves, submitted in 1792. He suggests there that industrious and sober Negroes be given Saturday or Friday off. Slaves or even free Negroes who are idle, disorderly, drunk, quarrelsome, or involved in gaming, are to be punished. [83]

In his *Letters on a Regicide Peace* Burke repeats the message of *Thoughts and Details on Scarcity.* Rain, tempest, frost, and blight raise havoc with nations. But there is nothing statesmen can do about their effects. The state is a limited state according to the ideology of bourgeois radicalism, and so, too, for Burke.

Let government protect and encourage industry, secure property, repress violence, and discountenance fraud, it is all that they have to do. In other respects, the less they meddle in these affairs the better; the rest is in the hands of our Master and theirs. [84]

Burke is upset at using the label poor for anyone who is in fact able-bodied. The poor are only the sick, the infirm, the orphans, and the aged, he insists. "When we affect to pity, as poor, those who must labor or the world cannot exist, we are trifling with the condition of mankind." To call a healthy laborer poor is to apply a term of pity to him, and to encourage dissatisfaction with his condition. Only the sick and aged and infirm need pity. To give it to vigorous laborers is "to teach them to seek resources where no resources are to be found, in something else than their own industry, and frugality, and sobriety." [85]

On the last pages of his *Letters on a Regicide Peace* Burke praises the wondrous unfolding of material progress. His task is to convince his reader that continued war with France will not impede English prosperity. His strategy is to parade the connections between war and commercial profit. His obsession with the Jacobins has brought him to this paradoxical juncture. Defending the age of chivalry requires dangling the temptations of the age of calculators and economists. The *Letters* gloat over an expansive English economy ever bigger and better. Burke thrills at the increase in the number of canals, the decline in bankruptcies, the flourishing of trade and manufacture, the clogging of noisy traffic in the Thames. He marvels at the shops "bursting with opulence" and a people "choked up by our riches." He offers proof of "our astonishing and almost incredible prosperity." [86] Few champions of the Industrial Revolution and bourgeois radicalism did better than Burke in describing the progress and improvement produced by the new age of calculation and economy in these pages of his *Letters on a Regicide Peace*. But, then, the likes of Wedgewood, Cooper, Price, and Priestley were not at the same time trying to revive the dying age of chivalry.

The contrast between bourgeois Burke sounding in 1795 much like the Smith of 1776 and Burke the more well-known apologist for the aristocratic order begs speculation on Burke's relationship to general ideological developments in the eighteenth and nineteenth centuries. To begin with, it should be noted that Burke's ambivalence need not involve any contradictions if read in the perspective of Frederick Engels' discussion of England in his essay *On Historical Materialism*. Engels suggested there that England's bourgeois revolution of 1640 ended with the setback of 1660 and that 1688 represented a carefully worked out compromise between the contending classes. The reactionary aristocratic classes retained political and social power while the progressive bourgeois class retained its commercial victory in the sense that the general principles of a bourgeois economy became the prevailing norms of English economic life. [87] From this perspective Burke's ambivalence could be understood as an effort to keep adamantly to the compromise against English radicals seeking to break it by demanding not only economic but political power as well. This might also explain Burke's historical preoccupation with 1688 and his constant claim that he embodies true Whig principles. This makes sense, then, if one accepts the notion of Whig principles as involving this compromise described by Engels. Using Engels' argument to make sense of Burke has some obvious appeal, but it suffers from what we now know about Burke. We know too much about his inner tensions over ambition, striving, and achievement to rest the case with a neat distinction between an economically bourgeois Burke and a politically aristocratic Burke.

Perhaps an even more interesting field for speculation is not how Burke might have fitted in to past ideological conflict but what his future ideological role would be. Here, too, one could argue that the ambivalence involved no contradiction, that is, if the defense of the status quo, privilege, subordination, and deference were divorced from aristocracy and transferred to capitalism. Burke becomes, as C. B. MacPherson has persuasively argued, a potentially crucial theorist for capitalism when read in this way as merely a theorist of hierarchy and class subordination. [88] In fact, he provides the new liberal capitalist order with what it would desperately need when it succeeded. Revolutionary bourgeois ideology in the eighteenth century was inherently critical and fluid; it attacked authority, status, and superiority. Successful capitalism, after it had replaced the aristocracy in the nineteenth century, rethought its attitudes to authority, subordination, and keeping to one's rank and assigned place. In response to attacks on these principles from its left, triumphant capitalism borrowed the old principles of hierarchy, class subordination, and keeping one's place from the ancien régime and restated them as once again the bulwarks of order, security, and civilization against all would-be challengers. The capitalist replaced the aristocrat, in the formula, and the upstart middle class, now fully arrived, was replaced by ambitious upstart workers who also had no respect for their betters. Read in these terms Burke is a critical capitalist ideologue, for he gave triumphant capitalism in the nineteenth century arguments from an older repressive and exploitive ideology to replace those of liberation and progress which it needed in the eighteenth century on its rise to power. And so one jumps forward easily to Burke becoming the prophet for the capitalist world in the cold war!

There is much to be said for this reading of Burke. He expressed himself often enough as a pure theorist of hierarchy and tradition so that the aristocratic dimension can often be overlooked. There are enough warnings against "corrupting the common people with the spoils of the superior classes" to fit him right into Victorian England or free-enterprise America.[89] And there are as many descriptions of subordination that deal with the servant and his master as with the money man and the broad-acred nobility. In an anachronistic reading Burke makes good sense from this perspective. The ambivalence fades away; he is a bourgeois theorist through and through, justifying the natural right of the superior capitalist class to rule. This could well be a legitimate reading of Burke's relevance for the nineteenth and twentieth centuries. It can be extrapolated, to a certain extent, from his writings, and it has been, especially in the context of America where the category of nobility is irrelevant. But Burke's bourgeois economics notwithstanding, this is a reading by no means true to Burke's intentions. It is historically unfair to him. Burke dealt with ascendent capitalism not triumphant capitalism. The precapitalist order and its values were very much a part of his frame of thought. This is not only a historical distortion of Burke, it is also a personal distortion, for the ambivalence between aristocratic principles and bourgeois principles was central to his personality and the dynamics of his private self and cannot be dismissed by replacing aristocratic with traditional. Aristocracy and aristocratic principles were very real to Burke. They were a critical part of his inner being and cannot be willed away by scholars two centuries later. His ideas are not timeless abstractions, nor are they universally applicable a priori truths unrelated to experiential data. When used by others they should be treated as products of historical and personal experience, which is, after all, only to follow Burke's own methodological advice.

OF PARTIES, POPES, AND POTENTATES

Before leaving Burke's obsession with Jacobinism, it is important to note the impact of the French Revolution on Burke the person, during these years. Here, too, one finds apparent contradiction, reflecting the basic ambivalence hidden within Burke. One result of the revolution, for example, was to undermine the peculiar device by which Burke had so successfully resolved the tensions involved in asserting himself and making his mark in a closed aristocratic society. The party of Rockingham and then Fitzwilliam and Portland was, as we have seen, critically important to Burke in terms of both his political principles and personal life strategy. It was, thus, a sad and lonely Burke who in 1791 disassociated himself from the group that for nearly three decades he had served and that in turn had served him so well. Burke's letters of these years make quite clear the extent of his personal loss.[90]

Burke left his beloved party and in so doing he played an important part in clearing the ideological air for future British party politics. In the demise of the Rockingham Whig party and in the wake of Napoleon's war there would rise the ideological parties of the nineteenth century. Burke sensed this future patterning of British public life and his own role in bringing it about. In writing to a friend he noted of his political views: "If they are Tory principles, I shall always wish to be thought a Tory." [91] But it is not Burke's public legacy that is our concern. Of more interest is how Burke could take this separation from his party in stride, indeed even contemplate it, if, in fact, it played so crucial a role in structuring the complex problems of his private identity. While Burke lamented the break with the Whigs he did recover after all. He was not ruined or incapacitated. How was this possible?

Burke could cope with this break from the party because he no longer needed the party as a vehicle to fame and fortune. Another impact of the French Revolution on Burke the person was to catapult him to world renown, far beyond the expectations of the ambitious young man fresh from Dublin seeking to make his mark for himself and his family. He might have no friends in Parliament, a fanciful exaggeration, or none in his old party, a somewhat more accurate assessment, but outside Westminster Burke acquired in the 1790s the importance he had sought since his youth. The cultural establishment (not the likes of youthful Coleridge and Wordsworth) were, as noted earlier, beside themselves with praise for the *Reflections*. Burke was very conscious of his sudden fame, as one might well expect. It was, to be sure, a bittersweet triumph. While the disapprobation of many of his party saddened him, he could still write with utter candor and great precision to a friend a few weeks after the publication of his *Reflections:* "The publick has been so favorable, that the demand for this piece has been without example; and they are now in the sale of the twelfth thousand of their copies." [92] Burke had always been a hero to bluestocking society from the days of his literary debut in the 1750s. What distinguished his triumph now was not their accolades but the tribute of the truly great—his betters. In the moment of alienating the party of his betters he opened the door to the truly superior circles of England and all Christendom. What years to savor for the upwardly mobile outsider! From 1791 to his death Burke's correspondence sparkled with letters to and from the great titled families of all Europe. His relationship with the opposition Whig magnates somewhat strained, he became the intimate of the aristocracy clustered around the Court and Throne. Visits were now to the Duke of Dorset and not the opposition peers. The king himself showered Burke with praise. How ironic, for in the early 1780s Burke had championed for Rockingham reforms of the king's very own household. George III had, in fact, been so infuriated then that he could not speak personally to Rockingham even though he had to tap him to be his minister. Now the king called Burke to his lévees and singled out his service to the cause of aristocracy. Burke had made it. The years of restless striving must have seemed worth it when he was received by George III on 3 February 1791. The details of that meeting are known thanks to the publication in 1967 of Jane Burke's letter to Will Burke.

I do not know whether he told you of his reception when he went to Court. . . . The King was talking to the Duke (of Portland), but his eyes were fixed on Ned who was standing in the crowd . . . The King went up to him, and, after the usual questions of how long have you been in town and the weather, he said you have been very much employed of late, and very much confined. Ned said, no, Sir, not more than usual—You have and very well employed too, but there are none so deaf as those that w'ont hear, and none so blind as those that w'ont see—Ned made a low bow. . . . You have been of use to us all, it is a general opinion, is it not so Lord Stair? who was standing near. It is, said Lord Stair;—your majesty's adopting it, Sir, will make the opinion general, said Ned—I know it is the general opinion, and I know that there is no man who calls himself a Gentleman that must not think himself obliged to you, for you have supported the cause of the Gentlemen—you know the tone of Court is a whisper, but the King said all this loud, so as to be heard by everyone at Court. [93]

Burke's support of "the cause of the Gentlemen" also brought him into close correspondence with George's peers in Europe. His correspondence includes letters to and from the king and queen of France, the king of Poland (who sent along a medal), the empress of Russia, and in 1793 from Pope Pius VI (who sent along a prayer to the Almighty to grant Burke "all such good things as the heart can desire"). Pius praised Burke's "defense of the cause of right" and urged him to "more and more exert yourself to protect the cause of civilization." This was, indeed, what Burke was doing, for by 1793 he had become the principal voice in Europe rallying the exiled émigrés and conservative governments to counterrevolution.[94] Thus these years also find him and his son Richard in daily communication with exiled nobility and military officials planning the strategy of the anti-Jacobin crusade. One suspects, however, that perhaps the sweetest victory for Burke was not this correspondence nor acceptance by the world's great but the news that the sentimental and chivalrous Burke received in a letter from a lady-in-waiting to the queen of France in January 1791.

. . . thro' the means of Miss Wilkes the Queen of France first saw the passage in your Book which relates to Her . . . this lady immediately carried it to the Queen, who before she had read half the lines, she burst into a flood of tears, and was a long time before she was sufficiently composed to peruse the remainder.[95]

CHAPTER 9

"Pain and Sorrows"

(1794–1797)

BURKE bore his fame with difficulty. In his last years his letters reflected the same insecurity and self-doubts of his adolescent letters to his friend Shackleton. Only fifty years later there was the added dimension of despair, despair of a life misspent, an existence meaningless and worthless. Burke spent some of his days attending Court on the queen's birthday, visiting Dorset's country house, and getting medals from kings and divine wishes from Popes. But as death drew near he seldom left his beloved estate in Beaconsfield. He never went into London and wrote to his friends of the miserable and sad debacle that was his life and career. In 1794 he wrote to Fitzwilliam thanking him for overlooking his "many faults and imperfections." The following year he described himself to his Irish friend Grattan as "in the mud of my obscurity and wretchedness." Writing in August 1796 to the Comte de Provence, then acknowledged by royalists as king of France, Burke characterized himself as "an obscure, broken and insignificant individual stranger." Nine months before his death he wrote to another Irish friend of his "pain and sorrows." Life itself was a trial; there was absolutely nothing "that I have the good fortune to be at all pleased with." And two months before his death, Burke wrote to Windham, his closest confidant, that his bodily pains were no match for his mental torture. "Grief, shame, indignation, and other despair, have so fermented in my mind, as to produce there a disorder, as strong, as the fermentation which my food undergoes in my miserable stomach." [1]

This despair was no postured melancholy designed to temper obvious

success and achievement. Alongside the glitter of the court and the correspondence with the great, Burke's last years were beset by a series of disas-
trous setbacks, reversals in areas ultimately much more meaningful and important to Burke the person than temporary renown. In these reversals lay
the basis for his wretchedness, pain, and sorrow; their effect would totally
dwarf the gratification derived from any kind words uttered, even loudly, by
George III.

"I AM PAST AND GONE BY"

Most of these setbacks were personal and manifestly painful only to him, but
two reversals were the result of general developments in the English political
scene which, had it not been for the personal obsessions we have traced
above, would not have so deeply depressed him. Burke was devastated by
Pitt's peace negotiations with Revolutionary France in late 1795 and early
1796. His personal crusade had failed; apparently no effort would be sustained to restore the ancien régime and lost property rights.[2] Burke had lost
on the Jacobins, he was convinced of that. And in 1796 he suffered a second,
and, to read his words, an even more stinging rebuff. In March, Hastings,
fresh with victory from his acquittal, was awarded his huge annuity and in-
terest-free loan by the House of Commons.[3]
    The peace and Hastings' victory were but the public tip of the iceberg
of private pain. Beneath the surface of these his last four years were numerous
private sources of pain and sorrow that shaped his sense of failure and his
"unhappy life." In June 1794, for example, there occurred a blow to his ego
which, while predictable, was nonetheless painful. He left Parliament. Later
generations would rank Burke with Walpole, Pitt (the elder), Disraeli, and
Churchill as House of Commons men. But for none of these other giants were
the years in the Commons alone as critical and decisive in shaping their historical identity as they were for Burke. The House of Commons had been
decisive in shaping Burke's personal identity as well. It was the arena for the
realization of his ambitions, where he made his mark, where he became an
independent man. His letters upon entering Parliament in 1765 come to
mind with their thrill of success, the exhilaration of a career and fortune to be
made, a family to be provided for. His first election victory in 1765 was of
such great moment in his life that it occasioned the only time (according to
his testimony) that he got drunk.[4] If leaving the party in 1790 had been difficult, even more sorrowful, then, was leaving Westminster in 1794. But in
the mood that pervaded his last years his taking leave of Parliament was also
tinged with melancholy and memories less of triumph than of defeat.[5]

Leaving the Commons was related to another mark of failure during his final years, the erosion of whatever financial security Burke had earlier achieved. As the Burke fortunes were made in conjunction with the arrival in Parliament, the departure from Parliament dramatized the shaky foundation of that wealth. His last years found Burke constantly in debt, a state of affairs bound to be of great embarrassment to such a prideful self-made man. The major source of his financial troubles came from the Burke common purse, for it was in helping to pay off William's large debt to Lord Verney in 1792 that Edmund's woes began. In 1780 William had agreed to pay Verney £20,000 in installments. Will spent most of the 1780s in India, partly because of this very debt, so the issue was never resolved. Verney died in 1791 and young Richard negotiated an agreement for Will with Verney's niece. William would pay £5,000 in 1792 and another £5,000 in 1795. What actually happened was that Fitzwilliam gave Burke £1,200 in 1792, for it was he, Edmund, who paid the first £5,000 due on William's debt. In 1795 William was arrested for failing to pay the second installment and Edmund secured his release on bond. Burke's debts by 1795 amounted to nearly £30,000, which included loans of over £5,000 from Fitzwilliam and £6,000 owed the estate of David Garrick.[6] In a letter to John King, brother of his close friend, Burke told of having

borrowed, as your Brother knows from some of my friends, in order to answer the most exigent of my debts, a sum of three thousand pounds; and I must borrow very speedily about a thousand or fifteen hundred more, or I sink.[7]

So gloomy were his prospects that Burke feared prison. In 1795 he wrote Walter King of his creditors' demands. "They are now directly upon me." One option that Burke seems to have considered was fleeing the country. "I might perhaps in America, Portugal, or elsewhere, have found a refuge and the sale of what I have, might have gone some way towards doing justice to my creditors." But there was no time for that; Burke concluded the letter confessing that "though I had conceived very few things could affect me after what has happened—I cannot quite reconcile my mind to a prison with great fortitude." [8]

This prospect of prison makes it easier to understand the mood of lamentation and despair found in Burke's last letters. This very letter to King on his financial plight began, in fact, with the sad note that "there is no longer anything on earth to hope, or even anxiously to wish for." The identity Burke had evolved for himself was inextricably bound up with success, achievement, place, wealth, and fame. To a man so driven by ambition, the lack of estates to pass on, the lack of even an heir, as we shall see, if only in the symbolic political sense, the prospect of ignominious financial disaster, all of these were as tantamount to failure as the public's apparent disregard for what he believed in.

One possibility seemed to hold out some relief from the immediate fi-

nancial bind as well as meet one of the deepest aspirations and personal needs
that had for so long been part of Burke's complex personality. Few things
could both provide Burke with ready cash and credit and also make him a
man of great and independent status and rank better than being elevated to
the peerage. And this is what seemed in the offing in 1794. But here, too,
there was painful reversal; the imprint of failure was once again the dominant
note. When Portland and his followers entered into coalition with Pitt in
1794 they asked that some provision be given Burke. Portland wrote, on 14
June, of "Pitt's idea of making Burke a peer." [9] Richard politicked
vigorously for his father. He wrote to Windham that "the peerage should be
given; since nothing else can be conceived to give a solid security or an earnest in public estimation of a future provision." Given what he described as
the "debt due from the country and due the opinion of Europe at large,"
nothing would do "less than the peerage." [10]

If they do not give it to him, for godsake for what kind of services is it reserved,
unless it is determined that it should never be given to civil service, or only follow in
the common line of official promotion? What do they mean to make peers of in future? I say nothing with regard to the past, tho I believe some might be found on the
list whose services are not more brilliant or their fortune more ample than his.
Indeed if it was a subject fit for me to discuss, I might compare his services for effect
and public benefit, with those of any single man, since the Restoration. [11]

Richard wrote the letter but it reflected Burke's own assessment of his worth.
He very much wanted the peerage as a public testimonial to the achievement
that was his life. He was not even above advertising himself. Informed that
Pitt was, as Burke put it, "so obliging as to think, that his humble industry
in his thirty years service may, without impropriety be recommended to his
Majesties gracious consideration," he sent Pitt a note outlining his claims
and comparing them with others such as Barré, Dunning, or Lord Auck-
land. [12] Even this was to no avail. The peerage never materialized. The king
would not agree. Perhaps the memory of an earlier Burke lay too heavy on
the king's now-lucid mind. The best that Pitt could get for Burke was a pension and annuity. The charmed aristocratic circle for so long the object of
Burke's love (and hate) was spared defilement by this Irish arrivé.

Even the pension brought grief. The £1,160-a-year grant and the yearly
annuity of £1,200 awarded in August 1795 were soundly criticized by the
Whig opposition. For some it confirmed their suspicion that Burke had been
paid by the ministry for his earlier anti-Jacobin bombast. For others, like
Bedford and Lauderdale, it seemed a repudiation of Burke's earlier principles
opposing royal patronage and corruption. Bedford's attack on the pension
was one of the cruelest reversals in these, Burke's last years, and prompted
the *Letter to a Noble Lord,* which has figured so prominently in this study.
Sensing himself near death Burke also saw himself a failure. Even this meager

public notice of his service was criticized by the great. Not only did they not welcome him into their sacred peerage, but in questioning the pension they were "not sensible of any desert of mine;" they "degrade what remains of myself." [13] It was in such a frame of mind that Burke wrote his reply to Bedford, and with it poured forth the repressed feelings of a lifetime. Not only did he deserve the pension but he was a success and worthy of more esteem than even the good duke was. That was, of course, if one applied the bourgeois criteria of value and virtue, criteria Burke no longer repressed. That they vied for his soul was at last out in the open, there for the few sensitive ones like Coleridge to note.

The criticism of his pension still pales, however, beside the most painful crisis of these years, the personal tragedy of his son's death. An only child's death is unnatural and tragic enough for any parent to bear, but the anguish of Richard's death was intensified for Burke because of all he had invested in his son and his son's future. Like many an arrivé, Burke was concerned that his achievement be perpetuated unto succeeding generations. This was one reason why the loss of a peerage loomed so painful. Above all else it was their secure ease in passing on wealth and fame that the bourgeoisie envied in the aristocracy. In his last years Burke was preoccupied with his inability to fulfill this aristocratic ideal of transmitting patrimony to his heir. "He will leave to his son a name of honour and dignity, that is a great thing to leave such a son, but more I fear, he never will inherit from his father," wrote Jane to Will in 1791. [14] Writing to Grattan in 1795, Burke made bitter jest of his inability to pass on a landed estate.

If it were not for the landed security I am able to give; much more surely, than any of them can do with their great real estates. The landed security I mean is the grave, which is too near to suffer me to prevaricate. Though not great in extent, it is lasting in its tenure, and above all objection in its title. All these things dispose me to it more and more. My inheritance is anticipated—my son is gone before me to take possession; and I linger here, for what it is not fit to be seen, either by the son, or by the father. [15]

By then Richard was dead, and with his death Burke's aspirations for aristocratic continuity were dashed. In his *Letter to a Noble Lord* Burke admitted as much. Had it only pleased God, his "hopes of succession" would have been fulfilled. He would have been a "sort of founder of a family." Nor could Burke resist a dig at Russell's lineage. Burke's family would have "in science, in erudition, in genius" been no "inferior to the Duke of Bedford, or to any of those whom he traces in his line." But such ambitions, the only ones remaining for the dying Burke, were forever doomed by the "Disposer," whose "wisdom it behooves us not at all to dispute." [16] How appropriate, then, that in writing about the failure of this ambition, Burke should use his favorite metaphor for aristocratic continuity—the oak tree.

The storm has gone over me; and I lie like one of those old oaks which the late hurricane has scattered about me. I am stripped of all my honors, I am torn up by the roots, and lie prostrate on the earth! There, and prostrate there, I most unfeignedly recognise the Divine Justice, and in some degree submit to it.[17]

The grieving Burke, all hope for future fame and glory through the foundation of a family gone, clings to the earth like the vine. The great Disposer has spoken. It is not Burke's place to soar like the great oaks and shade his country from generation to generation. His place is that of "annual plants that perish with our season and leave no sort of traces behind us."

Richard's death left Burke with a deep sense of guilt over his lifelong dealings with his son. Even as Burke wished success for himself, his driving ambition had been transferred to Richard whom he pushed forward with a passion that Burke lived to regret. Contemporaries noted how Burke, seemingly predisposed by nature to his kinsmen, doted particularly on his son. Wolfe Tone, no friend of Burke, spoke well of Richard as having "a considerable portion of talents from nature, and cultivated, as may be well supposed, with the utmost care by his father, who idolized him." [18] Burke had had extravagant expectations for his son. After Oxford and the Grand Tour, he studied law, but like himself it was into public life that the father pushed the son. In the late eighties and early nineties Burke arranged for his son to serve as agent for the Irish Catholics; in the early nineties he put him forward as liaison man with Europe's exiled nobility. More significantly, Burke obtained the position of legal advisor to Fitzwilliam for him in 1790. His most fervent wish, however, was that Richard serve in the House of Commons. Fitzwilliam had a vacant seat at his disposal in August 1793 but refused to give it to Richard for fear of alienating Fox. Edmund took this as a personal affront, indicative of his own failure. "I am past and gone by," he wrote to Elliot that September about Fitzwilliam's decision. Moreover, he sensed himself the cause of his son's failure. Guiltily, he wrote of his indignation "that my son, qualified in every way," was set aside "for the sins of his father." [19] Undaunted at this failure, Burke let it be known the following spring that he expected upon his retirement that his own seat would be offered to Richard by Fitzwilliam. He had little by way of broad-acred estates to leave his son but passing on his parliamentary seat was rich with aristocratic symbolism for the aging Burke. His friend, French Laurence, wrote Portland that "nothing would so wound him (Burke) to the soul as a disappointment in this respect." [20] Fitzwilliam agreed and wrote Richard that he would be his father's successor at Malton. Edmund replied that this was "by far the greatest favor which could possibly be conferred on me." Burke described the day when he had heard that Richard would follow him into the Commons as "the happiest of my life." [21]

Happiness turned immediately to deepest grief. The previous year Richard had shown symptoms of tuberculosis but neither he nor his father took them seriously. However, the very trip to Yorkshire and the exertions required by even the perfunctory campaign at Malton for the parliamentary seat brought on an acute and ultimately fatal attack. Three weeks after his formal election to Parliament as his father's successor Richard lay dead. Edmund's grief was fueled by bitter feelings of guilt. "I feel a thousand guilty pangs for my neglect in many many instances of such a son and such a friend." [22] What particularly bothered Burke was how he had driven his son. He realized that Richard's care and filial concern for him, his agreement to do whatever Edmund bade him, to serve him in Ireland, India, or Europe, to manage his affairs, left Richard little time to make his own mark. "This was among the causes of his being so little known to the world," he wrote Fitzwilliam.[23] Richard had always served his father's interests first, Burke wrote sadly. The election trip which had brought on the fatal attack was itself to serve the father's ambition and Richard had eagerly and energetically gone. The depths of his guilt are revealed in Burke's manuscript memorial for his dead son. The desire to immortalize his own achievements had led to this, the death of his beloved and dutiful son.

I cannot at this moment avoid many galling reflexions, when I look back and consider at what a price that unthinking and perhaps at my age unsuitable vivacity and that feverish energy was bought. . . . When I consider that his natural gay season of enjoyment was clouded with cares and solicitudes, which more fitly belonged to mine and were caused by my faults and that his talents which would have soared to an height immeasureable were chained down by these unworthy occupations (serving Burke's interests) I cannot help pressing it to all Parents who are but too apt to think more of what the children owe to them than what they owe to their children to consider with more than usual seriousness of everything which by self-indulgence dissipates and distracts their affairs.[24]

Throughout his life Burke had longed for what he felt his father owed but never gave him. Now he stood guilty of the same crime but with even more horrible consequences. "I threw him away by every species of neglect, and mismanagement," he wrote Fitzwilliam.[25] Such was the ultimate "pain and sorrow" of his last years, that he should do to his own son as his father had done to him.

"NOT ABOUT POPES BUT ABOUT POTATOES": THE RELEVANCE OF IRELAND

Facing death Burke was a broken man convinced of his failure, personal and public, but for an occasional prideful outburst, as in the *Letter to a Noble Lord*. In this mood his thoughts turned to his origins, his beloved Ireland, from whence youthful and ambitious he had fled nearly half a century earlier to make his mark and become his own man. His life and this study are brought full circle with Burke's melancholy reflections on Irish developments in the years before his death.

Burke never forgot his Irish roots (his opponents seldom allowed him to) and throughout his parliamentary career he championed its general interests as well as the particular concern of his mother's religion, Catholicism. But in the 1790s Burke's thoughts turned ever increasingly toward Ireland. Its Catholicism seemed the last virtuous bulwark against the anti-Christian toxin which had already spread from the French atheistic *philosophes* to Unitarian dissenters in England. Cherished memories of his mother and the warmth of her extended Catholic family buttressed its association with the warmth and security of traditional society. The last defenders of the age of chivalry, "the most effective barrier, if not the sole barrier, against Jacobinism" were the Catholics, Burke wrote in 1795 to William Smith.[26] Imagine then his acute pain in his last years when the dread disease of Jacobinism invaded even the body politic of Ireland. Here, too, he suffered in his decline. Not even a country, the repository of so much Catholic and chivalric virtue and good sense, was immune from the Jacobinism which had so quickly passed through the European system. March 1797 found Burke writing Fitzwilliam that Ireland like England "is going its own way to destruction."

The opposition, your Lordship's friends and let me add, my friends, have gone the full length of Jacobinism, and are doing all they can to pull up the land-marks of private property and public safety, and to disunite the two kingdoms; and that upon the falsest grounds both of fact and principle, which, I might easily prove, if I had heart or strength for such a task.[27]

But Burke had neither the heart nor the strength. He was sick with grief to learn that Grattan, his old friend and correspondent on Irish affairs, had moved left and begun to sound as radical as the United Irishmen, the group formed in 1791 to demand universal suffrage as well as Catholic emancipation.[28] All Ireland, urban Protestant radicals, poor Catholic peasants, and the well-to-do Catholic middle class, seemed to be turning to Jacobinism to express their grievances with English rule. Writing to Fitzwilliam two months before his death, Burke concluded:

The discontents of the Protestants and Catholics run into one common channel. All this is the more unhappy for both sides of the water, because all these discontents, without management, or disguise, unite in French Jacobinsim.[29]

There is more than just the nostalgic lament of a disappointed traditionalist in Burke's preoccupation with Irish affairs in the 1790s, however. Ireland was always capable of bringing some of Burke's deepest ambivalences to the surface and the 1790s were no exception. Burke's writings on Ireland in his declining years contain, in fact, some of the most crucial evidence of his deeply divided self. If they were sad defences of a doomed age of chivalry, they were also vicious attacks on the aristocratic principle that informed the traditional order. The ambivalence works its way from Burke's *Letter to Sir Hercules Langrishe, M.P.,* the first piece he wrote on Ireland in the 1790s, to the essays on the Irish question he wrote later in the decade.

The letter to his old friend, Langrishe, is a long, tortured inquiry on granting Irish Catholics the franchise in Irish parliamentary elections. What complicated the issue for Burke was the insistence by some radicals that the suffrage be extended to all Catholics. Burke was faced with the dilemma of his sympathies for the oppressed Catholic and his revulsion at the radical repudiation of social and political hierarchy. His preference was clearly for some Catholics to have the vote, "the rational, sober and valuable part," as opposed to the "low, thoughtless, wild and profligate." [30]

But in his *Letter to Richard Burke, Esquire,* written the following year, all the egalitarian and radical anger that lay within Burke rushed forth. The bourgeois Burke that would not surface publicly in England until the attack on Bedford in 1795 was always exposed by Ireland. If the *Letter* to Langrishe was primarily an assault on the Irish dissenters, then the *Letter* to his son was a condemnation of English aristocratic rule.

He writes to Richard that like himself he was involved in rescuing an oppressed people, and that as his father had done, Richard "must make enemies of many of the rich, of the proud, and of the powerful." Burke notes that he had for a very long time been struggling against the oppression of the great, with those who would confine "to a certain set of favored citizens" that which belongs to all. [31] It will be claimed that some are free, but, he replies, "partial freedom is privilege and prerogative, and not liberty." The Protestant leaders in Dublin claim a lofty "authority derived from their wisdom and virtue" enabling them to look after the happiness and freedom of the people. This is hypocrisy, Burke now notes.

It is neither more nor less than the resolution of one set of people in Ireland to . . . keep a dominion over the rest by reducing them to absolute slavery . . . and thus fortified in their power to divide the public state, which is the result of general contribution, as a military booty solely amongst themselves. [32]

Burke mocks a part of himself as he notes that the very word "ascendancy" is a soft and melodious euphemism, a pleasing illusion that covers a harsh reality. "In plain old English . . . it signifies *pride* and *dominion* on the one part of the relation, and on the other *subserviency* and *contempt*—and it signifies nothing else." [33] Burke reads here like the legions of radicals who attacked that passage in his *Reflections* where he thrilled to the dignified obedience of exalted subordination!

Once again Burke warns of pushing the Irish Catholics into the Jacobin camp, which holds out its arms to the oppressed and those who think they deserve more. The dread Jacobins, he warns the Protestant establishment, are the only ones who will benefit from the continued harshness of the aristocratic ascendancy. The ruling class fears that in every complaint of the Catholic there lurks the treasonous work of the Vatican, but it is only social and economic justice that the people seek, Burke proclaims. It is the angry radical Burke of *The Reformer,* of the *Vindication of Natural Society* who shouts, "it is not about popes but about potatoes, that the minds of this unhappy people are agitated." Isn't it possible, he asks, that they are tired of paying three pounds rent "to a gentleman in a brown coat," or fourteen shillings to someone else in a black coat for an acre of potatoes? Isn't it possible that these men are tired of being doubly taxed by landlords and priests, Burke asks? Their concern is their economic and legal burdens, while the aristocratic rulers of Ireland see only religious conspiracy.

All Burke's repressed resentment of the aristocracy expresses itself here in the Irish context. He was himself far from the misery of the Irish peasant; but it was all of a piece. Jacobinism attracted other victims of the aristocratic principle, as well. Men of talent and ambition thwarted by aristocratic privilege flocked to its tents. Burke never tired of noting that and he saw it at work in Ireland, too. Not just the poor were potential converts to the Jacobin creed. There was, he wrote in a letter of 1792, a new breed of Catholic in Ireland, "who have risen by their industry, their abilities, and their good fortune, to considerable opulence, and of course to an independent spirit." [34] Burke saw how easily Irish Catholics in Ireland could move from Catholicism, the bulwark of the traditional order, to Jacobinism, because he was well aware of how easy it was for himself to move from one principle to the other. He knew that the line between loving and deferring to traditional hierarchies and hating and overthrowing them was a thin one, and one most easily crossed under the weight of a particularly exclusive and/or oppressive "ascendancy."

In his letter to his son, Burke paid lip service to the Anglican establishment in Ireland. The religion of the prince and the leading proprietors must be the religion of the nation, he notes. Just as the people cannot be made Protestant so they cannot and ought not to get rid of Protestant government. All that can be done is to give the four-fifths Catholic majority representation through their more sober and distinguished chieftains. Burke ridiculed those Irish who insisted that if "the people" received the vote, there would be an end to property, that a Popish House of Commons in Ireland would confiscate all the estates of the Protestant aristocracy, who would be driven from their great houses and forced to "live by their wits." [35] Burke turns his satire on the fears he had been peddling himself with respect to English radical proposals for constitutional reforms or the evil ambitions of the confiscating dissenters. The aristocracy refuses to give in, Burke writes Richard. They insist they cannot listen to arguments of "equity or . . . constitutional policy" when "the sword is at their throats, beggary and famine at their door." One should not be moved by these pleadings, Burke cautions. "The same thing has been said in all times and in all languages. The language of tyranny is invariable." [36] How well Burke knew of what he wrote. How often had he conjured up nightmare visions of the House of Lords, the Commons and the king victimized by confiscatory mobs.

The full and savage fury of Burke was yet to come, for he next asks who is really robbing whom. Were the Catholics robbing the Protestant aristocracy or, in fact, had not the latter plundered the land that originally belonged to the Catholics? Three years before he would turn on Bedford, Burke accused the Protestant lords in Ireland of the same crime. That is what the aristocracy was everywhere, Burke notes, nothing more than older upstarts and usurpers who "would wish to let time draw his oblivious veil over the unpleasant modes by which lordships and demesnes have been acquired in theirs, and almost in all other countries upon earth." [37] Like the Jacobins in France (and Bedford's ancestors) the Irish lords had defiled and parceled out Church lands. What appears as utter theoretical confusion, the lumping together into the same despised package of the Protestant aristocracy in Ireland, Bedford in England, the Jacobins, and Hastings, is explained only by Burke's basic ambivalence. It is bourgeois Burke who reveals the hypocrisy of an aristocracy which pastes over its "melancholy and unpleasant title of grantees of confiscation" with the "sacred name of possession." They are the real thieves, usurpers, and plunderers. The passion with which Burke makes the case against the origins of the Protestant aristocracy in Ireland, as he would with Bedford, speaks volumes on what he felt or at least part of him felt about the aristocracy in 1793. It was, as Coleridge and others would note about the attack on Bedford, unusual, to say the least, from an avowed defender of the rights and privileges of nobility.

In two other essays on Ireland written in 1795 Burke's ambivalence is further revealed. In one he condemns the evil Irish Jacobins for rebelliousness and insubordination; [38] in another he confides to Langrishe that if he were treated the way the Catholics were in Ireland, he, too, would become a revolutionary.[39] The ambivalence that Burke so dramatically exposed in his *Letter to a Noble Lord* the very same year is found here in his writings on Ireland. All his sympathy for and identification with the outsider, the excluded, the oppressed but talented man who wants in and who is kept down by the great, is expressed in his defense of the Irish Catholics against the Protestant ascendency. His putting himself in the place of these people lies behind his recognition that there would be good reason for them to be rebellious Jacobins, for as in himself, too, so in the Irish Catholics the dread of Jacobinism is paralleled by an attraction to its ideological message. His identification with the Irish Catholics enables him to identify their common enemy. The Protestant ascendency which keeps down the Irish Catholic is the same Whig broadacred aristocracy which has irritated this talented Irishman, or part of him, for four decades, and which in these very years has sealed its verdict on him by excluding him and his progeny from their charmed inner circle, and kept him in his place.

Burke lived to write one more piece on Ireland, *A Letter on the Affairs of Ireland,* written in 1797 a few months before his death. As he did in the ultimate conclusion of the letter to Bedford, here, too, Burke retreated from the affirmation of his radical self. He ended with self-deprecating humility and fatalistic resignation. He denies the assertive Edmund Burke by cloaking himself with failure and irrelevance. He has, he writes, seldom been consulted about Irish policy. This is as it should be because, "the judgments of the eminent and able persons who conduct public affairs is undoubtedly superior to mine." [40] The essay sadly surveys the Irish scene, but all the fiery passion and vivid denunciation of the Protestant ascendency is gone. Anger has been replaced by respect and deference. The defeat of Catholic ambition in Ireland is received with stoic resignation; so, too, is Burke's defeat. His place was to accept the little platoon "in which God has appointed your station and mine." [41]

Irish affairs would haunt Burke to his deathbed. His last recorded conversation dealt with Ireland and fittingly enough its tone was melancholic ambivalence. He died shortly after midnight on 9 July 1797. The next day his friend, French Laurence, wrote to Fitzwilliam:

He talked of public affairs and private with his accustomed interest and vivacity. He asked me if I read Mr. Grattan's address. On being told that I had, he entered into a comment upon it, praising the brilliancy of some of the declarations, but censuring the false taste of the whole, particularly blaming, yet rather lamenting than blaming, more in sorrow than in anger the bad politics of beginning, continuing, and ending with what is called Parliamentary Reform. [42]

"THEY BARK AT ME": ON BURKE'S MADNESS

Burke's last years were particularly painful, to be sure, but on one level his entire adult life was one of "pain and sorrows." He often experienced deep depression, or as he put it in a letter to Rockingham, quoted earlier, "melancholy which is inexpressible." On many occasions, according to his own testimony, Burke dissembled and hid his pain, and bore up well. There were times, however, when the tortured state of his mind did surface. The depressed Burke was private Burke. In public it was manic Burke that his contemporaries were more likely to see, Burke "foaming like Niagra," as Boswell put it. [43] His parliamentary colleagues were often shocked by the verbal violence of Burke's attacks on Hastings or on the Jacobins. The sixth of May 1791 was just such a day. It saw the dramatic confrontation of Burke and Fox. Burke got increasingly angrier as the debate wore on, pouring out his words in torrents of rage. The members of Parliament were appalled and shouted him down. Burke turned on the Speaker declaring: "I am not mad, most noble Festus, but speak the words of truth and soberness." [44]

That Burke felt obliged to affirm his sanity indicates the extent to which many doubted it. Even while he screamed that Rousseau, Hastings, and the English reformers of the 1780s were deranged madmen, some of his contemporaries suggested that it was he who was possessed.[45] In reply to Boswell's assertion that "they represent him (Burke) as actually mad," Johnson answered "if a man will appear extravagant as he does, and cry, can he wonder that he is represented as Mad." A comment by Gibbon reveals the extent to which the subject was discussed. Praising the *Reflections,* the great historian wrote in 1791 that "poor Burke is the most eloquent madman that I ever knew." Wraxall, the diarist, recorded what he and many others took to be the strange transformation that overtook Burke when he rose to speak in Parliament.

Throughout his general manner and deportment in Parliament, there was something petulant, impatient, and at times almost intractable, which greatly obscured the lustre of his talents. His very features, and the undulating motions of his head, were eloquently expressive of this irritability, which on some occasions seemed to approach towards alienation of mind. Even his friends could not always induce him to listen to reason and remonstrance, though they sometimes held him down in his seat, by the skirts of his coat, in order to prevent the ebullitions of his anger or indignation. Gentle, mild, and amenable to argument in private society, of which he formed the delight and the ornament, he was often intemperate, and even violent in Parliament.[46]

It was after just such an extravagant outburst in 1789 that Burke's parliamentary colleagues warned him that if he did not restrain himself he risked being imprisoned as a madman.[47]

But Burke was no madman. To be sure, his last years were consumed with diabolical nightmares which he shared with his colleagues in Parliament and the readers of his essays. Jacobinism became the personification of Satan's forces and Burke and those he could rally were the troops of God. Jacobinism, he told the Commons in 1791, was "a shapeless monster, born of hell and chaos"; now was the time, he urged, "for crushing this diabolical spirit." [48] The English reformers in the 1780s were agents of the devil. Darkness loomed over England as "wild and savage men," "madmen," conducted "the death-dance of democratic Revolution." [49] Hastings, too, did the devil's work. The sufferings brought to India were all the furies of blackest hell.

He drew from every quarter whatever a savage ferocity could add to his new rudiments in the arts of destruction; and compounding all the materials of fury, havoc, and desolation into one black cloud, he hung for a while on the declivities of the mountains. Whilst the authors of all these evils were idly and stupidly gazing on this menacing meteor, which blackened all their horizon, it suddenly burst, and poured down the whole of its contents upon the plains of the Carnatic—then ensued a scene of woe, the like of which no eye had seen, no heart conceived, and which no tongue can adequately tell. All the horrors of war before known or heard of, were mercy to that new havoc. A storm of universal fire blasted every field, consumed every house, destroyed every temple. The miserable inhabitants flying from their flaming villages, in part were slaughtered; others, without regard to sex, to age, to the respect of rank, or sacredness of function, fathers torn from children, husbands from wives, enveloped in a whirlwind of cavalry, and amidst the goading spears of drivers, and the trampling of pursuing horses, were swept into captivity, in an unknown and hostile land. Those who were able to evade this tempest, fled to the walled cities. But escaping from fire, sword, and exile they fell into the jaws of famine.[50]

But it is really the Jacobins who were the devil incarnate. Rousseau was a demonic madman, wild and ferocious. The Jacobins were "foul, impious, monstrous things," "nefarious monsters." In *A Letter to a Noble Lord* the Jacobins were depicted as men who having "thrown off the fear of God" are the most "dreadful calamity" that can "arise out of hell to scourge mankind."[51] In the *Reflections* Burke has the Jacobins riot "in a drunken delirium from the hot spirit drawn out of the alembic of hell."[52] As one might suspect, however, it is in Burke's most unrestrained work, his *Letters on a Regicide Peace,* that he conjures up his most diabolical visions.

Out of the tomb of the murdered monarchy in France has arisen a vast, tremendous, unformed spectre, in a far more terrific guise than any which ever yet have overpowered the imagination, and subdued the fortitude of man. Going straight forward to its end, unappalled by peril, unchecked by remorse, despising all common maxims and all common means that hideous phantom overpowered those who would not believe it was possible.[53]

Burke had been preoccupied with the devil throughout his career. His diabolism is, indeed, yet another critical link between his public philosophy and his private world. In his earliest reference to the desirability of suppressing sexual passion, in the letter written at the age of fifteen to Shackleton, he spoke of sexuality as a devious plot organized by a crafty and subtle internal enemy that sought through using every bait imaginable to tempt the individual to destruction. Two years later he wrote to Shackleton of losing control to avarice and sensuality which "entirely take possession."[54] The demonic was by definition the opposite of restrained and suppressed passion. It was an evil and dangerous power free from civilized inhibitions with a will and direction of its own. Sublime objects in *The Sublime and Beautiful* were menacing and threatening with an internal power to evoke terror and fear in the beholder. But the demonic terror of the sublime also evokes admiration and awe. People are transfixed by the demonic, Burke wrote in 1756, terrified yet irresistibly drawn to it. So was he. He labeled this reaction "delightful horror," a simultaneous fascination and dread.

This was, in fact, his response four decades later to Jacobinism. While the demonic Jacobins filled him with loathing and disgust they also fascinated him; they evoked admiration, as we have seen, because he was himself in part so like them. In the *Letters on a Regicide Peace* Burke noted that so horrible is the monstrous Jacobin "we cannot bear to look that frightful form in the face." [55] Burke could not bear to see there the reflection of part of himself, although from the care with which he, in fact, did describe the frightful form, one might conclude that here, too, was "delightful horror."

The diabolical connection had a social and political referent, as well, in which Burke's ambivalence was also at work. Burke's diabolism is linked to the literary and philosophical use made of the devil in the Christian myth rendered most profoundly for Burke's world by Milton. In a speech to the House of Commons in 1794 Burke made quite specific the connection between his demonic vision and Milton's.

The condition of France at this moment was so frightful and horrible, that if a painter wished to portray a description of hell, he could not find so terrible a model, or a subject so pregnant with horror, and fit for his purpose. Milton, with all that genius which enabled him to excel in descriptions of this nature, would have been ashamed to have presented to his readers such a hell as France now was, or such a devil as a modern Jacobin. [56]

Part of Burke's preoccupation with the Jacobins as demonic is related to the devil's ambitious striving, his tampering with God's Chain of Being. It was as upstart and malcontent that Milton pictured Lucifer in *Paradise Lost*. Once the brightest and most promising of God's angels, Lucifer became unhappy with the subordinate station God had assigned him. In leading a revolt against God he repudiated the Chain of Being. Unsuccessful in this he was cast down to lowest hell where he continues his warfare against tyrannical God by tempting humanity. It is in this perspective that Burke's diabolism must also be read. Burke would be the last of the great English theorists to stress the Chain of Being. In the face of the bourgeois radical challenge he revived it in terms that would have pleased a Pope, an Elyot, a Raleigh, a Shakespeare. The Christian humanist Burke, then, condemns those restless and ambitious souls who tamper with the divine delegation of station, place, and platoon as satanic.

In his *Letter to a Noble Lord* Burke described the perfidious sans-culottes as "demoniacs possessed with a spirit of fallen pride, and inverted ambition," who in "breaking to pieces a great link of society . . . brought eternal confusion and desolation on their country." [57] The Jacobin was the devil for

Burke, because the devil was the rebel par excellence. Burke, in fact, restored the devil to his proper rebellious place. In the seventeenth century the Puritan revolutionaries demonized Charles I and the Royalist-Anglican establishment. In their holy revolution the Puritans were the saintly forces of God sent to purge England of its satanic ruling class, not unlike the conceptualization of the romantic poets at the turn of the nineteenth century. Burke reversed these roles; the ruling class became the saintly force defending God's Chain of Being, and the devil's camp was Jacobinism.

William Blake sensed Milton's unease as have most readers of *Paradise Lost* who marvel at the inspired and heroic speeches Milton gives Lucifer. Milton was "of the devil's party without knowing it," Blake noted in his "Marriage of Heaven and Hell." The same can be said of Burke. He wrestled with the devil to put down this great rebellious challenge to God's status quo throughout Europe. In so doing he struggled with a part of himself. We know enough of Burke to suggest that he, too, or at least part of him, was "of the devil's party without knowing it."

There is yet another dimension to Burke's diabolism beyond the Miltonic and that is its link to Burke's anality, his "excremental vision," by no means the order of Luther's or Swift's but there none the less and crucial to any understanding of Burke or appreciation of his importance. It is, of course, no surprise from a psychoanalytic perspective, since it fits the normal pattern of regression when oedipal problems are too overwhelming for the ego. As many commentators have noted the devil has about him unmistakable anal overtones.[58] Luther more than any one else in the Christian tradition has linked the devil with anality. His struggle with the devil, he wrote in his *Table-Talk*, was an encounter with something black and filthy.[59] According to Luther the devil's confrontation with God and his repudiation of God's order is symbolized by defiling that creation with excrement. The spiritual, the high and lofty is debased by the gross, the low, the offal of bottoms. At the center of the grand cosmic drama of redemption, the struggle between God and the devil, Luther puts feces.[60]

Burke it seems was just as specific in linking his devil, the Jacobins, and their murderous and wicked spirit to anal aggression. In the *Reflections* Burke describes their "black and savage atrocity of mind." Elsewhere he depicts them "all black with the smoke and soot of the forge of confiscation and robbery." [61] But Burke was capable of much more direct connections between diabolism and anality. In his *Letter to a Noble Lord*, for example, he compared the Jacobin to the "wicked spirit" of the devil—"the principle of evil himself, incorporeal, pure, unmixed, dephlegmated, defecated evil.:" [62] Excrement served Burke's devil as it had Luther's, dropping it on the great and good defiled and debased them. Thus, Burke portrays the Jacobin devil in his "synagogue of Anti-Christ . . . that forge and manufactory of all evil," where he is at work "to desecrate and degrade" all that is "holy and honourable." [63] Once the devil, his East India Company servants, and the Jacobins have finished with this world, this jewel, "once the delight and boast of the creation," would be "a bloated, putrid, noisome carcass, full of stench and poison, an offense, a horror, a lesson to the world." [64] In perhaps his most graphic vision of anal aggression Burke borrowed from Virgil and described the French Jacobins as filthy birds "sprung from night and hell." These foul birds fly from France and drop their filthy politics on England. They "flutter over our heads, and souse down upon our tables, and leave nothing unrent, unrifled, unravaged, or unpolluted with the slime of their filthy offal." [65]

Burke's *Letters on a Regicide Peace* contain his most horrific and demonic visions of the Jacobins and these are linked to anality. Paris is described as nothing less than hell with all the decent expectations of ordered civility turned upside down in a riot of wild and savage abandon. Children "cut the throats of their parents," and mothers cruelly abandon their offspring. While the courts of justice and churches are closed, scores of theaters are crowded day and night with blasphemous and lewd song and dance. There is everywhere "rankness," and "refuse and rejected offal." People are taught to "make no scruple to rake with their bloody hands in the bowels of those who came from their own." To this satanic portrait Burke adds cannibalism. The Jacobins devour "the bodies of those they have murdered," and "drink the blood of their victims." They carry out "nameless, unmanly, and abominable insults on the bodies of those they slaughter." These obscene and savage beasts of prey tender their opponents the ultimate disgrace. By eating them they reduce them to excrement.[66]

Luther was not the only predecessor in this preoccupation with anality, however, nor for that matter with its social connotations. There were also the more orthodox Christian humanists Swift and Pope. For them excrement was not only a symbol of man's bestial and lower self but also symptomatic of a deranged and disordered society. Excrement is also a useful metaphor for aggression and at this Swift was a master. Psychoanalytic theory, of course, makes much of the connection between anality and aggression, even calling this stage of infantile sexuality the anal-sadistic stage. In the symbolic control of excrement Freudian theory sees the origins of defiance, mastery, and the will to power. Burke's excremental vision shares both these motifs, the Augustan humanist and the Swiftian/Freudian notion. The Jacobins (and Hastings, as well) aggressively hurl excrement at those in higher stations to ridicule and humiliate them, in short, to lower them. When the Jacobins have done with their assault on the age of chivalry, have aggressively asserted their will to mastery, then true darkness, confusion, and chaos symbolize this inversion of social order. The world is putrid polluted slime, filthy offal, and defecated evil.

The excremental visions of Luther, Swift, and Burke are linked by another important similarity; each of them responds to anal aggression with anal counterattack. With Luther there is the manifestly anal response to the devil when the founder of Protestantism routs him "mit einem furz" or when he invites him to "lick my posterior" or threatens to "defecate in his face." [67] Swift, on the other hand, mediated his response through an anality sublimated in the written or printed word as in his letter to Arbuthnot where he wrote "let my anger break out at the end of my pen," or in his constant references to literary polemics as "dirt throwing." [68]

Modern psychoanalysis has gone beyond Swift to stress the theoretical connections between anal-sadism and the activity of speech and writing.[69] Few better proofs of this can be offered than the case of Burke, who responded to the anal aggression of the Jacobins and Hastings with an explosion of violent speeches and writings. His answer to the aggression and violence of his enemies was a verbal rage and violence never before heard on the floor of the Commons, and a printed violence that stands out to this day in the history of political thought with perhaps only Marx after him and John Knox before him as rivals. Burke manipulated and wielded colorful and charged language with a savagery as ruthless as any of his antagonists. He heaped scorn and ridicule on his enemies as they did on India, aristocratic women, or the age of chivalry. He debased and dehumanized Hastings and the Jacobins as they humiliated and bestialized the natives of India and the ancien régime in England or France. Burke's speech, according to contemporaries, was so fast that the parliamentary reporters could hardly keep track of him. Boswell wrote of one "Cavandish taking down while Burke foamed like Niagara." [70] If Rousseau and Hastings loomed as wild and violent men to Burke, then to his contemporaries the violent fits and torrents of written and spoken anger that flowed from Burke revealed if not a madman (they said this of Swift, too) then at best a hopeless enthusiast unable, fittingly enough, to control himself.

In modern psychoanalytic theory anality is also closely linked to money, the vision of filthy lucre. Things which are possessed and accumulated, property and money, are seen as essentially excremental in nature. They are retained by the stingy or given as gifts which bring joy and pleasure, an identity which, it is suggested, originates in infantile manipulation of the excremental product. Burke, too, is someone in whose subconscious the link is made between excrement, anal aggression, and the world of money. It is a theme, for example, that constantly reappears in his speeches and writings on Hastings and the English in India. Their palms itch, he claims in his *Speech on the Nabob of Arcot's Debts,* and "their bowels yearned for usury." [71] The financial manipulations of the Company and the great debt incurred by its servants "forms the foul, putrid mucus, in which are engendered the whole brood of creeping ascarides, all the endless involutions, the eternal knot. . . . Those inexpugnable tape-worms which devour the nutriment, and eat up the bowels of India." [72]

In a speech on the impeachment of Hastings, Burke offered a summary of the commercial operations of Hastings and his coplunderers on the make in India. He exposed in great detail the financial arrangements made by the Company, describing the inner workings of its system of "theft, bribery, and speculation." Luther could not have done better than Burke in condemning this rapacious capitalist system in excremental terms. The whole system, Burke told the Commons, was a series of vices "which gender and spawn in dirt, and are nursed in dunghills." These vices undermine the values of traditional society "and pollute with their slime that throne which ought to be a seat of dignity and purity." [73] Four days later, Burke said of Hastings that "for years he lay down in that sty of disgrace, fattening in it, feeding upon that offal of disgrace and excrement, upon everything that could be disgustful to the human mind." [74] Before Hastings and the English arrived in India, Burke once told the House of Commons, it was a clean, rich, well-cultivated country, the "Eden of the East." Into this "beautiful paradise" came the defilement of "the dirty and miserable interferences" of English politics and English avarice. "This delightful spot, the joint effect of nature and art, the united work of God and man was no more." [75] The fall from chivalric innocence, the death of the old order, is the victory of satanic calculation and temptation, not for an apple, not even for knowledge, but for filthy lucre.

Burke's scatology, the anal rage so evident in his speeches and writings, might well have contributed to the anger of the pack of contemporaries who hounded him at every turn in the 1790s. On that May day in 1791 when he broke with Fox, Burke reassured the House of his sanity and then he turned on those in the chamber who ridiculed him. He quoted the words of Lear, "the little dogs, and all,/Tray, Blanche, and Sweetheart. See, they bark at me!" This paranoia has not gone unnoticed. Copeland has written of Burke's "language of paranoia" and Namier of a "streak of persecution mania" running through Burke's life and writings. [76] A leitmotif of Burke's life is, in fact, his constant sense that enemies were out to get him. From his first arrival in politics he spoke of "attempts made to ruin me," a conspiracy "to pull me down," of efforts to defame him by those "known to be hired to that office by my enemies." [77] By 1791 Burke could claim in the Commons that he had always been hunted down, first by one party, then by another. [78] In the years between Richard's death and his own when Burke remained a virtual hermit, avoiding even his neighbors in Beaconsfield, he is reported to have insisted that he would not "show to the world the face of a man marked by the hand of God." [79]

Burke always sensed himself singled out, alone, deserted, and turned upon by former friends over Hastings, over France, over the dissenters. Conspiracies flourished everywhere; India men, Unitarians, Jacobins, money men, lurked behind every tree sowing seeds of unrest and chaos. Burke alone saw through their malevolent intentions. He once said, "I fear I am the only person in France or England, who is aware of the extent of the danger, with which we are threatened." [80] To his tortured mind the Jacobins were in fact out to get him, Burke. It takes a great deal of paranoia to envision an entire political movement directed at oneself. Burke did. He wrote to Fitzwilliam in November 1791:

I believe that having obtained one of their [the Jacobins'] objects, which, trivial as it is, they have had many years at heart, to drive me out of the publick service under obloquy, they may, in future, be a little more cool and guarded. [81]

Dogs did bark at Burke, and they were not always little. While much of his paranoia was a figment of his imagination, there was in fact enough real "persecution" to give it some basis in reality. His Irish origins were the source of countless attacks on him throughout his career. He was constantly slandered as a Catholic and caricatured in the press in Jesuit dress. His meteoric rise and opposition politics provoked the Court to serious efforts to undermine his success. In 1780 his house and life were threatened by anti-Catholic Gordon rioters; in 1793 he was burned in effigy by radicals in the town of Dronfield six miles south of Sheffield. [82] In only two instances, however, did Burke seek legal recourse against his persecutors. Both cases, as noted earlier, dealt with charges of homosexuality.

The notion of mad Burke has persisted. Lecky wrote a century later that Burke's "mind was profoundly and radically diseased." In his *History of Civilization in England* Buckle was even more certain. "Burke," he wrote, "during the last few years of his life, fell into a state of complete hallucination." It was the horrors of the French Revolution that broke him, according to Buckle. Because of it "the feelings of Burke finally mastered his reason; the balance tottered." [83] There is, however, no evidence that Burke's sanity succumbed to the Jacobins or to anything else, for that matter. Much of his withdrawal from public view in his last years is explained by his profound melancholy over the death of Richard, not by the fact, as some argued, that he was hiding actual madness. The evidence for the charges of insanity are apocryphal. There is, for example, the oft-told tale of Burke in his last years wandering aimlessly about the fields of his beloved Beaconsfield kissing his horses and cows. On the strength of such stories as these rumors spread of Burke's madness. The story, it turns out, is rooted in an actual incident, but one which says nothing to the question of his sanity. Walking in his field one day it seems that Burke came upon a horse that had been Richard's favorite. He threw his arms around the horse's neck and broke down in tears. [84] There is no doubt that throughout his life Burke was subject to periods of deep depression as well as to periods of manic explosion. There was also a clear streak of paranoia in him, and while paranoid and homosexual Burke might be grist for the Freudian mill, there is little evidence that he was actually mad. [85] It was, more likely than not, the fabrication of those enemies who, in Burke's words, were forever at work "finding some blot against me."

The dogs ultimately stopped barking, but not before persecuting Burke even for the minuscule pension given him in his old age. Neither the aristocracy nor the Jacobins would leave him be, so Burke literally took his paranoia to the grave. To this day no one knows the whereabouts of his true remains. His grave and the inscribed memorial slab in Beaconsfield Church are a ruse. He left instructions that his true burial place be kept secret, for he was convinced that when the Jacobins triumphed in England they would dig up his corpse and torment him even then.[86] He wrote:

I am not safe from them. They have tigers to fall upon animated strength. They have hyenas to prey upon carcasses. They pursue even such as me into the obscurest retreats. . . . Neither sex, nor age, nor the sanctuary of the tomb is sacred to them.[87]

CHAPTER 10

Epilogue:
Burke and His Age

B URKE'S life and thought bears lasting testimony to one of the great turning points in European civilization and to all the anguish, confusion, and even guilt found in that transition. Erikson's metaphor in his study of Luther seems appropriate. Here, too, in late eighteenth-century England a bridge was being forged between two great periods of western Christiandom. The aristocratic age was passing and the bourgeois epoch dawning. In such periods of fundamental change, according to Erikson, "men are swayed by alternating world moods." Burke was so swayed and, in turn, he became one of "the monopolists and manipulators of an era's opinions." Burke provided one of the best personifications of those alternating moods. That this happened may well be because, as Erickson claimed, crises in historical identity must be fixed on "the highly exploitative mood cycles inherent in man's psychological structure." [1] The identity crisis of Burke's early years was never completely resolved. His basic ambivalence persisted throughout his life, long after those six years in the 1750s, and matched most perfectly the historical identity crisis then being experienced by the advanced societies of England and France.

It is not exaggeration to suggest that Burke lived two quite different lives. To some he was the self-deprecating and dutiful servant of his betters, who could describe his service to Rockingham as a "situation of little rank and no consequence, suitable to the mediocrity of my talents and pretensions." This Burke denied any urges to better himself. "I have never been remarkable for a bold, active, and sanguine pursuit of advantages that are personal to myself," he told the electors of Bristol in 1780. Nor had he joined the party of the Savilles, the Wentworths, Manchesters, et al. to gratify "low, personal pride, or ambitious interest," he wrote in 1777. Another Burke proudly defended his ambition and his achievements, wrapping himself in the virtuous cloak of "new man" in 1770. It was this Burke who lashed out in Parliament at aristocrats who dismissed common freeholders as "base born" or "scum of the earth." This Burke could proudly proclaim that the "House of Commons was not a Court of Heraldry . . . birth and family had nothing to do with the question." The pride in his own achievements which he turned on Bedford in 1795 was evident years earlier when he told the Commons that though a common Irishman he had raised himself through his own merit "from an humble station, from obscurity, to a seat in the national great council." [2] It was a success that Will Burke noted had exceeded even the most sanguine hopes of their common ambitions.

Some of his contemporaries realized that there were two Burkes. The bluestocking Mrs. Thrale was perhaps the most astute observer of a public Burke and a quite different private Burke. What makes her observations all the more fascinating is that they describe the private Burke in the context of his household at Beaconsfield, so symbolic of Burke's retreat from public view. She, her husband, and Samuel Johnson had visited Burke's country house quite unexpectedly in 1774. Years later she described the scene as one of shocking paradox. This moral defender of Christian chivalry "was the first man I had ever seen drunk or heard talk obscenely," she wrote. The house was filled with great statues and fine paintings, yet there were dirt and cobwebs everywhere. A polite and liveried servant served tea "with a cut finger wrapped in rags." [3] Mrs. Thrale put into verse her conviction that Burke was not all he seemed; between the public figure and the private man stood the walls of Beaconsfield and the family Burke. On one side was the noble Cicero, on the other an avaricious boor wallowing in the muck of filthy friends.

> See Burke's bright intelligence beams from his face,
> To his language gives splendour, his action gives grace;
> Let us list to the learning that tongue can display,
> Let it steal all reflection, all reason away;
> Lest home to his house we the patriot pursue,
> Where scenes of another sort rise to our view;
> Where Av'rice usurps sage Economy's look,
> And Humour cracks jokes out of Ribaldry's book;
> Till no longer in silence confession can lurk,
> That from chaos and cobwebs could spring even Burke.
> Thus 'mong dirty companions conceal'd in the ground,
> And unnotic'd by all, the proud metal was found,
> Which, exalted by place, and by polish refined,
> Could comfort, corrupt, and confound all mankind. [4]

One need not be moved by such venomous spite to dwell on the contrast between the public and private Burke. His critics, to be sure, have spent much energy exposing his "turbulent schemes of ambition," but Burke himself was, as we have seen, well aware of this part of himself. Perhaps his most poignant moment of public introspection occurred in 1782 when he described for the House of Commons the mood of England in his age. He spoke of all Englishmen, but the one he knew best was himself. It was, he observed,

that particular period of men's lives when their ambitious views that had lain secretly in a corner of their hearts, almost undiscovered to themselves, were unlocked . . . when all their desire, their self-opinions, their vanity, their avarice and their lust of power . . . were set at large and began to show themselves.[5]

Burke's own life exemplified the restless ambition that in his age would totally transform English life. Adam Smith had linked this capitalist ambition to eros. His *Theory of Moral Sentiments* traces strident ambition, the restless urge to better oneself found in the middle classes, to the desire to be loved. It is not ease, he suggests, but vanity which preoccupies bourgeois man. The ambitious man seeks to be noticed, to be approved of, to be loved. In seeking the envy and admiration of others, he seeks to be adored. No one notices, no one cares for, no one loves the poor man, writes Smith. "He feels that it (his poverty) either places him out of the sight of mankind, or, that if they take any notice of him, they have, however, scarce any fellow-feeling with the misery and distress which he suffers." [6] The ambitious bourgeoisie covet fame and wealth, then, according to Smith, for the basic psychic solace it provides, the meaningfulness of self-identity it offers by the testimony of the attention and adoration of others.

Smith's insights into the bourgeois psyche compliment those offered later by Weber. The Protestant who has rejected the fatherhood of the papacy and of the priestdom in general wallows in anxiety over his worth. But business success, achievement, crowning ambition, are tokens of the ultimate father's—God's—love, of God's approval, of God's notice. But God may no longer be a loving God. He may be the stern and vengeful deity of Calvin. In this case, the love, the notice, the approval which He once provided must now come from the market, from the esteem of others who notice, value, and even love fame and wealth. Smith is thus also providing a valuable insight into the critical role of "marginal men" in ambitious enterprise and in capitalism in general. The outsider—the ascetic Protestant, the Quaker, the Jew, the Unitarian—through striving and achievement is noticed, accepted, and occasionally even perhaps loved.

Much of this applies to Burke. Lonely and smitten with tremendous feelings of paternal rejection, the young Burke sought love, notice, and approbation through ambition and success. Perhaps in this way he could become worthy as attested to by being noticed—i.e., famous. It could be argued that his marginality fed this ambition in his early years. Outsider, Irishman in the closed circles of English power, driven even perhaps by a sense of sexual marginality, Burke could well have found the approbation of fame symbolic of notice and acceptance in the nonmarginal world of conventionality, orthodoxy, and the establishment. Freed from the corporate fetters of the more traditional Ireland, where his notice, his place would have been self-evident, he would find his worth in the English market's assessment of his fame. Part of him screamed that this was as it should be—the bourgeois side that equated worth and identity with achievement and work.

If Burke's ambition and his desire to be noticed and loved was symptomatic of the new bourgeois age, so, too, was his ambivalence, and even more so. The transition from the aristocratic world to the bourgeois world was not easy, nor was it definitive. Men and women habituated to the dominant paradigms of aristocratic life and the prevailing values of aristocratic thought did not wake one day freed of this cognitive and normative universe to suddenly live good bourgeois lives along good bourgeois principles of thought and action. There was a long and confused period of transition when men and women were buffeted by the pulls and tugs of both the old and the new order. For sheer dramatic personification of this crisis in the western identity Burke dominates the period as a towering symbol of its "internal strife."

The aspect of this transition that Burke best embodies is the peculiar combination of love and hate that the bourgeoisie felt toward the aristocracy. The bourgeoisie despised the idleness and unproductivity of men of rank. They resented their unearned status and privileges; they were repulsed by their immorality and luxury. Yet the bourgeoisie also envied the wealth and power of their betters. As much as they resented their style of life they coveted it. Adam Smith, is here, too, the ablest chronicler of the bourgeois spirit. He has brilliantly captured this middle-class ambivalence, suggesting that while the self-made man hated his social betters and wished to turn them out he also loved them, indeed nearly worshipped them. Smith's description of ambivalent bourgeois man reads as if penned to describe Burke.

When we consider the condition of the great in those delusive colors in which the imagination is apt to paint it, it seems to be almost the abstract idea of a perfect and happy state. It is the very state which, in all our waking dreams and idle reveries, we had sketched out to ourselves as the final object of all our desires. We feel, therefore, a peculiar sympathy with the satisfaction of those who are in it. We favour all their inclinations and forward all their wishes. What a pity, we think, that anything should spoil and corrupt so agreeable a situation! We could even wish them immortal; and it seems hard to us that death should at last put an end to such perfect enjoyment.[7]

Smith's phrases evoke another relationship not unlike that of master class and subordinate class, the relationship of parent and child. The child, like Smith's middle class looking up at the aristocracy, sees adulthood as the perfect state at the end of his desires. Like the bourgeoisie's fantasies for the aristocracy, the child also wishes immortality for the parent, and cannot conceive of the death of the superior figure. What is particularly striking is how germane the analogy between class and family relations is when rebellion and revolution rip asunder the organic, harmonious, and natural order of supremacy and deference. Rebellious children are wracked with guilt at toppling the parent, which produces in turn a renewed love, worship, and even greater glorification of authority.

This relationship of hate and love, rebellion and guilt, was described by Adam Smith long before Freud's *Totem and Taboo*. The "doctrine(s) of reason and philosophy," Smith wrote, led a people to oppose, resist and punish kings and the aristocracy, "but the doctrine(s) of nature" teach men to tremble and bow down before the exalted station of the great. When a people contemplate or carry out violent acts against "those to whom they have been accustomed to look up to as their natural superiors," they soon cannot stand it, and "compassion soon takes the place of resentment." They forget past grievances and "then old principles of loyalty revive." They inevitably set up once again "the received authority of their old masters." An example of this cycle of hate and love cited by Smith was the murder of Charles I and the subsequent restoration of the Stuarts in the latter part of the seventeenth century.[8]

The bourgeoisie of the eighteenth century, rebellious children that they were, had, of course, been socialized by church, state, and culture in general, to respect and adore their betters, their superiors, their highnesses and their eminences. To contemplate toppling these betters provoked in some a deep sense of guilt that expressed itself in a restatement of love for the aristocracy that made more tolerable and legitimate the complimentary hatred. Any master-servant relationship could be expected to share these dynamics. The servant seeks to replace his master, indeed, hates his master, yet envies and often loves his master, all this the product of both irreducible socialization and newly acquired guilt. It would be a recurring historical problem for master-servant classes. Among the proletariat of a later age some would hate their masters, yet ape them and even love them. This would be a product of envy, socialization, and guilt.

If Smith was the theorist of this process then Burke was its most important embodiment. He was the prototypical rebellious son for his age. His life and personality mirrored the social and revolutionary problems of his age. His ambivalence, his hatred and love for the aristocracy, was the ambivalence of the revolutionary bourgeoisie. The psychic costs involved in embodying in one's own personality the ambivalence of an age's identity were tremendous. They produced all the pain, torment, self-hatred, depression, breakdowns and paranoia that was the private side of Burke's life. It was no easy chore to play out a public career while torn on basic social commitments. The rebellious son thus became neurotic and ill son, just as the revolutionary bourgeoisie destroying the secure world of ascribed status would produce a new world of neuroticism and mental disease. Once again it was Adam Smith who has best captured this tortured state of mind of the bourgeois man on the make. And, once again, the passage reads as if Smith were describing Burke.

The poor man's son, whom heaven in its anger has visited with ambition, when he begins to look around him admires the condition of the rich. He finds the cottage of his father too small for his accommodation, and fancies he should be lodged more at ease in a palace. . . . It appears in his fancy like the life of some superior rank of beings . . . With the most unrelenting industry he labours night and day to acquire talents superior to all his competitors. He endeavors next to bring these talents into public view, and with equal assiduity solicits every opportunity of employment. *For this purpose he makes his court to all mankind; he serves those whom he hates, and is obsequious to those whom he despises.* [9]

Burke's life was a set of variations on oedipal themes. He wrote often in his youth and in later years of replacing the great, a displacement of the fact that he had indeed replaced the one great, the father. But he was ambivalent on this score, for throughout his life he also worshipped and served the great, warding off their feared oedipal punishment. In his writings he vented this issue time and again with his invocation of the forbidden and repressed theme of parricide. His characterization of the bourgeoisie as ambitious and phallic and of the aristocracy as idle and feminine, and, in turn, his own vacillation between these two ideals echoes the oedipal dilemma. So, too, did the flavor and tone of his indictment of Hastings and the Jacobins. Decrying their aggressive masculinity represented the recurring need to deny his own masculine oedipal conquest.

The cornerstone of Burke's significance in western thought, his prophetic philosophy of conservatism, is closely bound up with his private self and personal needs. It is fitting that the oedipal theme should have played so significant a role, for as political theory his conservatism offers a profound legitimization of repression. Burke linked pessimism and repression, arguing that free, self-determining humanity is irrational and evil humanity. Within people, the conservative Burkean insists, are passions and inclinations which must be restrained, lest additional suffering, pain, and crime be unleashed on an already sinful world. Burke assigns part of this task of control, restraint, and repression to government, as have true conservatives ever since. This is clear in the important definition of government in his *Reflections*. Government, he writes there, provides that "power out of themselves" to which "the passions of individuals should be subjected." His terminology is a set of variations on the theme of repression. Government allows for "inclinations" to be "thwarted," "passions" to be "brought into subjection." Government has as "its office to bridle and subdue." [10] In his *Letter to a Member of the National Assembly* Burke wrote of government providing "moral chains upon

. . . appetites," and as "a controlling power upon will and appetite." This repression must be placed somewhere, he wrote, and "the less of it there is within, the more there must be without." [11] In these, his central statements of conservatism, the public Burke meets the private Burke. The public philosopher of Christian pessimism repudiating the optimism of liberal Enlightenment meets the private person for whom an entire life and identity has been constructed around thwarting and subduing two particular passions—avarice and sexuality.

Looming even larger in Burke's life and writings than this constant battle with avarice and sensuality and linked inextricably to it is the profound tension between a sense of self ascribed by birth, tradition, and custom and a sense of self as achieved by work and talent. This tension breathes through Burke's every action in public life, his every essay read to this day. But, ultimately this, his personal issue, was the principal public issue of his age. The ethos of ascription was rapidly being undermined by the ethos of achievement. This transformation was not without its guilt and pain. Some, like Burke, succumbed to this guilt and came down more often than not on the side of loving their betters. Others like Tom Paine and Mary Wollstonecraft repressed the guilt, swallowed the pain, and came down on the side of hate, proceeding forthwith to depose their betters. Hate won out and the age of chivalry would be buried along with the glory of Europe. Rail as he might against the new world of the bourgeoisie, a part of Burke was of that world. He, too, "was of the devil's party without knowing it."

NOTES

Introduction

1. Edmund Burke, *The Correspondence of Edmund Burke,* 9 vols. (Chicago and Cambridge: 1958–1971), vol. 6, pp. 238–39, Jane Burke to William Burke (21 March 1791); vol. 7, p. 421, Pope Pius VI to Burke (7 September 1793).

2. Ibid., vol. II, p. 377, Burke to the Duke of Richmond (post 15 November 1772).

3. Edmund Burke, "A Letter to a Noble Lord" in *The Works of the Right Honourable Edmund Burke* (London: 1877–1884), vol. V, pp. 124–134. Emphasis is Burke's. To avoid confusion, the citation policy of Burke's works should be made clear here. The Bohn Standard Library edition of Burke's *Works* (London, 1877–1884) is used throughout this book as the source for quotations from his *Works.* However, this six-volume collection omits a good many of Burke's India speeches. They are found, however, in the Little, Brown & Co. edition (Boston, 1869) and in the Nimmo edition (London, 1887). Where these are cited, information will be given on the specific edition in detail. Unless otherwise indicated, then, citations from Burke's published works noted merely as *Works* will refer to the Bohn edition (London, 1877–1884).

4. *Letters of William Wordsworth,* selected by P. Wayne (London: 1954), p. 149.

5. Beaumarchais, *The Marriage of Figaro,* Act V.

6. *Monthly Review,* vol. XIX (London: 1796), p. 317.

7. Burke, *The Correspondence,* vol. 1, p. 28, Burke to Shackleton (7 July 1744).

8. Ibid., vol. 4, p. 80 (25 May 1779).

9. Ibid., vol. 1, p. 89 (21 March 1746).

10. Ibid., vol. 3, p. 35 (25 September 1774).

11. G. M. Young, *Today and Yesterday: Collected Essays and Addresses* (London: 1948), pp. 88–89.

12. Burke, "Reflections on the Revolution in France" in *Works,* vol. 2, p. 333.

Chapter 1 *Mythic Burke*

1. *Aristocratic Government and Society in Eighteenth Century England,* ed. Daniel A. Baugh (New York: 1975), p. 3.

2. Everett E. Hagan, *On the Theory of Social Change* (Homewood, Illinois: 1962), pp. 261–309. See also Witt Bowden, *Industrial Society in England Towards the End of the Eighteenth Century* (New York: 1925); T. S. Ashton, *Iron and Steel in the Industrial Revolution (Manchester:*

1924); G. Unwin, *Samuel Oldknow and the Arkwrights* (Manchester: 1924); A. E. Musson and Eric Robinson, *Science and Technology in the Industrial Revolution* (Manchester: 1969); D. G. C. Allen, *William Shipley: Founder of the Royal Society of Arts* (London: 1968); Raymond V. Holt, *The Unitarian Contribution to Social Progress in England* (London: 1938); Betsy Rodgers, *Georgian Chronicle: Mrs. Barbauld and Her Family* (London: 1958); C. M. Elliot, "The Political Economy of English Dissent 1780–1840" in *The Industrial Revolution,* ed. R. M. Hartwell (Oxford: 1970); Neil McKendrick, "Josiah Wedgewood and Factory Discipline," *Historical Journal,* 4 (1961); R. B. Rose, "The Priestley Riots of 1791," *Past and Present,* 18 (November 1960); E. P. Thompson, "Time, Work—Discipline and Industrial Capitalism," *Past and Present,* 38 (December 1967), p. 97.

   3. Quoted in Robert E. Schofield, *The Lunar Society of Birmingham* (Oxford: 1963), p. 353.

   4. Joseph Priestley, *Proper Objects of Education in the Present State of the World* (London: 1791), pp. 22, 39.

   5. Joseph Priestley, *An Account of a Society for Encouraging the Industrious Poor to Which Are Prefixed Some Considerations on the State of the Poor in General for the Use of J. Wilkinson's Iron Works at Bradley* (Birmingham: 1789), pp. 5, 7.

   6. Joseph Priestley, *Letters on History and General Policy,* 4th ed. (London: 1826), lecture xxxviii, pp. 290–305. In addition, see his article in the American newspaper *Aurora* (27 February 1798) in which he insists that the "fundamental maxim of political arithmetic" is the "state's not interfering in the economy." See also Joseph Priestley, *Letters to the Right Honourable Edmund Burke* (Birmingham: 1791), p. 55.

   7. Joseph Priestley, "On the Repeal of the Test and Corporation Acts" in *Familiar Letters to the Inhabitants of the Town of Birmingham* (Birmingham: 1790–92), letter IV, pp. 19–20.

   8. See Anna L. Barbauld, *Address to Opposers of the Repeal of the Corporation* and *Test Acts* (London: 1790), pp. 17–18; John Aikin, *Letters from a Father to His Son on Various Topics Relative to Literature and the Conduct of Life* (Philadelphia: 1794), p. 205; Thomas Walker, *A Review of Some of the Political Events Which Have Occurred in Manchester During the Last Five Years* (London: 1794), pp. 46–47; Adam Smith, *The Theory of Moral Sentiments* (Edinburgh: 1813), vol. 1, pp. 188, 136.

   9. Joseph Priestley, *Memoirs of Dr. Joseph Priestley to the Year 1795* (London: 1806), p. 3.

   10. John Aikin, *Address to the Dissenters of England on Their Late Defeat* (London: 1790), p. 18.

   11. Anna Barbauld, *Address to Opposers of the Repeal of the Corporation and Test Acts* (London: 1790), p. 18.

   12. Mary Wollstonecraft, *Vindication of the Rights of Woman,* ed. Miriam Brody Kramnick, Pelican Classics Edition (New York: 1975), pp. 147–48, 171, 181.

   13. Richard Price, *Observations on the Importance of the American Revolution and the Means of Making It a Benefit to the World* (London: 1784), p. 69.

   14. Joseph Priestley, *Memoirs,* p. 82.

   15. Robert Hall, *Miscellania* (Cambridge: n.d.), p. 205.

   16. Joel Barlow, *Advice to the Privileged Orders in the Several States of Europe* (London: 1792), pp. 97–98.

   17. Thomas Cooper, *A Reply to Mr. Burke's Invective Against Mr. Cooper and Mr. Watt* (London: 1792), p. 16.

   18. Ann Finer and George Savage, eds., *Selected Letters of Josiah Wedgewood* (London: 1965), p. 44. See also Robert Schofield, *Lunar Society of Birmingham;* S. H. Jeyes, *The Russells of Birmingham in the French Revolution and America 1791–1814* (London: 1911); L. S. Marshall, *The Development of Public Opinion in Manchester 1780–1820* (Syracuse: 1946); Eric Robinson, "The Derby Philosophical Society," *Annals of Science,* 9 (1953); J. Taylor, "The Sheffield Constitutional Society," *Transactions of the Hunter Archaeological Society* 5, (1943); W. H. Chaloner, "Dr. Joseph Priestley, John Wilkinson and the French Revolution 1789–1802," *Transactions*

of the Royal Historical Society, series 5, vol. 8 (1958); Eric Robinson, "The English Philosophes and the French Revolution," *Annals of Science,* 9 (1953).

19. Burke, "Letters on a Regicide Peace" in *Works,* vol. 1, p. 395.
20. Tom Paine, *The Rights of Man,* ed. Henry Collins, Pelican Classics Edition (Baltimore: 1969), p. 72.
21. Tom Paine, *Common Sense,* ed. Isaac Kramnick, Pelican Classics Edition (London: 1976), p. 83.
22. Paine, *Rights of Man,* pp. 105, 128.
23. Ibid., p. 249.
24. Ibid., p. 168.
25. Ibid., p. 220. For an interesting discussion of Paine's laissez-faire attitudes, see Eric Foner, *Tom Paine and Revolutionary America* (New York: 1976).
26. Paine, "Dissertation on First Principles of Government" (Paris, 1795) in *The Writings of Tom Paine,* ed. M. D. Conway and C. Putnam (New York: 1906), vol. 3, p. 268.
27. Burke, "Speeches on Fox's Motion for Repeal of Certain Penal Statutes Respecting Religious Opinions," *Parliamentary History,* 29 (1791–1792), p. 1389.
28. Burke, "Several Scattered Hints Concerning Philosophy and Learning Collected Here From My Papers" in *A Notebook of Edmund Burke,* ed. H. V. F. Somerset (Cambridge: 1957), pp. 90, 91.
29. *The Letters of Horace Walpole,* ed. Paget Toynbee (Oxford: 1903–1925) vol. 5, p. 86; D. C. Bryant, *Edmund Burke and His Literary Friends* (St. Louis: 1939), p. 258.
30. Burke, "A Vindication of Natural Society" in *Works* (London: 1883), vol. 1, pp. 3–5.
31. For the background of this concept, see Arthur O. Lovejoy, *The Great Chain of Being* (Cambridge, Mass.: 1936); E. M. W. Tillyard, *The Elizabethan World Picture* (New York: 1956); Isaac Kramnick, *Bolingbroke and His Circle* (Cambridge, Mass.: 1968).
32. Burke, "Vindication," p. 4.
33. See Alfred Cobban, *Burke and the Revolt Against the Eighteenth Century* (London: 1929). See John Morley, *Burke* (London: 1879), p. 17, for a somewhat dramatic, but generally perceptive reading of Burke's "Vindication."
34. Burke, "Thoughts on the Cause of the Present Discontent" in *Works,* vol. 1, p. 375.
35. Ibid., pp. 337, 367.
36. *The Correspondence of Edmund Burke,* (Chicago and Cambridge, 1958–1971), vol. 2, p. 150. Burke to Richard Shackleton (5 June 1770), vol. 2, p. 157; Burke to Marquess of Rockingham (7, 8 June 1770); See also Macaulay's attack on Burke in her *Observations on a Pamphlet Entitled Thoughts on the Cause of the Present Discontents* (London: 1770).
37. Burke, *Thoughts,* p. 368.
38. Burke, "Speech on American Taxation" (1774) in *Works,* vol. 1, pp. 382–438 and "Speech on Moving His Resolutions for Conciliation with America" (1775) in *Works,* vol. 1, pp. 456–512. See also *Parliamentary History,* 17 (1771–4), p. 1183; *Parliamentary History,* 18 (1774–1777), p. 190; *Parliamentary History,* 22 (1781–2), p. 1134; *Parliamentary History,* 19 (1777–1778), p. 694; *Letter to the Sheriffs of Bristol* in *Works,* vol. 2, pp. 8–11; *Parliamentary History,* 20 (1778–1780), p. 1207; *Parliamentary History,* 18 (1774–1777), p. 854.
39. Burke, "Speech on American Taxation," in *Works,* vol. 1, p. 432; "Speech on Conciliation with America" in *Works,* vol. 1, p. 483; "Speech on American Taxation" in *Works,* vol. 1, p. 418.
40. Burke, "Speech on American Taxation" in *Works,* vol. 1, p. 432; "Speech on Conciliation" in *Works,* vol. 1, pp. 464, 500–01.
41. "A Letter to the Sheriffs of Bristol on the Affair of America" (1777) in *Works,* vol. 2, pp. 29–31.
42. Burke, "Speech on Conciliation" in *Works,* vol. 1, pp. 490–91.
43. See my *Bolingbroke and His Circle,* pp. 172 ff, for the development of this notion.

44. Burke, "Speech at Mr. Burke's Arrival at Bristol" (1774) in *Works,* vol. 1, p. 447; See also "Two Letters to Gentlemen in the City of Bristol" (1778) in *Works,* vol. 2, p. 49; and "Speech at the Guildhall in Bristol" (1780) in *Works,* vol. 2, pp. 130, 136–37, 167.

45. Burke, "Speech on a Motion Made in the House of Commons, 7 May 1782, for "A Committee to Inquire into the State of the Representation of the Commons in Parliament" in *Works,* vol. 6, pp. 144–147.

46. In rising to speak in 1783 in favor of Fox's bill to reform the East India Company, Burke told of his extensive research into Indian affairs which he dated from 1780. See "Speech on Mr. Fox's East India Bill" in *Works,* vol. 2, p. 173. It might be noted that nearly half of Burke's published works is material (speeches, reports, etc.) on India or Hastings.

47. *Parliamentary History,* 24 (1783–1785), pp. 1265, 1255, 1272.

48. *Parliamentary History,* 24 (1783–1785), p. 1259.

49. Burke, "Speeches in the Impeachment of Warren Hastings—First Day Saturday, February 16, 1788," in *Works of the Right Honorable Edmund Burke* (Boston: 1869), vol. 9, p. 383.

50. Burke, "Speeches on the Impeachment of Warren Hastings, Speech on the Sixth Article of Charge" (First Day, April 21, 1789) in *Works* (Boston: Little, Brown & Co., 1869), vol. 10, p. 217.

51. Burke, "Speech on Mr. Fox's East-India Bill" in *Works,* vol. 2, p. 222.

52. Ibid., vol. 2, p. 221.

53. Burke, "Letters on a Regicide Peace" (1776–77) in *Works,* vol. 5, p. 155. "Out of the Tomb of the Murdered Monarchy in France has arisen a vast, tremendous, unformed spectre."

54. Hugh Cecil, *Conservatism* (London: 1937).

55. Quoted in M. H. Abrams, *Natural Supernaturalism* (New York: 1971), p. 328.

56. *The Correspondence of Robert Southey with Caroline Bowles,* ed. Edward Dowdeen (Dublin: 1881), p. 52.

57. William Blake, "The French Revolution," in *The Poetry and Prose of William Blake,* ed. David Erdman (New York: 1970), p. 11–12.

58. Quoted in Abrams, *Natural Supernaturalism,* p. 331.

59. Richard Price, *Evidence for a Future Period of Improvement in the State of Mankind with the Means and Duty of Promoting It: An Address to Supporters of New Academical Institutions Among Protestant Dissenters* (London: 1787), pp. 5, 22, 25.

60. Ibid., p. 53.

61. Joseph Priestley, *Letters to the Right Honourable Edmund Burke* (Birmingham: 1791), letter 14, p. 25. In contrast to this mood of optimism found in late eighteenth-century radicalism there exists, it should be noted, a strain of pessimism associated with criticism of and lamentation over the national debt. See, for example, Richard Price's *An Appeal to the Public on the Subject of the National Debt* (London: 1771) and *London Society For Constitutional Information* (London: 1782). Paine wrote critically of the national debt on some occasions and on others he defended it.

62. Burke, "Reflections on the Revolution in France," in *Works,* vol. 2, pp. 327, 322, 320.

63. Ibid., p. 320.

64. Ibid., p. 310.

65. Ibid., p. 333. The italics are Burke's.

66. Ibid., p. 334.

67. Ibid., p. 335.

68. Ibid., p. 348.

69. Ibid.

70. Ibid., p. 349.

71. Ibid., p. 359.

72. Ibid., p. 351.
73. Ibid., pp. 350–51, 357.
74. Ibid., p. 368.
75. *Parliamentary History*, 30 (1792–1794), p. 646.
76. Burke, "Reflections," in *Works*, vol. 2, p. 368.
77. Ibid., p. 369. Burke saw first in his *Reflections* what countless conservatives would point to after him. The madness and confusion of the levelling which "crushed together all the orders," (p. 456) and which eliminated all "the diversity of interests," (p. 455) that existed in the complex (read pluralistic) corporate and hierarchical world would produce mass society. "They have attempted," he wrote, "to confound all sorts of citizens, as well as they could, into one homogeneous mass. . . . They reduce men to loose counters, merely for the sake of simple telling, and not to figures whose power is to arise from their place in the table." (p. 455). Tocqueville's fears and that of latter-day critics of mass society were already expressed by Burke in his lament that "all the indirect restraints which mitigate despotism are removed." (p. 456). The intellectual source for Burke and Tocqueville, and for these modern writers as well, is, of course, Montesquieu. See, in fact, vol. 2, p. 455.
78. Burke, "An Appeal from the New to the Old Whigs" in *Works*, vol. 3, p. 79.
79. Ibid., pp. 86–87.
80. Burke, "Speech on the Petition of the Unitarians" in *Works*, vol. 6, p. 121.
81. Ibid., p. 120.
82. Ibid., p. 114.
83. Burke, "Letters on a Regicide Peace" in *Works*, vol. 5, pp. 216, 219.
84. Ibid., p. 200.
85. Ibid., p. 209.
86. Ibid., pp. 210–11. Burke had for many years defended the family as a conservative institution. See, for example, his 1765 "Tracts on the Popery Laws" in *Works*, vol. 6, pp. 7–11. See also *Correspondence*, vol. 3, p. 457. To Edmund Sexton Perry, 16 June 1778. In a parliamentary debate of 1780 Burke quoted Thomas Aquinas against breaking the law of nature by which parents had full rights over their children. *Parliamentary History*, 21 (1780–1781), p. 720. In 1781 Burke spoke against Fox's proposal to lower the age of marriage allowed without parental consent, acknowledging that he defended "the avaricious principle of fathers" and sought to protect children from "their ignorance and inexperience." "Speech on a Bill for Repealing the Marriage Act" (1781) in *Works*, vol. 6, pp. 171–72.
87. Burke, "A Letter to William Elliot, Esq." in *Works*, vol. 5, pp. 69, 77–78.
88. Ibid., pp. 78–81.
89. Woodrow Wilson, *Mere Literature and Other Essays* (Boston: 1896), p. 160.
90. People have even learned to write good English by reading Burke, for some time in the late nineteenth century his *Speech on Conciliation with the Colonies* was made a part of the basic high school English curriculum. Generations of Americans deep into the twentieth century learned how to construct topic sentences and to write extended outlines of prose on the model of Edmund Burke's works. It was no accident, of course, that of the master's works this particular piece was chosen. Until the Cold War of the 1950s it was as an opponent of the American War that Burke was primarily known in America. And even this older identification still lingers. The week of 22 March 1975 found the *Christian Science Monitor* and the *Philadelphia Bulletin* using Burke in their editorials on the bicentenary of his great speech. On the day itself the CBS television network chose Ronald Reagan (a subtle and all too clever choice) to read Burke's words from the speech on their nightly "200 Years Ago Today."
91. For details on these circles, see Chauncey B. Tinker, *The Salon and English Letters* (New York: 1915) and Donald C. Bryant, *Edmund Burke and His Literary Friends* (St. Louis: 1939).
92. See William B. Todd, "The Bibliographical History of Burke's *Reflections on the Revolution in France*," in *The Library* (1951–52), series 5, vol. 6, pp. 100–08. See also James T.

Boulton, *The Language of Politics in the Age of Wilkes and Burke* (London: 1963), pp. 80–82.

93. Mrs. Henry Baring, ed., *The Diary of the Right Honourable William Windham 1784–1810* (London: 1866), pp. 212–213.

94. Quoted in Sir Philip Magnus, *Edmund Burke* (London: 1939), p. 195.

95. Quoted in Boulton, *Language of Politics,* p. 80.

96. *The Times* (30 November 1790).

97. R. E. Prothero, ed., *The Private Letters of Edward Gibbon* (London: 1897), vol. 2, pp. 237, 251.

98. Samuel Taylor Coleridge, *Religious Musings* (1794), *Table Talk* (London: 1835), vol. 5, p. 18; vol. 2, p. 147; see also T. W. Copeland's *Our Eminent Friend Edmund Burke* (New Haven: 1949), p. 4.

99. William Wordsworth, *The Prelude.* Some of the radicals of the 1790s would only years later pay their debt to Burke, and not always by acknowledging it. In the 1820s William Godwin published his *History of the Commonwealth of England* (London: 1824–1828). It is a Godwin much more conservative than in his *Inquiry Concerning Political Justice* (1793) that one meets here. He does not mention Burke but some of Godwin's passages could only have been inspired by Burke. See vol. 3, pp. 16–17, 117, 515; vol. 4, pp. 579–580.

100. Robert Bisset, *The Life of Edmund Burke* (London: 1898), vol. 1, p. 8.

101. See William Hazlitt, *The Spirit of the Age,* Everyman ed., (London: 1964), p. 185; DeQuincey, "Essay on Rhetoric," *Blackwood's Magazine* (December 1828); Lord Macaulay, "On Southey's Colloquies on Society," *The Edinburgh Review* (January 1830) and "Essay on Warren Hastings" in *Critical Historical and Miscellaneous Essays* (New York: 1871), vol. 5, p. 106; Matthew Arnold, "The Function of Criticism," *The National Review* (November 1864); see also T. W. Copeland, "The Reputation of Edmund Burke," *Journal of British Studies,* no. 2 (1962), p. 82; John J. Fitzgerald, "Burke's Reputation in the Nineteenth Century," *The Burke Newsletter,* 5 (1964), pp. 331–335.

102. Thomas MacKnight, *History of the Life and Times of Edmund Burke* (London: 1858), p. xii; James Prior, *Memoirs of the Life and Character of the Right Honourable Edmund Burke* (London: 1824), vol. 1, pp. 364, 564.

103. George Croly, *A Memoir of the Political Life of the Right Honourable Edmund Burke: With Extracts From His Writings* (London: 1840), vol. 1, pp. 145–146; vol. 1, p. viii; vol. 1, p. 24; vol. 1, p. 3.

104. John Morley, *A Historical Study* (London: 1867), p. 123.

105. John Morley, *Burke* (London: 1888), p. 210.

106. Henry T. Buckle, *The History of Civilization in England,* ed. John Robertson, (New York: 1904), pp. 259–260, 263; Sir Leslie Stephen, *English Thought in the Eighteenth Century,* 1st ed., 1876, (New York: 1949), vol. 2, p. 219; William Lecky, *A History of England in the Eighteenth Century* (New York: 1891), vol. 5, p. 476.

107. Lecky, *History of England,* vol. 3, p. 197.

108. Cited in Copeland, "Reputation," p. 83. See also Morley, *Burke,* pp. 81–82.

109. Woodrow Wilson, *Mere Literature,* p. 107.

110. Ibid., pp. 128, 141, 158.

111. Ibid., p. 155.

112. Arthur Baumann, *Burke the Founder of Conservatism* (London: 1929), pp. 37, 46; Robert Murray, *Edmund Burke: A Biography* (London: 1931), p. 407.

113. Alfred Cobban, *Edmund Burke and the Revolt Against the Eighteenth Century* (New York: 1929), p. 12.

114. Sir Lewis Namier, "King George III; A Study of Personality" in *Crossroads of Power* (New York: 1962), p. 140. The major works of Namier were *The Structure of Politics at the Accession of George III* (London: 1929) and *England in the Age of the American Revolution* (London: 1930).

115. Namier, "Monarchy and the Party System" in *Personalities and Powers* (London: 1955), p. 143.

116. Namier, "The Character of Burke," *The Spectator* (19 December 1958). See also Lucy Sutherland, "The City of London in Eighteenth Century Politics" in *Essays Presented to Sir Lewis Namier* (London: 1956); John Brook, "Party in the Eighteenth Century" in *Silver Renaissance: Essays in Eighteenth Century English History* (London: 1961); Robert Walcott, "Sir Lewis Considered—Considered," *Journal of British Studies,* 3 (May 1964).

117. Namier, "King George III" p. 140.

118. Jeffrey Hart, "Burke and Radical Freedom," *The Review of Politics,* 29 (April 1967), p. 221. See also Donald C. Bryant, "Edmund Burke: A Generation of Scholarship and Discovery," *Journal of British Studies,* 2, no. 1, NN (1962), pp. 91–115.

119. Russel Kirk, "Edmund Burke and Natural Rights," *The Review of Politics,* 13, no. 4 (October 1951); "Burke and the Philosophy of Prescription," *Journal of the History of Ideas,* 14, no. 3 (June 1953); *The Conservative Mind from Burke to Santayana* (New York: 1953); *Edmund Burke: A Genius Reconsidered* (New Rochelle, N.Y.: 1967). Ross J. S. Hoffman and Paul Levack, eds., *Burke's Politics* (New York: 1959). Ross J. S. Hoffman, "Burke as a Practical Politician," in Peter J. Stanlis, ed., *The Relevance of Edmund Burke* (New York: 1964). Francis Canavan, S.J., *The Political Reason of Edmund Burke* (Durham, N.C.: 1960); "Edmund Burke," in *History of Political Philosophy,* eds., L. Straus and J. Cropsey (Chicago: 1963); "Burke as a Reformer," in Stanlis, ed., *The Relevance of Edmund Burke.* Louis I. Bredvold, *The Brave New World of the Enlightenment* (Ann Arbor: 1961); ed. with Ralph G. Ross, *The Philosophy of Edmund Burke* (Ann Arbor: 1960); "Introduction" in Stanlis, ed. *The Relevance of Edmund Burke.* Peter J. Stanlis has for many years been the editor and guiding hand behind the *Burke Newsletter,* now *Studies in Burke and His Times.* He is author of *Edmund Burke and the Natural Law* (Ann Arbor: 1958); "Edmund Burke in the Twentieth Century" in Stanlis, ed., *The Relevance of Edmund Burke;* editor of *Edmund Burke: Selected Writings and Speeches* (New York: 1963); author of "Edmund Burke and the Scientific Rationalism of the Enlightenment" in Stanlis, ed. *Edmund Burke: The Enlightenment and the Modern World* (Detroit: 1967). C. P. Ives was for many years coeditor of *The Burke Newsletter.* He is the author of "Edmund Burke and the Legal Order" in Stanlis, ed. *The Relevance of Edmund Burke.*

120. Hoffmann and Levack, eds., *Burke's Politics,* pp. xiii, xii.

121. Kirk, *Edmund Burke,* p. 16.

122. Ibid., pp. 21, 209, 211.

123. Kirk, *The Conservative Mind,* p. 61.

124. Stanlis, "Edmund Burke in the Twentieth Century" in *The Relevance of Edmund Burke,* ed. Stanlis, p. 53.

125. Stanlis, *Edmund Burke and the Natural Law,* pp. 247–49.

126. Ibid., p. 249. See also Canavan, *The Political Reason of Edmund Burke,* and "Edmund Burke"; Leo Straus, *Natural Right and History* (Chicago: 1953).

127. Stanlis, *Edmund Burke and the Natural Law,* p. 48.

128. This point is intelligently argued in A. Cobban's "Review of F. P. Canavan's *Political Reason," History,* 45 (1960).

129. Peter Stanlis teaches at Rockford and for many years *Studies in Burke and His Times* was published there. It was then published in Alfred, New York and now in Lubbock, Texas by Texas Tech. University. The *Burke Newsletter* began in Detroit (at the Jesuit University) and much of Russel Kirk's material comes out of Michigan or New Rochelle, New York.

130. Nathan Glazer, "On Being Deradicalized," *Commentary,* 50, no. 4, (October 1970), p. 75.

131. Glazer's "Confessions" in *Commentary* is a moving example of the Burkean realism in the new conservatism.

132. Irving Kristol, *On the Democratic Idea in America* (New York: 1972), pp. ix, 69, 149, 144.

133. Ibid., pp. 62–63.

134. See E. C. Banfield, *The Unheavenly City* (Boston: 1970).

135. See, for example, James Q. Wilson, *Thinking About Crime* (New York: 1975) as well as his numerous articles in *The New York Times Magazine* and *Commentary*.

136. Allen Bloom, "The Democratization of the University" in *How Democratic Is America,* R. Goldwin, ed. (Chicago: 1969), pp. 115, 121.

137. See Jeffrey Hart, "Burke and Radical Freedom," *Review of Politics,* 29 (April 1967), pp. 224–229, 236–238.

138. Burke, "Thoughts on the Cause of the Present Discontents," (1770) in *Works,* vol. 1, p. 337.

139. Andrew Hacker, "On Original Sin and Conservatives," *New York Times Magazine* (25 February 1973), p. 13; Alexander Bickel, "Edmund Burke: A Retrospective," *The New Republic* (17 March 1973), pp. 30–35.

140. Edward Banfield, "In Defense of the American Party System" in *Political Parties U.S.A.,* Robert Goldwin, ed. (Chicago: 1964), pp. 37–38.

Chapter 2 *Tory Prophet*

1. Burke, *The Correspondence,* vol. 1, p. 62. Burke to Richard Shackleton (26 April 1746).

2. Ibid., p. 273. Burke to Richard Shackleton (28 October 1766).

3. There is some controversy over whether Burke's father had in fact always been a Protestant or had only conformed in 1722 to the established church in order to practice law. It should be noted that if he did conform that this is not evidence in itself that he was previously a Catholic, since dissenting Protestants would have had to, also. For details, see *The Correspondence* vol. 1, p. 274, note, and also Conor Cruise O'Brien's introduction to *Reflections on the Revolution in France,* pp. 29, 81. Professor Copeland has written to O'Brien that Richard Burke was a common name and that there is no certainty that the Burke on the conforming rolls was Edmund's father. Basil O'Connell, a direct descendent of Burke, has written in *The Burke Newsletter,* 8, no. 3 (Spring 1967), pp. 14–15, that "Richard Burke had conformed to the established church on 13 March 1722." There seems in turn no doubt that Mary Nagle continued as a practicing Catholic. Mr. O'Connell speculates that Edmund's subsequent marriage to the Catholic Jane Nugent (1757) infuriated his father and was seen as letting the family down.

4. James Prior, *Memoir of the Life and Chracter of the Right Honourable Edmund Burke* (London: 1839), p. 4.

5. Burke, *The Correspondence* vol. 1, p. 125.

6. Prior, *Memoir,* p. 9.

7. Burke, *The Correspondence,* vol. 1, p. 66, note 2.

8. Ibid., p. 71. Burke to Richard Shackleton (19 August 1746).

9. Ibid. p. 74. Burke to Richard Shackleton (5 December 1746).

10. Ibid., p. 121.

11. Ibid., pp. 119–20. Burke to Richard Shackleton (11 March 1755).

12. Ibid., p. 67. Burke to Richard Shackleton (12 July 1746).

13. See Philip Magnus, *Edmund Burke: A Life* (London: 1939), p. 11; Dixon Wecter, "The Missing Years in Edmund Burke's Biography," *P.M.L.A.,* (December 1938), p. 1123.

14. Arthur P. I. Samuels, *The Early Life, Correspondence, and Writings of the Rt. Hon. Edmund Burke* (Cambridge: 1923), p. 8.

15. Cited in Prior, *Life of Burke* (London: 1854), p. 97.

16. Burke, *The Correspondence,* vol. 1, p. 67. Burke to Richard Shackleton (12 July 1746).

17. Ibid., p. 274. Burke to Richard Shackleton (28 October 1766).

18. Samuels, *The Early Life,* pp. 405–07.

19. Burke, *The Correspondence,* vol. 1, p. 136. Burke to Agmondesham Vesey (10 September 1760).

20. Ibid., VII, 592.

21. Prior, *Life of Burke,* p. 4.

22. Burke, *The Correspondence,* vol. 1, p. xvi.

23. Ibid., p. 18. Burke to Richard Shackleton (14 June 1744).

24. Ibid., p. 24 (5 July 1744).

25. Ibid., p. 32 (15 October 1744).

26. Ibid., p. 2 (14 April 1744); p. 65 (1 June 1746); p. 77 (24 January 1747).

27. Ibid., pp. 19–20 (21 June 1744).

28. Ibid., p. 21 (26 June 1744).

29. Ibid., p. 86 (5 March 1746).

30. Ibid., p. 87 (12 March 1746).

31. Ibid., p. 39 (25 January 1745).

32. Ibid., p. 86 (5 March 1746).

33. The uncertainty of success and the unpredictability of fortune are persistent themes in the bourgeois literature of the eighteeneth century. Nowhere is this seen more dramatically than in the rapidly burgeoning literature for children where long-lost poor sons constantly turn up rich merchants and in turn children of successful farmers become paupers. See, for example, *Goody Two-Shoes* (London: 1764) and *Sandford and Merton* (London: 1783). Rousseau sensed how critical this uncertainty was to bourgeois man in his *Emile.*

> You reckon on the present order of society, without considering that this order is itself subject to inscrutable changes, and that you can neither foresee nor provide against the revolution which may affect your children. The great become small, the rich poor, the king a commoner. Does fate strike so seldom that you can count on immunity from her blows? *Emile,* Everyman ed. (London: 1961), p. 157.

34. Burke, *The Correspondence,* vol. 1, p. 59. Burke to Richard Shackleton (28 December 1745).

35. Ibid., p. 62 (15 February 1746).

36. Ibid., p. 111. (31 August 1751).

37. Ibid., vol. 2, p. 26. Burke to Charles O'Hara (31 May 1769).

38. Ibid., vol. 1, p. 111. Burke to Richard Shackleton (31 August 1751).

39. Ibid., p. 79.

40. Ibid., p. 102.

41. Ibid.

42. *The Reformer,* number 1 (28 January 1748). Reproduced in Samuels, *The Early Life,* pp. 297–98.

43. Ibid., no. 7 (10 March 1748), pp. 316–317.

44. Ibid.

45. Ibid. Italics are Burke's.

46. Ibid.

47. One thinks immediately of Burke's later *Vindication of Natural Society* (1756), a radical critique of government and political society, which Burke described as a satire of Bolingbroke. See chapter four, for discussion of this.

48. On this last point see O'Brien's introduction to the Pelican classic edition of Burke's *Reflections,* for a discussion of Burke's reverential attitudes to the papacy during the French Revolution.

49. Burke, "Speech on A Motion Made in the House of Commons, the 7th of May 1782, for a committee to inquire into the state of representation of the Commons in Parliament" in *Works,* vol. 6, p. 153.

50. Burke, "Letters on a Regicide Peace" in *Works,* vol. 5, pp. 148, 211.

51. Burke, "Reflections on the Revolution in France" in *Works,* vol. 2, p. 368. Burke's language implies a classical allusion to Medea, but this in no way lessens the dramatic linking of patricide and rebellion.

52. Boswell recorded this passage from a Burke conversation. *Boswell's Life of Johnson,* ed. G. B. Hill, rev. L. F. Powell (Oxford: 1934–50), vol. 3, p. 390.

53. Burke, *The Correspondence,* vol. 1, pp. 27–28. Burke to Richard Shackleton (7 July 1744).

54. Ibid., p. 31 (14 July 1744).

55. Ibid., p. 57 (12 November 1745).

56. We know of this from *Memoirs of Richard and Mary Shackleton,* ed. M. Leadbeater (Dublin: 1849).

57. Burke, *The Correspondence,* vol. 1, p. 56. Burke to Richard Shackleton (2 November 1745).

58. Ibid., p. 58 (7 November 1745).

59. Ibid., p. 60 (16 January 1746).

60. Ibid., p. 63 (15 May 1746).

61. Ibid., p. 64 (24 May 1746).

62. Ibid., p. 82 (21 February 1747).

63. Ibid., p. 85 (5 March 1747).

64. Ibid., p. 87 (12 March 1747).

65. Ibid., p. 97 (17 October 1747).

66. Copeland, *Our Eminent Friend Edmund Burke* (New Haven: 1949), p. 36.

Chapter 3 *Burke's "Missing Years"*

1. Morley, *Edmund Burke* (London: 1867), p. 8; Burke, *The Correspondence* vol. 1, p. xvii.

2. Magnus, *Edmund Burke,* p. 10.

3. E. Erikson, *Young Man Luther* (New York: 1962), pp. 14, 262, 44–45.

4. Burke, *The Correspondence* vol. 1, p. 111. Burke to Richard Shackleton (31 August 1751).

5. *A Notebook of Edmund Burke,* ed. H. V. F. Somerset (Cambridge: 1957). Philip Magnus, perhaps Burke's most definitive biographer, had seen the notebook in the Wentworth manuscript collection, but in his magisterial biography of 1939 he merely mentioned it in passing. Dixon Wecter's articles on Burke, "The Missing Years in Edmund Burke's Biography," *P.M.L.A.* (December 1938) and "Edmund Burke and His Kinsmen," *The University of Colorado Studies* (Boulder, 1939), also discuss the notebook material, then in manuscript. He quoted from the manuscript, often in detail, but his interest was bibliographical and not biographical or interpretive. The most recent biographer of Burke, C. P. Cone in his *Burke and the Nature of Politics* (Kentucky: 1957) had also seen the notebook material, but he, too, passed over it quickly with no effort at analyzing the material found there.

6. Burke, *The Correspondence* vol. 1, p. xvii.

7. There is some evidence that "cousin" in the eighteenth century was conventionally used to characterize close male friendships. See, for example, the letter from Josiah Wedgewood to his partner Bentley in 1772 where he writes of a mutual acquaintance falling in with "half a dozen young bloods whom he calls cousins." *Selected Letters of Josiah Wedgewood,* ed. by Finer and Savage (London: 1965), p. 133.

8. Burke, *The Correspondence* vol. 1, p. 113. Burke to Richard Shackleton (28 September 1752).

9. Ibid., vol. 3, p. 348. Burke to Philip Francis (9 June 1777).

10. Ibid., vol. 4, p. 431. Burke to William Burke (27 March 1782).

11. Ibid., p. 273. Burke to The Duke of Portland (3 September 1780); vol. 5, p. 214. Burke to George Leonard Staunton (27 July 1785).

12. Burke, *A Notebook,* p. 27.

13. Prior, *Life of Burke,* p. 491.

14. Burke, *The Correspondence,* vol. 4, p. 287. William Burke to The Duke of Portland (23 September 1780).

15. Ibid., p. 290.

16. Ibid., vol. 2, p. 274. Burke to William Markham (post 9 November 1771).

17. Quoted in Wecter, "Edmund Burke and His Kinsmen," p. 48.

18. This phrase used by Laetitia Hawkins is quoted in Donald C. Bryant, *Edmund Burke and His Literary Friends* (St. Louis: 1939), p. 197.

19. Wecter, "Edmund Burke and His Kinsmen," p. 11.

20. Ibid., p. 88.

21. Magnus, *Edmund Burke,* p. 9; Wecter, "Edmund Burke and His Kinsmen," p. 95; Copeland, *Our Eminent Friend,* p. 47.

22. The notebook was published in 1957 by Cambridge University Press with the title *A Notebook of Edmund Burke,* subtitled, *Poems, Characters, Essays and Other sketches in the Hands of Edmund and William Burke Now Printed for the First Time in Their Entirety.*

23. Burke, *The Correspondence* vol. 1, p. 111. Burke to Richard Shackleton (31 August 1751).

24. Ibid., pp. 103–107 and *A Notebook of Edmund Burke,* pp. 21–27.

25. Italics are Burke's.

26. "An Epistle to Dr. Nugent by E. B." in Burke, *The Correspondence* vol. 1, pp. 115–118 and *A Notebook of Edmund Burke,* pp. 35–39.

27. Burke, *The Correspondence* vol. 2, p. 130. Burke to Richard Shackleton (19 April 1770).

28. Ibid., vol. 1, p. 273. Burke to Richard Shackleton (28 October 1766).

29. Ibid., vol. 4, p. 80. Burke to Richard Shackleton (25 May 1779).

30. *A Notebook of Edmund Burke,* pp. 53–54.

31. Fanny Burney, *The Journal and Letters,* ed. Joyce Hemlow (Oxford: 1972), vol. 1, p. 194.

32. Ibid., pp. 57–59.

33. Ibid., pp. 49–52.

34. Ibid., pp. 60–62.

35. *Parliamentary History,* 22 (1781–1782), p. 1228.

36. Gordon Rattray Taylor, *Angel Makers: A Study in the Psychological Origins of Historical Change 1750–1850* (New York: 1974), pp. 98–99; see also his *Sex in History* (New York: 1970).

37. Claire Tomalin, *Life and Death of Mary Wollstonecraft* (London: 1974), p. 72.

38. *Parliamentary History,* 21 (1780–1781), pp. 389–90.

39. *Morning Post,* 13 April 1780. Italics are in original.

40. Details on this are in Burke, *The Correspondence* vol. 4, p. 351.

41. See *The Annual Register* (1784), p. 197. In 1792 Thomas Cooper, it might be noted, wrote of Burke's "feminine lamentation" in his essay *A Reply to Mr. Burke's Invective Against Mr. Cooper and Mr. Watt* (London: 1792). Taylor in his *Angel Makers* observes that the term Corinthian, a particular favorite of Burke's, (see for example, *"Reflections,"* in *Works,* vol. 3, p. 409) had become in the late eighteenth century a code word for effeminacy, p. 272.

42. Woodrow Wilson, *Mere Literature,* p. 109.

43. Burke, *The Correspondence,* vol. 1, p. 103.

44. Magnus, *Edmund Burke,* p. 10.

45. Sigmund Freud, "Some Psychological Consequences of the Anatomical Distinction Between the Sexes" (1925) in Phillip Rieff, ed., *Freud—Sexuality and the Psychology of Love* (New York: 1974), p. 185; see also Freud, "Psycho-Analytic Notes on an Autobiographical Account of a Case of Paranoia (Dementia Paranoides)" (1911) in Freud, *Standard Edition*, vol. 12 (1958), (also known as the 'Schreber Case'); "Analysis of a Phobia in a Five-Year Old Boy," (1909), *Standard Edition*, vol. 10 (1955) (also known as "Little Hans"); "The Passing of the Oedipus-Complex" (1924) in *Freud—Sexuality and the Psychology of Love*.

46. See Freud, "Notes Upon a Case of Obsessional Neurosis" (1909) *Standard Edition*, vol. 10 (1955), (also known as 'The Case of the Rat Man').

47. In an aside to Boswell at tea one day Burke was somewhat ambiguous on the roles of activity or passivity in a marriage. Similarly there is ambiguity on the importance of sexuality itself. "He declared it as his opinion that keeping separate beds was a certain sign of corruption. A woman in that case never went to bed to her husband but with a gross purpose; and if she slept with him constantly, that might happen or not, as inclination prompted." Quoted in Bryant, *Edmund Burke and His Literary Friends*, p. 123.

Chapter 4 *The New Burke*

1. Prior, *Life of Burke*, pp. 33–35.

2. Kirk, *Edmund Burke, A Genius Reconsidered*, pp. 30–31; Peter Stanlis, *Edmund Burke and the Natural Law*, p. 125; *Edmund Burke Selected Writings and Speeches*, ed. Stanlis, p. 40; Stanlis, "Edmund Burke and the Scientific Rationalism of the Enlightenment," pp. 105–110; Copeland, *Our Eminent Friend*, p. 133.

3. Godwin, *Political Justice*, p. 88; Elie Halevy, *The Growth of Philosophical Radicalism* (New York: 1928), pp. 215–216; and J. B. Bury, *The Idea of Progress* (New York: 1932), pp. 181–182. Halevy and Bury offer anarchist readings of Burke's *Vindication*. The former suggests that it was, in fact, the source of inspiration for Godwin.

4. See Murray N. Rothbard, "A Note on Burke's Vindication of Natural Society," *Journal of the History of Ideas*, 19 (1958), pp. 114–118; John C. Weston, Jr., "The Ironic Purpose of Burke's *Vindication* Vindicated," *Journal of the History of Ideas*, 19 (1958), pp. 435–41.

5. Burke, "Vindication," in *Works*, vol. 1, pp. 7, 24, 26, 41, 42. The italic is mine.

6. Ibid., pp. 26, 41, 44, 41–42, 29.

7. For these similar passages in *The Reformer*, see above, pp. 60–62.

8. Burke, "Vindication," in *Works*, vol. 1, p. 28.

9. Ibid., pp. 38–39, 41, 46.

10. See "A Body of Anonymous Writing" in Copeland, *Our Eminent Friend*, pp. 130–132.

11. "An Abridgement of English History" in *Works*, vol. 6, p. 414.

12. *Parliamentary History*, 16 (1765–1771), pp. 1267–1268.

13. Burke, *Works*, vol. 1, p. 407.

14. *Parliamentary History*, 18 (1774–1777), p. 1361.

15. *Parliamentary History*, 28 (1789–1791), p. 146. In addition, see the almost Gilbertian zest with which Burke lampooned lawyers in 1791 during the Hastings trial, *Parliamentary History*, 28 (1789–1791), pp. 1135–1169. See also his scorn for the Jacobin advocates and attorneys who governed France in his "Reflections" in *Works*, vol. 3, p. 315.

16. Burke, "An Abridgement" in *Works*, vol. 6, p. 414.

17. "Tracts on the Popery Laws" in *Works*, vol. 6, pp. 19, 21.

18. Ibid., p. 29.

19. Ibid., pp. 22, 26.

20. Burke, "Vindication," in *Works*, vol. 1, p. 2.

21. For these comments, see J. T. Boulton's introduction to his edition of Edmund Burke's *A Philosophical Inquiry into the Origin of Our Ideas on the Sublime and Beautiful* (London: 1958), p. ix.

22. Burke, "On the Sublime and Beautiful," in *Works*, vol. 1, p. 74.

23. Ibid., pp. 74–77.

24. Ibid., pp. 100, 108.

25. Ibid., pp. 141–42.

26. Ibid., pp. 88, 94.

27. Ibid., p. 95.

28. Ibid., pp. 96–97.

29. Ibid., p. 100.

30. Ibid., p. 132.

31. Ibid., pp. 133–140, 160.

32. Ibid., p. 134.

33. Ibid., pp. 82–83. For themes very similar to this discussion see Simon de Beauvoir *The Second Sex* (New York: 1974), pp. 72, 74.

34. Ibid., p. 84.

35. Ibid., pp. 130–31.

36. Ibid., p. 168.

37. See Neal Wood, "The Aesthetic Dimension of Burke's Political Thought," *Journal of British Studies*, 4, no. 1 (November 1964) for an interesting discussion of Burke's "On the Sublime and Beautiful." I came upon it after I had written most of this section, and was struck by how compatible his excellent piece is with my reading of the essay.

38. Burke, "On the Sublime and Beautiful," p. 101.

39. Burke, *The Correspondence*, vol. 1, p. 39. Burke to Richard Shackleton (25 January 1745). One might note that according to Prior (*Life of Burke*) p. 36, Burke told contemporaries that he had begun "On the Sublime and Beautiful" in Dublin in the late 1740s and worked on it after he had come to England.

40. "On the Sublime and Beautiful," p. 167.

41. Burke, *The Correspondence*, vol. 1, p. 131. Burke to Mrs. Montagu (24 September 1759).

42. Quoted in ibid., vol. 1, p. xix.

43. Quoted in Samuels, *The Early Life*, p. 17.

44. Burke, *The Correspondence*, vol. 1, pp. 24, 34, 51. Burke to Richard Shackleton (29 June, 15 October, 1744, and 4 July 1745).

45. Quoted in Samuels, *The Early Life*, p. 178.

46. Burke, *The Correspondence*, vol. 1, pp. 164–65. Burke to W. G. Hamilton (March 1763).

47. Ibid., p. 180. Burke to W. G. Hamilton (ante 12 February 1765).

48. Ibid., p. 195. Burke to John Monck Mason (post 29 May 1765).

49. Ibid., p. 199. Burke to John Healy Hutchinson (May 1765). Italics are Burke's.

50. Ibid.

51. Coleridge, *The Friend* in K. Coburn ed. *The Inquiring Spirit* (London: 1951), p. 268.

52. For what it is worth Hamilton, like Will Burke, never married. Bertram D. Sarason, "A Sketch of Burke by Single Speech Hamilton" in *The Burke Newsletter*, 5, nos. 3 and 4 (Spring, Summer 1964), pp. 327–330. According to the *Dictionary of National Biography* Fanny Burney wrote of him: "He is extremely tall and handsome, and he has an air of haughty and fashionable superiority." Hamilton's notes are in Burke, *The Correspondence*, vol. 1, pp. 189–191.

53. Cited in Burke, *The Correspondence*, vol. 1, p. 237.

54. Ibid., pp. 241, 286 (4 March 1766 and 23 December 1766).

55. Ibid., p. 269. William Burke to Charles O'Hara (4 October 1766).

56. Ibid., p. 272. Burke to Charles O'Hara (21 October 1766).
57. Ibid., p. 245. William Burke to James Barry (23 March 1766).
58. Ibid., p. 351. Burke to Shackleton (1 May 1768).
59. Ibid., p. 238. Richard Burke Sr. to James Barry (11 February 1766).
60. See Wecter, "Edmund Burke and His Kinsmen," *passim* and Burke, *The Correspondence,* vol. 1, p. 351 and vol. 2, pp. 548–51.
61. Burke, *The Correspondence,* vol. 1, p. 222. Burke to George Macartney (post 23 December 1765). The italics are Burke's.
62. Ibid., p. 239. Burke to Charles O'Hara (1, 4 March 1766).
63. Ibid., p. 350. Burke to Shackleton (1 May 1768).
64. Ibid., p. 340. Burke to Charles O'Hara (11 December 1767).

Chapter 5 *Present Discontents*

1. See Burke, *The Correspondence,* vol. 2, pp. xii, xv; vol. 2, p. 211. Burke to Garrett Nagle (6 May 1771); vol. 2, p. 321. Burke to the Duke of Richmond (4 August 1772).
2. See ibid., vol. 2, p. 26–29, 31, 111, 140.
3. Ibid., p. 29. Burke to Charles O'Hara (1 June 1769).
4. Ibid., p. 409. Burke to the Marquess of Rockingham (10 January 1773).
5. Ibid.
6. Cited ibid., p. 80.
7. Ibid., pp. 127–28. William Burke to William Dennis (6 April 1770). The italicized Latin phrase reads "You hate the industry of self-made men." (Cicero, *In Verrem,* vol. 3, 4). Italics are Burke's.
8. Ibid., p. 131. Burke to Richard Shackleton (19 April 1770).
9. Ibid., p. 116. Burke to the Marquess of Rockingham (5 December 1769).
10. Ibid., p. 57. Burke to Charles O'Hara (28 August 1769).
11. See ibid., p. 251.
12. Ibid., p. 249. Burke to Charles Townsend (17 October 1771).
13. Ibid., p. 253–286. Burke to Dr. William Markham (post November 1771). These 33 pages amount to approximately 15,000 words.
14. Ibid., pp. 253, 254, 263, 268, 267. Italics are Burke's.
15. Ibid., p. 150. Burke to Richard Shackleton (5 June 1770); vol. 2, p. 157. Burke to the Marquess of Rockingham (7, 8 June 1770).
16. See Catherine Macaulay, *Observations on a Pamphlet Entitled Thoughts on the Cause of the Present Discontents* (London: 1770).
17. Burke, *The Correspondence,* vol. 2, pp. 150, 157.
18. Ibid.
19. On this subject see Caroline Robbins, *The Eighteenth-century Commonwealthman* (Cambridge, Mass.: 1959); my *Bolingbroke and His Circle* (Cambridge, Mass.: 1968); Harvey Mansfield, Jr., *Statesmenship and Party Government* (Chicago: 1965).
20. These debates and controversies are to be found, in part, in the following works: L. B. Namier, *Avenues of History* (London: 1952), *The Structure of Politics at the Accession of George III,* (London: 1957), *England in the Age of the American Revolution* (London: 1930), *Monarchy and the Party System* (Oxford: 1952); Herbert Butterfield, *George III and the Historians* (London: 1957); Richard Pares, *King George III and the Politicians* (Oxford: 1953); John Brooke, *The Chatham Administration* (London: 1956); H. Mansfield, Jr. *Statesmanship and Party Government;* "Sir Lewis Namier Considered," *Journal of British Studies,* 2 (November 1962).
21. Burke, "Thoughts on the Cause of the Present Discontent" in *Works,* vol. 1, pp. 373–74.
22. Ibid., p. 379.

23. Ibid., pp. 374, 380.

24. Ibid., p. 375.

25. Ibid.

26. *Parliamentary History,* 29 (1791–1792), p. 388.

27. *Parliamentary History,* 30 (1792–1794), p. 180.

Chapter 6 *Recovery*

1. Burke, *The Correspondence,* vol. 3, p. 35. Burke to the Marquess of Rockingham (18 September 1774).

2. Ibid., vol. 2, p. 40. Burke to the Duke of Richmond (29 September 1774).

3. Ibid., p. 78. Burke to Richard Champion (19 November 1774).

4. Ibid., vol. 4, p. 74. Burke to the Marchioness of Rockingham (21 May 1779), p. 170. Burke to William Eden (23 November 1779).

5. Ibid., vol. 2, p. 86. Burke to Charles O'Hara (27 September 1769).

6. Ibid., vol. 3, p. 107. Burke to the Marquess of Rockingham (24 January 1775).

7. Ibid., p. 192–93 (22, 23 August 1775). The reference here is to Rockingham's repeal of the Stamp Act in 1766; see also, ibid., p. 312 (6 January 1777).

8. Ibid., pp. 312, 400 (5 November 1777).

9. Ibid., vol. 2, p. 372. Burke to the Duke of Richmond (post 15 November 1772).

10. Ibid., vol. 3, p. 388. Burke to William Baker (12 October 1777).

11. Ibid., p. 381. Burke to Charles James Fox (8 October 1777).

12. Ibid., p. 186. Burke to Charles O'Hara (17 August 1775). The aide-de-camp was, of course, Hamilton.

13. Ibid., p. 190. Burke to the Marquess of Rockingham (23 August 1775).

14. Burke, "Letter to the Sheriffs of Bristol," in *Works,* vol. 2, pp. 31–32.

15. Burke, "Speech on Conciliation with America," in *Works,* vol. 2, pp. 462, 460.

16. Burke, "Letter to the Sheriffs of Bristol," p. 32.

17. On this subject see my *Bolingbroke and His Circle,* and Bernard Bailyn, *Ideological Origins of the American Revolution* (Cambridge: Mass., 1967).

18. Burke, "Speech on American Taxation" in *Works,* vol. 1, p. 403.

19. *Parliamentary History,* 18 (1774–1777), p. 233.

20. Burke, "Speech on American Taxation," pp. 403–404.

21. Burke, *The Correspondence,* vol. 1, p. 229. Burke to Charles O'Hara (31 December 1765).

22. "Letter to the Sheriffs of Bristol," pp. 41, 31–32.

23. Wentworth Woodhouse ms. 127h. Quoted in Bertram D. Sarasan, "Burke's Two Notes on America," *Burke Newsletter,* 6, no. 1 (Fall 1964). Italics are Burke's.

24. "Speech on American Taxation," p. 401.

25. Ibid., p. 433.

26. "Letter to the Sheriffs of Bristol," p. 41.

27. Burke, *The Correspondence,* vol. 2, p. 138. Burke to Charles O'Hara (21 May 1770); See also ibid., vol. 3, p. 273. Burke to the Marquess of Rockingham (1 October 1775).

28. Ibid., vol. 3, p. 218. Burke to the Duke of Richmond (26 September 1775); p. 381. Burke to Charles James Fox (8 October 1777); vol. 4, p. 153. Burke to the Duke of Portland (16 October 1779).

29. Ibid., vol. 2, p. 156. Burke to the Marquess of Rockingham (8 September 1770); vol. 3, p. 192. Burke to the Marquess of Rockingham (23 August 1775); p. 384. Burke to Charles James Fox (8 October 1777).

30. See Burke, "Speech to the Electors of Bristol," (13 October 1774), in *Works,* vol. 2, pp. 85–88.

31. Burke, *The Correspondence*, vol. 3, p. 224. Burke to the Duke to Portland (2 October 1775).

32. For letters between Burke and his constituents, see *The Correspondence*, vol. 3, pp. 207, 224, 259, 356, 361, 429, 430, 434, 436, 438, 440, 442.

33. Ibid., vol. 4, p. 274. Burke to the Marquess of Rockingham (8 September 1780).

34. Burke, "Speech on the Economical Reform," in *Works*, vol. 2, p. 124.

35. Ibid., vol. 3, p. 398. Draft letter from Burke to the stewards of the Bell Club (1 November 1777).

36. Burke, "Speech on a Motion Made in the House of Commons, the 7th of May 1782, for a Committee to Inquire into the State of the Representation of the Commons in Parliament," in *Works*, vol. 6, p. 151.

Chapter 7 *Obsession One*

1. Burke, *The Correspondence*, vol. 4, p. 430. Burke to Will Burke (27 March 1782).

2. Ibid., vol. 6, p. 192. Burke to John Haly Hutchinson (18 December 1790).

3. Ibid., vol. 5, p. 253.

4. Ibid., p. 337. Burke to Dr. Samuel Parr (9 June 1787).

5. Ibid., p. 468. Burke to Frederick Montagu (1 May 1789), p. 477. Burke to Lord Charlemont (26, 27 May 1789), p. 468.

6. Ibid., vol. 4, p. 33. Burke to Philip Francis (24 December 1778).

7. Ibid., vol. 5, p. 255. Burke to Miss Mary Palmer (19 January 1786).

8. Ibid., vol. 8, pp. 424–25. Burke to Lord Loughborough (17 March 1796). Burke's concerns with the East India Company and its mismanagement of Indian affairs, even its cruelty, were anticipated in Smith's *Wealth of Nations*, pp. 600 ff.

9. Burke, *The Correspondence*, vol. 3, p. 458. Burke to Edmund Sexton Perry (24 June 1778); "Speech on the East India Bill" in *Works*, vol. 2, pp. 218, 221.

10. Burke, "Speech on the Impeachment of Warren Hastings" (3rd Day, 18 February 1788) in *Works*, (Boston, 1869), vol. 7, pp. 43–45.

11. Burke, *The Correspondence*, vol. 5, p. 255. Burke to Miss Mary Palmer (19 January 1786).

12. Ibid., p. 243. Burke to Philip Francis (10 December 1785).

13. *Parliamentary History*, 23 (1782–1783), p. 797; Burke, "Speech in General Reply," (3 June 1794) in *Works* (Boston, 1869), vol. 11, p. 304.

14. Burke, "Speech in General Reply," (5 June 1794) in *Works* (Boston, 1869) vol. 11, p. 442.

15. Burke, "Speech on the Impeachment of Warren Hastings" (3rd Day, 18 February 1788), in *Works* (Boston, 1869), vol. 10, pp. 28, 43–47; *The Correspondence*, vol. 5, p. 468. Burke to Frederick Montagu (1 May 1789); "Ninth Report from the Select Committee Appointed to take into Consideration the State of the Administration of Justice in the Provinces of Bengal, Bahar, and Orissa" (25 June 1783), in *Works*, vol. 4, pp. 51, 29, 40; "Speech on Mr. Fox's East India Bill" in *Works*, vol. 2, pp. 163, 194; "Speech on the Nabob of Arcot's Debts" in *Works*, vol. 3, p. 150.

16. Burke, "Speech on the Nabob of Arcot's Debts" in *Works*, vol. 2, p. 146; "Speech on Mr. Fox's East India Bill" in *Works*, vol. 2, p. 195.

17. *Parliamentary History*, 24 (1783–1785), pp. 939, 1265.

18. Burke, "Speech on the Sixth Article of Change" (7 May 1789) in *Works* (Boston, 1869), vol. 10, p. 450.

19. Burke, *The Correspondence*, vol. 5, p. 136. Burke to Sir William Lee (27 March 1784).

20. Burke, "Speech on the Sixth Article of Change" (7 May 1789) in *Works* (Boston, 1869), vol. 10, p. 450.

21. Burke, *The Correspondence,* vol. 5, p. 314. Burke to Henry Dundas (25 March 1787).

22. Ibid., vol. 7, p. 279 (28 October 1792). See also vol. 5, p. 323 and vol. 8, p. 441.

23. Burke, "Motion Relative to the Speech from the Throne" in *Works,* vol. 2, p. 272; "Speech on the Nabob of Arcot's Debts" in *Works,* vol. 3, p. 157; "Articles of Charge Against Warren Hastings" in *Works,* vol. 4, p. 412.

24. Burke, "Speech on Mr. Fox's East India Bill" in *Works,* vol. 2, p. 221.

25. "Speech on the Sixth Article" (5 May 1789), in *Works* (Boston, 1869), vol. 10, p. 372.

26. Ibid. (21 April 1789), pp. 179–276.

27. Burke, "Speech in General Reply" (7 June 1794), in *Works* (London: Nimmo, 1887) vol. 12, p. 25. "Speech on the Nabob of Arcot's Debts," pp. 188–189.

28. Burke, "Report of a Committee on the Affairs of India" in *Works,* vol. 4, p. 138; "Speech in Opening the Impeachment" (15 February 1788) in *Works* (Boston, 1869), vol. 9, p. 381; "Speech on the Sixth Article" (25 April 1789) in *Works* (Boston, 1869), vol. 10, p. 252; ibid. (21 April 1789), p. 163; Ibid. (5 May 1789), p. 347.

29. Burke, "Speech in General Reply" (7 June 1794) in *Works* (London, 1887), vol. 12, pp. 10, 11; Ibid. (16 June 1794), pp. 395 ff.

30. Burke, *The Correspondence,* vol. 7, p. 553. Burke to Earl Fitzwilliam (24 June 1794); ibid., vol. 8, p. 372 (11 January 1796). Fitzwilliam was the nephew and heir of Rockingham. He served as patron to Burke, though on a much more distant level than had his uncle. See also, ibid., vol. 6, p. 395. Burke to the Duke of Dorset (14 September 1791).

31. Ibid., vol. 8, p. 432. Burke to Lord Loughborough (17 March 1796).

32. Burke, "Speech in General Reply," (7 June 1794) in *Works* (London, 1887), vol. 12, pp. 23–24.

33. Burke, "Speech on Mr. Fox's East India Bill" in *Works,* vol. 2, pp. 205 ff; "Speech in Opening the Impeachment" (15 February 1788) in *Works* (Boston, 1869), vol. 9, p. 377; See also, "Speech on the Nabob of Arcot's Debts" in *Works,* vol. 3, p. 157.

34. Burke, "Speech in Opening the Impeachment" (19 February 1788) in *Works* (Boston, 1869), vol. 10, p. 125; "Speech on the Sixth Article" (5 May 1789), ibid., p. 367.

35. Burke, "Speech on the Nabob of Arcot's Debts," pp. 175, 138, 187.

36. Burke, "Speech in Opening the Impeachment," (18 February 1788) in *Works* (Boston, 1869), vol. 10, pp. 71–74; ibid., vol. 9, p. 398.

37. *Parliamentary History,* 23 (1782–1783), p. 797; *Parliamentary History,* 24 (1783–1785), p. 1258.

38. "Appendix to the Speech on the Nabob's Debt" in *Works,* vol. 3, pp. 265–66.

39. Burke, "Speech in Opening the Impeachment" (18 February 1788) in *Works* (Boston, 1869), vol. 10, pp. 83–89.

40. Ibid., p. 83; "Speech on the Sixth Article" (5 May 1789), ibid. p. 324.

41. Ibid., p. 83.

42. Ibid. (19 February 1788), pp. 140, 141; Articles of Charge Against Warren Hastings" in *Works,* vol. 4, p. 267.

43. Burke, "Articles of Charge Against Warren Hastings," p. 289.

44. Ibid., pp. 279–335; See also, "Speech in General Reply" (30 May 1794) in *Works* (Boston, 1869), vol. 11, pp. 291–94.

45. *Parliamentary History,* 24 (1783–1785), p. 1258.

46. *Parliamentary History,* 25 (1785–1786), pp. 1393, 1398.

47. Burke, "Speech in General Reply" (11 June 1794) in *Works* (London, 1887), vol. 12, p. 103; (12 June 1794), ibid., pp. 144, 156.

48. Burke, "Speech in General Reply" (12 June 1794), ibid., pp. 163–64.

49. *Parliamentary History,* 17 (1771–74), p. 671.

50. Ibid., p. 673.
51. Burke, *The Correspondence,* vol. 1, p. 28. Burke to Shackleton (7 July 1744).
52. Ibid., p. 86 (5 March 1747).
53. *Parliamentary History,* 18 (1774–1777), p. 45.
54. *Parliamentary History,* 23 (1782–1783), p. 612.
55. Ibid., p. 918.
56. *Parliamentary History,* 24 (1783–1785), p. 939.
57. *Parliamentary History,* 26 (1786–1788), p. 489.
58. See Erik Erikson, *Childhood and Society* (New York: 1950), p. 90.
59. Burke, "Speech in General Reply" (7 June 1794) in *Works* (London, 1887), vol. 12, p. 31.
60. Ibid., pp. 52–53, 70.

Chapter 8 *Obsession Two*

1. Burke, *The Correspondence,* vol. 9, p. 170. Burke to the Rev. Thomas Hussey (post 9 December 1796).
2. Ibid., vol. 4, p. 71. Thomas Paine to Edmund Burke (17 January 1790).
3. Ibid., vol. 6, p. 451. Burke to Earl Fitzwilliam (21 November 1791). Italics are Burke's.
4. Ibid., vol. 7, p. 60. Burke to William Weddel (31 January 1792).
5. Burke, "Letter to a Member of the National Assembly" in *Works,* vol. 2, pp. 533, 520, 545; see also, *The Correspondence,* vol. 6, p. 173; *Reflections,* vol. 2, p. 316. This disdain for money men, jobbers, and Jews was nothing new. Indeed, it was a staple of the early aristocratic response to financial and commercial capitalism. See, for example, my *Bolingbroke and His Circle, passim.*
6. Ibid., vol. 7, p. 62. Burke to William Weddel (31 January 1792).
7. Ibid., vol. 8, p. 362. Earl Fitzwilliam to Burke (17 December 1795).
8. Burke, *Reflections,* vol. 2, p. 324; see also, "Thoughts on French Affairs," vol. 3, p. 353.
9. Burke, "Remarks on the Policy of the Allies" in *Works,* vol. 3, p. 437. Italics are Burke's.
10. Burke, *The Correspondence,* vol. 8, p. 242. Burke to Earl Fitzwilliam (15 May 1795), vol. 8, p. 254. Burke to Sir Hercules Langrishe (26 May 1795); see also, vol. 9, p. 123. Burke to Earl Fitzwilliam (20 November 1796).
11. Burke, *Works,* vol. 3, p. 528; vol. 5, pp. 76–77. "Letters on a Regicide Peace," ibid., vol. 5, p. 207, 259.
12. Ibid., vol. 5, p. 191; vol. 3, p. 502.
13. Ibid., vol. 3, p. 448. Italics are Burke's.
14. Burke, "Observations on the Conduct of the Minority" in *Works,* vol. 3, p. 492.
15. Burke, "Preface to M. Brissot's Address to His Constituents" in *Works,* vol. 4, p. 492.
16. Burke, *Works,* vol. 5, p. 257.
17. Burke, "A Letter to William Elliot, Esq." in *Works,* vol. 5, p. 71.
18. Burke, "Remarks on the Policy of the Allies" in *Works,* vol. 3, p. 417; "Observations on the Conduct of the Minority," ibid., p. 469.
19. Burke, "A Letter to a Noble Lord," ibid., vol. 5, p. 114.
20. Ibid., p. 131.
21. Ibid., pp. 147, 127. Italics are Burke's.
22. Paine, *Dissertation on the First Principles of Government* (Paris: 1795), vol. 3, p. 270.

23. "A Letter to a Noble Lord," p. 141.

24. Burke, *The Correspondence,* vol. 6, p. 141. Burke to Charles-Alexandre de Calonne (25 October 1790).

25. Ibid., vol. 6, p. 92. Burke to Philip Francis (20 February 1790).

26. Burke, "Speech on the Acts of Uniformity" in *Works,* vol. 6, p. 92; "Speech on a Bill for the Relief of Protestant Dissenters," ibid., p. 111.

27. Ibid., vol. 5, pp. 47 ff, and vol. 6, pp. 82 ff.

28. Burke, "Speech on Fox's Motion for Repeal of Certain Penal Statutes Respecting Religious Opinions." *Parliamentary History,* 29 (1791–1792), p. 1389.

29. See Burke, *Reflections on the Revolution in France,* ed. Conor Cruise O'Brien, Pelican Classics (London: 1968), pp. 9–77.

30. See Joseph Berrington, *An Address to the Protestant Dissenters* (Birmingham: 1787); *Rights of Dissenters from the Established Church in Relation Principally to English Catholics* (Birmingham: 1789).

31. Burke, "Speech on Fox's Motion for Repeal of Certain Penal Statutes Respecting Religious Opinions." *Parliamentary History,* 29 (1791–1792), p. 1393.

32. Burke, "Speech on the Petition of the Unitarians" in *Works,* vol. 6, pp. 121, 122–23; see also, *The Correspondence,* vol. 7, p. 56. Burke to William Weddel (31 January 1792); "An Appeal from the New to the Old Whigs," vol. 3, pp. 44, 91.

33. Burke, *The Correspondence,* vol. 7, p. 415. Burke to William Windham (23 August 1793).

34. *Parliamentary History,* 29 (1791–1792), p. 1382 (11 May 1792).

35. Burke, *The Correspondence,* vol. 6, p. 91. Burke to Philip Francis (20 February 1790).

36. *Reflections,* vol. 2, p. 352.

37. Ibid., p. 343.

38. Ibid., p. 344.

39. *Memoirs of Madame de la Tour du Pin,* ed. Felice Harcourt (London: 1970), pp. 131–137.

40. *Reflections,* vol. 2, p. 363.

41. Ibid., p. 349.

42. Ibid., pp. 349, 359.

43. Ibid., p. 282. The weekly *Anti-Jacobin Review* picked up this theme from Burke as it did so much of its propaganda. In 1798 it described the Jacobins as setting individual men against each other—"insulated and individual,—and every man for himself (stripped of prejudice, of bigotry, and of feeling for others) against the remainder of his species;—and there is then some hope of a totally new order of things—of a radical reform in the present corrupt system of the world." *Poetry of the Anti-Jacobin,* ed. Leonard Rice-Oxley (Oxford: 1924), p. 130.

44. *Reflections,* vol. 2, p. 349.

45. Ibid., p. 352.

46. Ibid., p. 349.

47. Ibid., pp. 344, 366, 413.

48. Ibid., pp. 432–33, 472.

49. Burke, "A Letter to a Member of the National Assembly" in *Works,* vol. 2, p. 535.

50. Ibid., p. 540.

51. Burke, *The Correspondence,* vol. 6, p. 91. Burke to Philip Francis (20 February 1790).

52. Burke, "A Letter to a Member of the National Assembly" in *Works,* vol. 2, p. 538, 541.

53. *Edmund Burke: Selected Writings and Speeches,* ed. Peter J. Stanlis, p. 94.

54. Burke, "Letter to a Member," pp. 538–39.

55. Ibid., p. 540.

56. Jean-Jacques Rousseau, *The Confessions* (London: 1953), bk. 8, p. 362. In his *Discourse on the Arts and Sciences,* Rousseau repeated his identification of nakedness with genuineness, freedom, and equality. See Everyman Edition (New York: 1950), pp. 147–148.

57. Burke, "Letter on a Regicide Peace" in *Works,* vol. 5, pp. 208–209, 213.

58. Burke, "An Appeal from the New to the Old Whig," in *Works,* vol. 3, p. 104.

59. Burke, "Speech on the Petition of the Unitarians," in *Works,* vol. 6, p. 125. Emphasis is Burke's.

60. *Parliamentary History,* 30 (1792–1794), p. 53; *Parliamentary History,* 30 (1792–1794), p. 189. For Sheridan's criticism, see *Parliamentary History,* 30 (1792–1794), p. 554.

61. *Parliamentary History,* 19 (1777–8), p. 698.

62. Burke, *The Correspondence,* vol. 6, p. 42. Burke to Charles-Jean-Francois Dupont (November 1789).

63. Ibid., vol. 7, p. 359. Burke to Sir Lawrence Parsons (7 March 1793); vol. 6, p. 266. Burke to Claude-François de Rivarol (1 June 1791).

64. Ibid., vol. 6, pp. 93, 95. Burke to Captain Thomas Mercer (26 February 1790).

65. Burke, "Thoughts on Scarcity," rep. in *Edmund Burke,* Great Lives Observed Edition, ed. Isaac Kramnick (Englewood Cliffs, N.J.: 1974), p. 84.

66. Ibid., pp. 85, 87.

67. Cited in C. B. Cone, *Burke and the Nature of Politics* (Lexington, Kentucky: 1957), p. 326.

68. Burke, "Thoughts on Scarcity," p. 87.

69. Burke, *The Correspondence,* vol. 9, pp. 361–62. Burke to Arthur Young (23 May 1797).

70. See Joseph Priestley, "The General Principles of Good Government" in *Priestley's Writings on Philosophy, Science, and Politics,* ed. John Passmore, (New York: 1965), pp. 177–185.

71. For Paine's views on the Poor Laws see his *Rights of Man,* Pelican Classics Edition, ed. Henry Collins, (London: 1969), part II, pp. 260 ff. For Priestley's, see his *Writings.* Needless to say, Adam Smith also opposed the Poor Laws as obstructions of "The Free Circulation of Labor," and as an "evident violation of natural liberty and justice." See his *Wealth of Nations,* pp. 135, 141.

72. Burke, "Thoughts on Scarcity," p. 84.

73. Ibid., p. 85. For similar views see Burke's 1772 Speech to the Commons, *Parliamentary History* 17 (1771–1776), p. 481 or his 1785 speech, *Parliamentary History* 28 (1789–1791), p. 366.

74. Mary Wollstonecraft, *Vindication of the Rights of Men* (London: 1790), p. 256.

75. Burke, *The Correspondence,* vol. 4, p. 93. Burke to Garret Nagle (Post, 24 June 1779).

76. *Parliamentary History* 21 (1780–1781), p. 237.

77. Burke, "Speech on the Economical Reform," in *Works,* vol. 2, pp. 60, 68, 74, 81.

78. Ibid., p. 83.

79. Ibid., pp. 85, 87, 109, 115, 102.

80. Burke, "Letters on a Regicide Peace," vol. 5, pp. 312–313.

81. Ibid., pp. 314–315.

82. Karl Marx, *Capital* (Moscow: 1954), vol. 1, p. 760, footnote 2.

83. Burke, "Sketch of the Negro Code" in *Works,* vol. 5, pp. 542–54.

84. Burke, "Letters on a Regicide Peace," ibid., p. 321.

85. Ibid., p. 322.

86. Ibid., pp. 327–350.

87. Frederick Engels, "On Historical Materialism" in *Marx and Engels Basic Writings in Politics and Philosophy,* ed. Lewis Feuer (New York: 1959), pp. 47–68.

88. C. B. MacPherson, "Edmund Burke" rep. in *Edmund Burke,* Great Lives Observed Edition, pp. 154–163.

89. Burke, *The Correspondence,* vol. 7, p. 383. Burke to General Dalton (6 August 1793).

90. Ibid., vol. 6, pp. 274–75. Burke to Earl Fitzwilliam (5 June 1791); vol. 7, p. 308. Burke to Earl Fitzwilliam (29 November 1792); vol. 6, p. 275. Burke to Earl Fitzwilliam (5 June 1791); ibid., p. 450. Burke to Earl Fitzwilliam (21 November 1791); vol. 7, p. 52. Burke to William Weddel (31 January 1792); vol. 6, p. 273. Burke to Earl Fitzwilliam (5 June 1791).

91. Ibid., vol. 9, p. 446. Burke to Dr. Richard Brocklesby (no date).

92. Ibid., vol. 6, p. 177. Burke to Sir Gilbert Elliot (29 November 1790). Paine's *Rights of Man,* written as a reply to Burke's *Reflections,* would soon far outsell even this impressive number.

93. Ibid., pp. 238–39. Jane Burke to William Burke (21 March 1791). See also, vol. 6, p. 363 and vol. 7, p. 514 for other mention of Burke's attendance at court.

94. Ibid., vol. 7, p. 421. Pope Pius VI to Burke (7 September 1793).

95. Ibid., vol. 6, pp. 203–204. Edward Jerningham to Burke (ante 18 January 1791).

Chapter 9 *"Pain and Sorrows"*

1. Burke, *The Correspondence,* vol. 7, p. 558. Burke to Earl Fitzwilliam (28 June 1794); vol. 8, p. 207. Burke to Henry Grattan (20 March 1795); vol. 9, p. 69. Burke to the Comte de Provence (25 August 1796); ibid., p. 113. Burke to John Keogh (17 November 1796); ibid., p. 347. Burke to William Windham (16 May 1797).

2. Ibid., vol. 7, p. 435. Burke to Sir Gilbert Elliot (22 September 1793); vol. 8, p. 76. Burke to William Burke (14 November 1794); see also, ibid., p. 380. Burke to John Coxe Hippisley (22 January 1796); ibid., vol. 9, p. 347. Burke to William Windham (16 May 1797); ibid., p. 370. Burke to Earl Fitzwilliam (18 June 1797).

3. Ibid., vol. 8, p. 437; ibid., p. 424. Burke to Lord Loughborough (circa 17 March 1796); ibid., p. 436; ibid., p. 422.

4. Ibid., vol. 1, p. 222. Burke to Charles O'Hara (24 December 1765).

5. Ibid., vol. 7, p. 453. Burke to Earl Fitzwilliam (21 June 1794).

6. For these details see ibid., vol. 6, p. 271, vol. 7, pp. 141, 151.

7. Ibid., vol. 8, p. 13. Burke to John King (14 September 1794).

8. Ibid., p. 280. Burke to Walter King (30 June 1795).

9. Ibid., vol. 7, p. 550.

10. Ibid., p. 557. Richard Burke Jr. to William Windham (circa 27 June 1794); ibid., p. 550. Richard Burke Jr. to William Windham (19 June 1794).

11. Ibid.

12. Ibid., pp. 557–58.

13. Ibid., vol. 8, p. 340. Burke to William Windham (ante 17 November 1795).

14. Ibid., vol. 6, p. 237. Jane Burke to William Burke (21 March 1791).

15. Ibid., vol. 8, p. 206. Burke to Henry Grattan (20 March 1795). Many years earlier Burke had complained of his own lack of inherited estates. He would make an easier mark in the world, he noted on his arrival in London, "if Providence had blessed me with a few paternal acres." Ibid., vol. 1, p. 360. Burke to Michael Smith.

16. Burke, "Letter to a Noble Lord," *Works,* vol. 5, pp. 135–36.

17. Ibid., p. 137.

18. Burke, *The Correspondence,* vol. 7, p. xix.

19. Ibid., p. 429. Burke to Gilbert Elliot (16 September 1793). In pushing his son to

the fore, Burke was not above employing methods which he himself had often criticized. As Paymaster General, while busy reforming abuses, he tried to obtain for his son a most valuable sinecure on the Exchequer. Horace Walpole noted: "Can one but smile at the reformer of abuses reserving the second greatest abuse for himself." Quoted in Philip Magnus, *Edmund Burke*, p. 116.

20. Ibid., p. 556.
21. Ibid., p. 558. Burke to Earl Fitzwilliam (28 June 1794); ibid., p. 568.
22. Ibid., p. 583. Appendix.
23. Ibid., p. 568. Burke to Earl Fitzwilliam (7 August 1794).
24. Ibid., pp. 591–93. Appendix.
25. Ibid., p. 568. Burke to Earl Fitzwilliam (7 August 1794).
26. Burke, "Letter to William Smith, Esq." (1795) in *Works,* vol. 6, p. 53.
27. Burke, *The Correspondence,* vol. 9, p. 283. Burke to Earl Fitzwilliam (15 March 1797).
28. Ibid., p. ix–xxvi.
29. Ibid., p. 331. Burke to Earl Fitzwilliam (7 May 1797).
30. Burke, "A Letter to Sir Hercules Langrishe, M.P.," vol. 3, p. 300.
31. Burke, "Letter to Richard Burke, Esq.," vol. 6, p. 62–63.
32. Ibid., vol. 6, p. 66.
33. Ibid. Emphasis is Burke's.
34. Ibid., vol. 9, p. 9. Burke to Richard Burke, Jr. (post 3 January 1792).
35. Ibid., vol. 6, pp. 72–74.
36. Ibid., vol. 6, p. 75.
37. Ibid., vol. 6, pp. 75–76.
38. Burke, "Letter to William Smith, Esq." (1795) in *Works,* vol. 6, p. 52.
39. Burke, "A Second Letter to Sir Hercules Langrishe" (1795), vol. 6, pp. 58–59.
40. Burke, "Letter on the Affairs of Ireland" (1797), p. 82.
41. Ibid., p. 88.
42. Ibid., vol. 9, p. 373. French Laurence to Earl Fitzwilliam (10 July 1797).
43. Cited in Copeland, *Our Eminent Friend,* p. 13.
44. *Parliamentary History,* 29 (1791–1792), p. 388.
45. The reference to the Reformers of the 1780s is in *A Letter to a Noble Lord,* vol. 5, p. 116.
46. *Private Letters of Edward Gibbon,* ed. R. E. Prothero (London: 1899), vol. 2, p. 251; G. Wraxall, *Historical Memoirs of My Own Time* (London: 1815) vol. 2, pp. 33–34.
47. *Parliamentary History* 27 (1788–1789), p. 1249.
48. *Parliamentary History* 29 (1791–1792), pp. 419, 386.
49. Burke, "Letter to a Noble Lord" in *Works,* vol. 5, p. 115.
50. Burke, "Nabob of Arcot's Debts" in *Works,* vol. 3, p. 160.
51. Burke, "Letter to a Member of the National Assembly," vol. 2, p. 538; "An Appeal," vol. 3, p. 8; "Thoughts," vol. 5, p. 108; "A Letter to a Noble Lord," vol. 5, p. 141.
52. Burke, *The Reflections,* vol. 2, pp. 363, 344; See also "The Conduct of the Minority," vol. 3, p. 509.
53. Burke, "Letters on a Regicide Peace," vol. 5, p. 155.
54. Burke, *The Correspondence,* vol. 1, pp. 28, 86.
55. Burke, "Letters on a Regicide Peace," vol. 5, p. 374.
56. *Parliamentary History* 31 (1794–1795), p. 379.
57. Burke, "A Letter to a Noble Lord," vol. 5, p. 148; see also, "Letter on a Regicide Peace," ibid., p. 259; "The Policy of the Allies," vol. 3, p. 437.
58. N. O. Brown's *Life Against Death* (Middleton, Conn.: 1959); M. Murray, *Witch Cult in Western Europe* (Oxford: 1921); M. J. Rudwin, *The Devil in Legend and Literature* (Chicago: 1931).

59. Rudwin, *The Devil*, pp. 51, 110 and Brown, *Life Against Death*, p. 208.

60. Cited in Brown, *Life Against Death*, p. 226.

61. Burke, *Reflections*, vol. 2, p. 424; "Letter . . . ," vol. 2, p. 526. See Burke's discussion of blackness in his "On the Sublime and Beautiful," vol. 1, pp. 155–160.

62. Burke, "Letter to a Noble Lord," vol. 5, p. 141.

63. Burke, "Letter on a Regicide Peace," ibid., pp. 209–210.

64. Burke, "The Nabob of Arcot's Debts," vol. 3, p. 194.

65. Burke, "A Letter to a Noble Lord," vol. 5, pp. 120–121.

66. Burke, "Letter on a Regicide Peace," ibid., pp. 211–213.

67. Cited in Brown, *Life Against Death*, p. 208.

68. See P. Greenacre, "The Mutual Adventures of Jonathan Swift and Lemuel Gulliver," *Psychoanalytic Quarterly* 24 (1955), pp. 20–62 for this interpretation. See also Swift's "Letter of Advice to a Young Poet" in *Prose Works of Jonathan Swift* (London: 1907) vol. 11, p. 108, where he describes the Grub Street of Writers as one of "filth and excrement."

69. See the discussion in Brown, *Life Against Death*, p. 199.

70. Quoted in Copeland, *Our Eminent Friend*, p. 13.

71. Burke, "The Nabob of Arcot's Debts," vol. 3, p. 165.

72. Ibid., p. 173.

73. Burke, "Speech on the Sixth Article" (21 April 1789), in *Works* (Boston, 1869), vol. 10, p. 163.

74. Ibid. (25 April 1789), p. 163.

75. *Parliamentary History* 24 (1783–1785), p. 1259.

76. Burke, *The Correspondence*, vol. 1, p. 88; Namier, "The Character of Edmund Burke," *The Spectator* (19 December 1958), p. 89.

77. Burke, *The Correspondence*, vol. 1, p. 340. Burke to Charles O'Hara (11 December 1767); vol. 2, p. 267. Burke to Dr. William Markham (post 9 November 1771) vol. 2, p. 130. Burke to Richard Shackleton (22 April 1770). See also ibid., vol. 5, p. 214. Burke to George Lenard Staunton (post 27 July 1785); vol. 4, p. 431. Burke to William Burke (4 April 1782).

78. *Parliamentary History* 29 (1791–1792), p. 374.

79. Cited in John Campbell, *Lives of the Chancellors* (Philadelphia: 1851), vol. 6, p. 214.

80. Cited in Charles Butler, *Reminiscences*, 4th ed. (London: 1824), vol. 1, p. 171.

81. Burke, *The Correspondence*, vol. 6, pp. 451–52. Burke to Earl Fitzwilliam (21 November 1791).

82. Ibid., vol. 4, pp. 240–46; vol. 7, p. 340.

83. William E. H. Lecky, *A History of England in the Eighteenth Century* (New York: 1887), vol. 5, p. 131; T. H. Buckle, *History of Civilization in England* (New York: 1858), vol. 2, p. 334.

84. John Timbs, *Anecdote Biography* (London: 1860), p. 348.

85. For the Freudian linkage of paranoia and latent homosexuality, see S. Freud, "Psychoanalytic Notes Upon an Autobiographical Account of a Case of Paranoia (Dementia Paranoides)" in *Sigmund Freud—Collected Papers* (New York: 1959), vol. 3, p. 431. See also vol. 2, "Certain Neurotic Mechanisms in Jealousy, Paranoia and Homosexuality."

86. See Bertram Sarson, "Edmund Burke's Burial Place," in *Notes and Queries*, (Jan.–Dec. 1955), pp. 69–70; see also British Museum Additional Manuscript 3256. In a letter to Windham (*The Correspondence*, vol. 8, p. 339, ante 17 November 1795) Burke wrote of the Jacobins: "they tear our corpses from the tombs to turn the coffin lead which preserves the departed into bullets to assassinate the living."

87. Burke, "A Letter to a Noble Lord," vol. 5, p. 112.

Chapter 10 *Epilogue*

1. Erik Erikson, *Young Man Luther,* pp. 15, 75.

2. Burke, "Speech at Bristol on Declining the Poll," (1780), vol. 2, p. 170; *Parliamentary History,* 20 (1778–80), pp. 919, 674; *Parliamentary History,* 21 (1780–1781), pp. 1210, 1296.

3. Charles Hughes, *Mrs. Piozzi's "Thraliana"* (London: 1913), pp. 33–34.

4. Hester Lynn Piozzi, *Autobiography, Letters, and Library Remains of Mrs. Piozzi (Thrale)* ed. A. Hayward, 2 vols. (London: 1861), vol. 2, pp. 17–18.

5. *Parliamentary History,* 22 (1781–1782), p. 1224.

6. Adam Smith, *The Theory of Moral Sentiments,* vol. 1, p. 109.

7. Ibid., p. 111. For a beautiful fictional representation of this love-hate ambivalence see the character of Falkland in William Godwin's *Caleb Williams.*

8. Ibid., pp. 114–115.

9. Ibid., pp. 411–12. Italics are mine.

10. Burke, *Reflections,* vol. 2, p. 333.

11. Burke, "Letters to a Member of the National Assembly," vol. 2, p. 555.

INDEX